Intellectual Sacrifice
and Other Mimetic Paradoxes

STUDIES IN VIOLENCE, MIMESIS, AND CULTURE

Intellectual Sacrifice
and Other Mimetic Paradoxes

Paolo Diego Bubbio

Michigan State University Press · *East Lansing*

∞ The paper used in this publication meets the minimum requirements
of ANSI/NISO Z39.48-1992 (R 1997) (Permanence of Paper).

Michigan State University Press
East Lansing, Michigan 48823-5245

Printed and bound in the United States of America.

27 26 25 24 23 22 21 20 19 18   1 2 3 4 5 6 7 8 9 10

LIBRARY OF CONGRESS CATALOGING-IN-PUBLICATION DATA IS AVAILABLE
ISBN 978-1-61186-273-7 (paperback)
ISBN 978-1-60917-555-9 (PDF)
ISBN 978-1-62895-322-0 (ePub)
ISBN 978-1-62896-322-9 (Kindle)

Book design by Charlie Sharp, Sharp Des!gns, East Lansing, Michigan
Cover design by David Drummond, Salamander Design, www.salamanderhill.com.
Cover art is a detail from "Ocean Code" ©2017 Mauro De Giorgi.
Used with permission of the artist. All rights reserved. Www.maurodegiorgi.com.

Michigan State University Press is a member of the Green Press Initiative and is committed to developing
and encouraging ecologically responsible publishing practices. For more information about the Green
Press Initiative and the use of recycled paper in book publishing, please visit *www.greenpressinitiative.org.*

Visit Michigan State University Press at *www.msupress.org*

Contents

Preface

I n 1993, I was a first-year undergraduate student in the Faculty of Literature and Philosophy at the University of Turin, Italy, and I was enrolled in an aesthetics course mostly focused on the notion of myth. Each student was expected to select and study two monographs from a long list of books dealing with the subject matter. As a freshman, I was completely in the dark about which ones to choose. I talked to a friend of mine who was in second year, and he recommended a few books. I was particularly intrigued by the title of one of them: *Violence and the Sacred.*

I started reading *Violence and the Sacred*, and I was immediately fascinated by it. It was nothing like the other philosophy books that I had read in high school or that I was reading for my other university courses. The words of Jacques Guillet perfectly describe the excitement that I felt reading that book:

> There is something fascinating in the work and in the way of proceeding of René Girard. A coherent perspective, capable of explaining the first processes of hominization in the animal realm up to the refinements of snobbism in which Marcel Proust took delight, an exceptional ability to compare and enlighten with one another the most diverse disciplinary

domains: animal behaviors and the history of myths, Freudian analyses and the great literary works of our civilization, from Genesis to Dostoyevsky. There is also a passionate concern for humanity, a deep sense of the threats that loom over it, the need to find the right point, the effective word that enlightens and solves. One cannot remain indifferent to this passion for the human being, to this need to convince her, to save her.[1]

Two years later, when I had to choose a topic for my dissertation (*tesi di laurea*), I had no hesitation: I was going to write a thesis on the work of René Girard in the discipline I was most passionate about, that is, philosophy of religion. I spent months reading Girard's works, consulting the university library, and using (when possible) the few computers at the university that were connected to the Internet, in a time when this was a rare opportunity and the material available through the World Wide Web very limited. I still cherish that time as one of the most intellectually exciting periods of my life. I frequently met with my supervisor, Marco Ravera, to discuss my findings. During my research, I had become aware that an internationally recognized philosopher who also taught at my university had recently become very fond of Girard's work: Gianni Vattimo. I had attended Vattimo's lectures in my first year, but now I wanted eagerly to discuss mimetic theory with him. Despite his busy schedule, Vattimo was kind enough to find the time to talk to a very young student and to share his thoughts with me. The thesis I was working on was a provocative and bold one: that it was possible to consider philosophy and religion as subjects engaged in a mimetic process, situated at the intellectual level. Thanks to a PhD student who had also written his MA thesis on Girard's mimetic theory, I managed to acquire Girard's postal address, and I wrote a letter to him in which I briefly explained, in my faltering French, my main argument. Months later, and two days before my thesis defense, I received a letter with Girard's reply. He endorsed my argument and encouraged me to take part in the activities of the Colloquium on Violence and Religion. That letter, which is included in this volume, was the beginning of a marvelous correspondence between us.

I graduated summa cum laude in 1997, receiving an honorable recommendation for publication (*dignità di stampa*). Two years later, a revised and shorter version of the thesis was published in Italian by the imprint of a small scholarly press, with the title *Il sacrificio intellettuale: René Girard e la filosofia della religione* [Intellectual sacrifice: René Girard and the philosophy of religion].

Part 1 of the current volume, which charts my journey with mimetic theory, is the English translation of that short book. I hesitated before republishing it. That book was, after all, the work of a twenty-three-year-old student. To read it twenty years later has been an interesting experience. Surely that work is not devoid of naïvetés. And yet I can recognize in it a *tension* between mimetic theory and philosophical hermeneutics that I think can be regarded as a characteristic feature of all my subsequent work on the topic. Of course, in *Intellectual Sacrifice* that tension was explored internally, that is, from a point of view that is very much *within* Girard's mimetic theory. Also, I retrospectively realized how much I had been influenced, in my emphasis on the intellectual violence embedded in philosophy and religion, by the Turin school of hermeneutics in general, and by Vattimo's arguments on the violence of metaphysics in particular—despite the fact that, back then, I thought that I was distancing myself from the suspected relativism of Vattimo's "weak thought" (in time, my philosophical positions have actually become closer to his—and his, I suspect, closer to mine!). The emphasis on intellectual violence can, perhaps, be guilty of some excesses; but I still think that the central thesis expressed there is fundamentally valid. While I was in the process of editing the current volume, I came across an interesting article written by Matthew Edward Harris in 2012. Among several thoughtful insights, Harris advances some criticisms against Vattimo: "By bringing the violence of metaphysics too close to the physical violence of the natural sacred," Harris writes, "Vattimo runs the risk of trivialising the latter"; later in the article, he argues that Vattimo's hermeneutics "cuts him off from being able to conceptualise the origins of physical violence in the way evolutionary biology and anthropology can. This leads Vattimo to place undue weight on metaphysics as an explanation for physical violence."[2] I can easily imagine such criticisms being raised against my *Intellectual Sacrifice* as well. However, at least in my case—but, I suspect, in the case of Vattimo as well—one thing does not exclude the other. Of course we should conceptualize the origins of physical violence through evolutionary biology and anthropology. And of course the physical violence involved in, say, scapegoating heretics or political opponents by burning them alive is a more serious and dangerous matter than the intellectual violence involved in scapegoating them by silencing them or expelling their writings or ideas. Nobody—neither Vattimo nor certainly I—denies that. The point here is that we are too familiar with the dynamic according to which we easily pass from the latter to the former situation. I appreciate that when Vattimo talks about the violence of metaphysics, or when I talk about the mutual violence of religion and philosophy, the discourse might sound too abstract: after all, one might object, it is one thing to talk about the intellectual violence exercised by a concrete human being over another, and quite a different thing to talk about the intellectual violence exercised by one *cultural form* over another. However, as I strove to show in *Intellectual Sacrifice*, the two situations are less distant from each other than is usually conceded. We constitutively are cultural beings, and we have a perpetual tendency to project our inclinations into the cultural forms that we produce. The violence of metaphysics is always the violence of the concrete human beings who *use* metaphysics to impose a supposedly "objective" reality over other human beings. The violence of religion or of philosophy that I talk about in *Intellectual Sacrifice* is, no differently, the violence of concrete human beings who use those cultural forms to express their violence—and, less rarely than is expected, to justify acts of *physical* violence or psychological oppression.

As I read *Intellectual Sacrifice* twenty years later, I realize that it features arguments that could be better sustained, passages that could benefit from more mindful and cautious judgments, and discussions that could take into consideration more, and perhaps more appropriate, secondary sources. I felt the temptation to rewrite the text entirely—but I resisted it. The project of this book was built around the idea of presenting my personal scholarly (but also existential) journey through mimetic theory. In a real journey, you do not always walk at the same pace, and you do not always take the most linear path: sometimes, to reach your destination, you take a detour, and sometimes you stumble. And this was (and still is) a real journey. I therefore decided to leave my original text as it was. I have made only very few, limited revisions, most notably when a literal translation from the original Italian failed to render the actual meaning of my thought; in a very few cases I added some sentences, especially when I thought the text was in desperate need of clarification. Similarly, the references to the secondary literature are the original ones, although I realize that a lot has been written in the meantime and that therefore several important works, especially in English, were not mentioned, because of my limited familiarity at the time with the relevant literature in English.

In 1999 and 2000 I wrote three articles on mimetic theory, all published in Italian journals.[3] They are not included in this volume, because they mostly elaborated on questions that I had already considered in *Intellectual Sacrifice*. In the meantime, I had enrolled in the doctoral program in philosophy at the University of Turin. My research project concerned the notion of sacrifice in contemporary philosophy. I was impelled to investigate this topic by an emotional—even before it was an intellectual—lack of satisfaction with the account of sacrifice provided by Girard in his major works. I had the feeling that such an account did not do justice to the altruistic dimension of sacrifice. I therefore devoted my doctoral research to a hermeneutic analysis of the notion of sacrifice, addressing the ambiguity between "suppressive" sacrifice and what I came to identify as the kenotic sacrifice of the Christian tradition. One of the chapters of my dissertation was devoted to the notion of sacrifice in Girard's thought, its potential ambiguities, and the corrections that Girard himself made to his original conception of sacrifice. A revised version of my doctoral dissertation was published in Italian in 2004, with the title *Il sacrificio: la ragione e il suo altrove* [Sacrifice: reason and its other], whereas a shorter version of the dissertation's chapter devoted to Girard's thought was published in the form of a journal article.[4] The translation of the most significant portion of that article features in this volume as the first essay in part 2, "Transition: Corrections and Paradoxes." Although it does not contain particularly innovative ideas, I wanted to include it in this volume because it records my admiration for Girard, who had not hesitated to amend his conception of sacrifice when he had realized its insufficiency, and because, at the same time, it marks the transition from, and my personal struggle between, loyalty to his thought on one hand, and my incipient resolution to actively provide my own contribution to the development of mimetic theory on the other. Such resolution marks a kind of *rupture* between the tension connecting mimetic theory and philosophical hermeneutics, which I explored in *Intellectual Sacrifice* from an angle that was still very much internal to Girard's thought, and my subsequent work, in which I strived—not always linearly or straightforwardly—to thematize such tension more explicitly. While the continuity with themes and insights that were present in *Intellectual Sacrifice* does not disappear in my subsequent work, the intention to develop mimetic theory forward becomes, from that essay onward, more prominent. I think both elements are evident in that piece.

In the academic year 2004–5 I was based at Heythrop College, University of London, and in October I was fortunate enough to contribute to the organization of the conference "René Girard: A Celebration," which was hosted by the college. On that occasion, I had the opportunity to meet René Girard face to face for the first time. The three days of the conference were, for me, electrifying. On the second day, I presented a paper that was meant to express the central thesis of my *Intellectual Sacrifice* (with particular emphasis on hermeneutics), and I was at the same time pleased and terrified when I noticed that René Girard had picked up my session and was sitting in the front row.[5] On the evening of the third day, as I was sitting next to him at dinner, I finally found the courage to ask him a question that I had often held back from asking him in our correspondence. I told him that I was working on the thought of the French existentialist philosopher Gabriel Marcel (whom, I had discovered the previous day, Girard had met in France many years earlier) and on philosophical hermeneutics, and that I thought the encounter between mimetic theory and philosophical hermeneutics could generate a form of nonsacrificial philosophy; and then I asked him what he thought about such a project. René remained silent for a few seconds (but it seemed a much longer time to me), and then, in a style that was so typical of him and that his friends and colleagues will not find difficult to recognize, he told me: "Honestly, I don't know. But if you think this is a path that is worth pursuing, I think you should do it."

Retrospectively, I think that the effect of René's words on me was deeper than I expected. Without those words, I do not know whether I could have decided to write the piece that is included as the next chapter of this volume. Originally written as a paper to be presented at the conference "Questioning the Absolute: New Readings of Traditional Arguments for God's Existence," which was hosted by the International Institute for Hermeneutics at Mount Allison University, New Brunswick, in August 2006, and later published in the form of a journal article, this was the first piece in which I was openly critical of an aspect of Girard's thought—specifically, his argument for the divinity of Christ.[6] In the meantime, and without ceasing to research and publish in the field of mimetic theory,[7] I had also started to actively work on a larger project concerning the notion of sacrifice. By then, I was convinced

that mimetic theory had to be complemented with an account of kenotic sacrifice; but I also came to the conclusion that the analyses that I had performed
in my book *Il sacrificio* were not sufficient: I had to retrieve the historical
and theoretical sources of the kenotic conception of sacrifice. I devoted several years to such a project, which eventually resulted in the publication, in
2014, of my book *Sacrifice in the Post-Kantian Tradition*.[8] In the course of
that research, I became convinced of the nexus between kenotic sacrifice and
the perspectivism of the post-Kantian tradition. Simultaneously, it became
inevitable for me to reassess mimetic theory in the light of such analysis, and
to address directly an intuition that I had had for a very long time, namely,
that mimetic theory has its theoretical roots in the tradition of Kantian and
post-Kantian perspectivism. I accomplished that project in a paper entitled
"Mimetic Theory's Post-Kantian Legacy," which I presented at the 2011
meeting of the Colloquium on Violence and Religion, and which is included
in this volume. During all this time, I never forgot my overarching project
of an encounter between mimetic theory and philosophical hermeneutics.
Already present in the form of a tension in my *Intellectual Sacrifice*, and later
invoked in order to contextualize a reinterpretation of Girard's argument for
the divinity of Christ, that project became very prominent again in the context of my analysis of the post-Kantian legacy of mimetic theory. There I felt
the need to go back to the distinction between a theological (or "religious")
hermeneutics and a profane (or "sacred") hermeneutics, and reconsider it in
light of my research on kenosis and (post-Kantian) perspectivism.

Despite my strengthening conviction of the need of an encounter
between mimetic theory and philosophical hermeneutics, I remained hesi-
tant to address that need directly. I must be grateful to my friend and colleague Chris Fleming who, along with his coeditors Joel Hodge and Scott
Cowdell, invited me to contribute papers to two collections on mimetic
theory—the first having an emphasis on politics, the second an emphasis on
the media. Prompted by such invitations, I could test my approach in two
"applied" fields. In 2014 I wrote an essay discussing the book *Hermeneutic
Communism* by Gianni Vattimo and Santiago Zabala (which had appeared
in 2011) and the compatibility of such a project with mimetic theory; and
in 2015 I wrote an essay that addressed the crisis of the self through the
analysis of two American TV series (*Mad Men* and *Homeland*). Such essays,
included in this volume, gave me the opportunity to address more explicitly

the encounter between mimetic theory and philosophical hermeneutics and (especially in the latter) the need for a mimetic hermeneutics of the self. Putting this volume together, I wondered whether I had to rewrite such essays in order to "distill," as it were, their more theoretical content while reducing or even dropping the works from which the discussions of that theoretical content emerged. Eventually, I concluded that this would not be consistent with the true spirit of mimetic theory. Girard taught us that it is often through an analysis of fictional works like the novels of the nineteenth century, or of political/military treatises like Clausewitz's *On War*, that we can achieve the most interesting insights on human nature and cultural transformations. In all humility, I tried to approach the subjects of the encounter between mimetic theory and philosophical hermeneutics on a political level, and of the need for a mimetic hermeneutics of the self, along similar lines.

In the last essay in this volume, I finally address directly and explicitly the encounter between mimetic theory and philosophical hermeneutics. I use the notion of paradox as an entry point for such discussion because, as I was rereading all the other chapters and essays of this volume, it became apparent to me that what I have been trying to do all along has been to make sense of some of the paradoxes stemming from mimetic theory. To make sense, not "to solve" or "to fix" them: there is, in fact, a form of paradox that is the evidence that thought is trying to think something that cannot be thought; a paradox is, therefore, the sign that thought is fulfilling its mission. Hence, the subtitle of this volume: *And Other Mimetic Paradoxes*. In this final essay, I also advance my project of what I call *hermeneutic mimetic theory*, or HMT. I do that not without trepidation, and with the awareness that this contribution to the discipline, regardless of its value (on which it is not up to its proponent to express a judgment), is made possible by standing on the shoulders of a giant—the giant being, of course, Girard himself. But I do that also with the feeling that, in arguing for such a position, I am doing what René recommended to me twelve years ago. I consider HMT to be not an individual but a collective enterprise: something that I would like to develop with all the scholars who think that there is something worth pursuing in this proposal.

René left us on November 4, 2015. The sad news caught me while I was working on this volume. I felt that I had lost an intellectual guide; and I also felt, with sadness but also with determination, that mimetic theory, his great legacy, should now continue its development without him—a feeling that, I am sure, is shared by many, if not all, mimetic theory scholars around the world.

This book is essentially the diary of a journey—my intellectual and existential journey through mimetic theory. It is my hope that, during this journey, I have been able to offer some valuable contribution to the advancement of the discipline. However, as I now reread the final chapter of this book, I realize that even that is nothing but a preliminary account of what HMT could become, or—at best—its research agenda. The work of HMT has just started. But this is consistent with the essence of a true journey. After all, the only true journeys are those in which the destination is only the starting point for a new journey.

NOTES

1. Jacques Guillet, "René Girard et le sacrifice." Études 351 (July 1979): 91–102, 91 (my translation).

2. Matthew Edward Harris, "Metaphysics, Violence and the 'Natural Sacred' in Gianni Vattimo's Philosophy," *Humanicus* 8 (2013), 1–21, 1, 19.

3. Paolo Diego Bubbio, "Il sacrificio intellettuale: René Girard filosofo della religione" [Intellectual sacrifice: René Girard as philosopher of religion], *Filosofia e Teologia* 13, no. 3 (1999): 545–61; Paolo Diego Bubbio, "Ermeneutica: Ancora pensiero sacrificale? Heidegger, Derrida e Ricoeur secondo il pensiero di René Girard" [Hermeneutics: Still sacrificial thought? Heidegger, Derrida and Ricoeur according to René Girard's thought], *Annuario filosofico* 15 (2000): 449–81; Paolo Diego Bubbio, "Il circolo auto-referenziale del Logos sacrificale: Spunti gnoseologici del pensiero di René Girard" [The self-referential circle of sacrificial logos: Gnoseological elements of René Girard's thought], *Filosofia* 51, no. 1 (2000): 36–63.

4. Paolo Diego Bubbio, "Oblazione e paradosso: L'evoluzione del pensiero di René Girard" [Oblation and paradox: The evolution of René Girard's thought], *Iride* 41 (2004): 151–61.

5. Later, that paper was published as "Mimetic Theory and Hermeneutics," *Colloquy: Text Theory Critique* 9 (2005). I am happily surprised to see that, more than ten years later, that paper is still being cited.

6. Paolo Diego Bubbio, "Girard and Anselm: Ontological Argument and Mimetic Theory," *Analecta Hermeneutica* 2 (2010), http://journals.library.mun.ca/ojs/index.php/analecta/article/view/165/108.

7. In 2007, I published a paper entitled "Literary Aesthetics and Knowledge in René Girard's Mimetic Theory," *Literature and Aesthetics* 17, no. 1 (2007): 35–50. This paper basically expanded upon the idea of the self-referentiality of reason, already introduced in my *Intellectual Sacrifice*, but the matter was approached from an aesthetic standpoint. In 2008 I coedited with Silvio Morigi a collection of essays in Italian, *Male e redenzione: Sofferenza e trascendenza in René Girard* [Evil and redemption: Suffering and transcendence in René Girard] (Turin: Edizioni Camilliane, 2008), for which I wrote a chapter entitled "Secolarizzare il male: La teoria mimetica

e *L'adolescente* di Dostoeveskij" [Secularizing evil: Mimetic theory and Dostoyevsky's *The Adolescent*], 17–39. I decided not to include a translation of that piece in the current volume, because it is an essay explicitly devoted to a literary work, and because the theoretical insights that are present in it are more fully developed in "Mimetic Theory's Post-Kantian Legacy" (included in this volume).

8. Paolo Diego Bubbio, *Sacrifice in the Post-Kantian Tradition: Perspectivism, Intersubjectivity, and Recognition* (Albany: SUNY Press, 2014).

Acknowledgments

This book could be considered to be the diary of my twenty-year-long intellectual and existential journey through mimetic theory. During this journey, I have met several mentors, colleagues, and friends who have been great travel companions. It would be impossible to list them all; but I want to mention at least a few of them to whom I feel particularly grateful.

I cannot but start with René Girard himself. As all his friends, colleagues, and even acquaintances know very well, René was not only a great intellectual—an actual genius—but also a wonderful human being. I treasure every letter and every phone call that we exchanged, and every second I was fortunate enough to spend in his company. His ability to listen to everyone, no matter how young or inexperienced, taking into serious consideration what "the other" had to say, was a rare and marvelous gift. I would like to think of this book as being my own tribute to this great man.

Many people played a role in the early stages of my journey through mimetic theory. My friend Stefano Ferrando encouraged me to read *Violence and the Sacred*—and for that I will be eternally grateful to him. Marco Ravera supervised my MA thesis, which was later revised and published as *Il sacrificio intellettuale*. Piero Burzio introduced me to the secondary literature and discussed with me the various conceptual steps of such book, providing numerous insights. Gianni Vattimo found the time to explain his view on Girard's thought to me when I was a very young student; he read my dissertation and encouraged me to submit it for publication.

During the following years, I frequently exchanged ideas with the mimetic theory scholars active in Italy. These include Luigi Alfieri, Federica Casini, Giuseppe Fornari, Alice Gonzi, Silvio Morigi, Alberto Signorini, and Claudio Tarditi. I am particularly grateful to Federica, for her intellectual passion, humor, and grace.

I spent the academic year 2004–5 as Research Fellow at Heythrop College (University of London). I am very grateful to Michael Kirwan for his friendship and for allowing me to contribute to the organization of the conference "René Girard: A Celebration," which, as I mentioned earlier, took place in October 2004. It was a wonderful intellectual experience.

In 2006, I moved to Sydney and I met Chris Fleming. Since then, Chris has been a discussion partner, a friend, and—since I joined Western Sydney University in 2012—a collaborative colleague. I want to thank Chris for his humor and for his generosity in sharing thoughts, ideas, and feedback on my work. Chris was very encouraging when I had doubts about the opportunity to republish my twenty-year-old work *Il sacrificio intellettuale*; he was a very careful reader of its English translation, and he was very helpful in pointing out opacities and hazards that needed to be clarified or overcome.

I thank all the friends of the Australian Girard Seminar, and in particular Joel Hodge and Scott Cowdell, for organizing intellectually challenging events around Australia and for promoting mimetic theory in Australia.

I am also grateful to all the other mimetic theory scholars around the world with whom I have, in some form or another, collaborated in all these years. I cannot name them all, but let me at least mention Jeremiah Alberg, Paul Dumouchel, Eric Gans, and Sandor Goodhart.

I want to express my gratitude to my friend and colleague Dimitris Vardoulakis, who was the first to encourage me to publish a translation of my *Il sacrificio intellettuale* and who, in his capacity as Chair of the Philosophy Research Initiative at Western Sydney University, supported my request for funding so that the translation could be done; and to Professor Peter Hutchings, Dean of the School of Humanities and Communication Arts at Western Sydney University, for approving such a request.

Theodore Ell, in his capacity as translator, has done a marvelous job in rendering my—sometimes convoluted—Italian prose into English. I am grateful for the patience and care he devoted to the translation.

Thanks are also due to William A. Johnsen, editor of the book series Studies in Violence, Mimesis, and Culture at Michigan State University Press, for welcoming this project, for supporting my decision to present it in the form of an intellectual journey, and for his incredible patience in dealing with my multiple delays in delivering the manuscript.

Last but not least, I am grateful to my friends and family, for whom mimetic theory has often become—and not always willingly—an everyday topic of conversation. My wife Silvia, and my children Sofia and Alessandro, are and remain a genuine blessing in my life.

. . .

The chapters that follow recast material that has appeared earlier, often in a different form and language, in other settings. I thank the following journals and publishers for allowing me to republish or draw on that material.

"Part 1: Intellectual Sacrifice" is the translation from the Italian (with small revisions and additions) of my book *Il sacrificio intellettuale: René Girard e la filosofia della religione* (Turin: Quadrante, 1999).

"Transition: Corrections and Paradoxes" is a translation from the Italian of a significant portion of the journal article "Oblazione e paradosso: Fascino e ambiguità nell'evoluzione del pensiero di René Girard," *Iride* 41 (2004): 151–61.

"Girard's Ontological Argument for the Existence of God" is an altered and expanded version of "Girard and Anselm: Ontological Argument and Mimetic Theory," *Analecta Hermeneutica* 2 (2010). A slightly different version of it appeared in Italian as "La teoria mimetica e la prova ontologica dell'esistenza di Dio," in *La pietra dello scandalo: La sfida antropologica del pensiero di René Girard*, edited by Umberto Cocconi and Martino Presenti Gritti (Massa: Transeuropa, 2013), 303–22.

"Mimetic Theory's Post-Kantian Legacy" draws from ideas included in "Prospettivismo e secolarizzazione: L'eredità post-kantiana della teoria mimetica," in *Religioni laicità secolarizzazione: Il cristianesimo come "fine del sacro" in René Girard*, edited by Maria Stella Barberi and Silvio Morigi

(Massa: Transeuropa, 2009), 107–29. In its current form, the chapter is an expanded version of a conference paper in English that I presented at the 2011 meeting of the Colloquium on Violence and Religion, in Salina, Italy.

"Mimetic Theory and Hermeneutic Communism" appeared in *Violence, Desire, and the Sacred*, vol. 2, *Rene Girard and Sacrifice in Life, Love, and Literature*, edited by Joel Hodge, Scott Cowdell, and Chris Fleming (New York: Bloomsbury Academic, 2014), 45–56.

"The Self in Crisis" appeared as "The Self in Crisis: Watching *Mad Men* and *Homeland* with Girard and Hegel," in *Violence, Desire, and the Sacred*, vol. 3, *Mimesis, Movies, and Media*, edited by Joel Hodge, Scott Cowdell, and Chris Fleming (New York: Bloomsbury Academic, 2015), 171–88.

The second section of "Hermeneutic Mimetic Theory," entitled "Mimetic Hermeneutics of the Self," expands on some ideas that also appear in "The Development of the Self," in *Palgrave Handbook of Mimetic Theory and Religion*, edited by James Alison and Wolfgang Palaver (London: Palgrave, 2017).

Abbreviations

Page numbers in citations refer to the English translations.

BE *Achever Clausewitz: Entretiens avec Benoît Chantre* (Paris: Carnets Nord, 2007). Translated by Mary Baker as *Battling to the End: Conversations with Benoît Chantre* (East Lansing: Michigan State University Press, 2010).

DBB *"To Double Business Bound": Essays on Literature, Mimesis and Anthropology* (Baltimore: Johns Hopkins University Press, 1978).

DDN *Mensonge romantique et vérité romanesque* (Paris: Grasset, 1961). Translated by Yvonne Freccero as *Deceit, Desire, and the Novel* (Baltimore: Johns Hopkins University Press, 1965).

ISS *Je vois Satan tomber comme l'éclair.* (Paris: Grasset, 1999). Translated by James G. Williams as *I See Satan Fall Like Lightning.* (Maryknoll, NY: Orbis Books, 2001).

J *La route antique des hommes pervers* (Paris: Grasset, 1985). Translated by Yvonne Freccero as *Job: The Victim of His People* (London: Athlone Press, 1987).

RU   *Dostoevskij: Du double à l'unité* (Paris: Plon, 1963). Translated by
       James G. Williams as *Resurrection from the Underground: Feodor
       Dostoevsky* (East Lansing: Michigan State University Press, 2012).

S   *Le bouc émissaire* (Paris: Grasset, 1982). Translated by Yvonne
       Freccero as *The Scapegoat* (Baltimore: Johns Hopkins University
       Press, 1986).

TE   *Shakespeare: Les feux de l'envie* (Paris: Grasset, 1990). English ver-
       sion, with revisions, by Girard, *A Theater of Envy: William Shake-
       speare* (Oxford: Oxford University Press, 1991).

TH   *Des choses cachées depuis la fondation du monde: Recherches avec
       Jean-Michel Oughourlian et Guy Lefort* (Paris: Grasset, 1978).
       Translated by Stephen Bann and Michael Metteer as *Things
       Hidden since the Foundation of the World: Research Undertaken
       in Collaboration with Jean-Michel Oughourlian and Guy Lefort*
       (Stanford, CA: Stanford University Press, 1987).

VS   *La violence et le sacré* (Paris: Grasset, 1962). Translated by Patrick
       Gregory as *Violence and the Sacred* (Baltimore: Johns Hopkins
       University Press, 1977).

WTTB   *Quand ces choses commenceront . . . Entretiens avec Michel Treguer.*
       (Paris: Arléa, 1994). Translated by Trevor Cribben Merrill as
       When These Things Begin: Conversations with Michel Treguer (East
       Lansing: Michigan State University Press, 2014).

PART 1

Intellectual Sacrifice

1999

Translated from the Italian by Theodore Ell

CHAPTER 1

Intellectual Expulsion

1. The Mechanism of Mimetic Victimage

The theoretical unity of René Girard's mimetic theory relies on the fundamental tenet that every person feels as though she or he is missing "something," a *being* with which others, by contrast, seem to be endowed by nature.

If the subject desires to be something *more*, it is because there is a model, an *other* who seems to personify this *being* of which the subject feels deprived. The best metaphor for expressing this triple relation of disciple-model-object is the triangle. Indeed, according to Girard, the preliminary stage of every subjective behavior moves via a "third element," an object, which will determine the target of the subject's desire. The corners of the resulting triangle are occupied by the subject, by the object, and by this "third element," the model, which, by virtue of its own potentiality, Girard calls the "mediator."

The object appears to the subject-disciple to constitute the sign of success; this, however, is an illusion, generated by the fact that the object is possessed, or at least desired, by the model-mediator, and thus has no value beyond its relation to that model. The disciple will therefore remain disappointed, for it is not the possession of the object that can bestow the *being* that the subject feels she or he lacks. However, this will almost never cause the subject to question the model. If anything, it will intensify the subject's sense of inferiority: she will conclude that she has made some sort of error, having not imitated the model well enough, and will convince herself that a perfect imitation will unquestionably endow her with this *being*. The subject, wishing to be what the model is, will wish to have what the model has, and will desire what the model desires. This confluence of desires onto identical objects will generate rivalry between disciple and model.

It is therefore possible to speak of *metaphysical desire* insofar as desire no longer has an object—or at least the object endures only as a sign that leads back to the mediator—and aspires to nothing specific, transcending instead the objective dimension to refer exclusively to the *being* of the model. Metaphysical desire is extraordinarily contagious: every individual may become the mediator of her or his neighbor without realizing the role she or he is performing, and can therefore find her- or himself being a rival without having done anything—apparently—to provoke this rivalry.[1] In short, the model is an object of hatred, qua persecutor, and indissolubly also an object of love, qua possessor of the desired *being*.

The subject desires the object because the object is also desired by the rival: the rival is the subject's model on the plane of desire; and it is this mimetic desire that produces conflict. The significance of the *being* that everybody seeks, but that nobody possesses, is violence. In the convergence of mimetic desires, each subject equates the *being* that is at stake with the violence of every other subject (the violence with which everybody defends the possessed object). In the course of this process, there arises what Girard calls, using a psychiatric expression, *cyclothymia*: each subject lives her or his own moment too intensely to comprehend reciprocity. Every subject feels able to master violence, insofar as she or he feels extraneous to it; but on the contrary, it is violence that masters every subject and generates violent reciprocity. Each subject sees in the other the sole perpetrator of the crisis, while in reality everybody is responsible for it. At the paroxysm of crisis, how is it possible to restore a unity that has been completely undone?

If violence renders everyone the same, anyone may become the double of any other, and thus an object of universal hatred. Thus, human beings choose a scapegoat or victim. It is important that the victim be similar to those she substitutes, without leading to a catastrophic confusion caused by pure assimilation. This extraneousness of the scapegoat, although it originates from some distinguishing characteristics of the victim, only becomes established in the act of expulsion itself. The scapegoat is therefore fully loaded with violence and expelled, and if all truly believe the scapegoat to be solely responsible for the violence that is threatening the community, all are effectively liberated from that violence through the scapegoat's expulsion.

Since the expulsion of the victim restores peace, it is the victim—the scapegoat—who is credited with the beneficial ending of the crisis. The victim therefore becomes a kind of supernatural creature, sowing violence to reap peace. If discord causes disgrace, and sacrifice restores lost peace, then sacrifice is the source of all fruitfulness.

The set of actions aimed at preventing violence constitutes the sphere of religion. Thus, violence coincides with the sacred. This is the explanation for the paradoxical nature of sacrifice, at once a culpable and deeply sacred act. The religious moment liberates human beings from the suspicions that would poison them if they were to recall the crisis as it really unfolded. Violence and the sacred fundamentally coincide.

Religious rites are attempts to provide a "technique" for catharsis. The ritual victim is a substitute neither for a sole member of the community nor for all members, but for the victim of the original expulsion. There is, in other words, a first substitution, which we may call original, in which the victim does substitute for the whole community, and a second substitution, which we may call ritual, in which the place of the original victim is taken by a member of some sacrificeable category. Ritual substitution is aimed at perpetuating the beneficial effects of the original expulsion. Human beings would not succeed in placing their own violence outside themselves if there were no expiatory victim to expel, and indeed they could not expel the victim if they were conscious of the *transfer* of violence from them onto the victim. The effectiveness of any sacrifice therefore depends on misrecognition (*méconnaissance*).

If mimetic victimage lies at the basis of all cultures, then it is also possible to trace all myths back to it. Common to many myths is the negative connotation of the scapegoat (the "eliminated fragment"), and the positive connotation of elimination itself, which generally takes the form of a collective expulsion. Indeed, more or less organized forms of lynching feature in the majority of myths. In fact the true project of mythology is to collectively recall foundational crises and lynchings, that is, the sequence of events that constitute or reconstruct a cultural order.

If behind all mythical and ritual meanings it is possible to trace the violence that we may rightfully call foundational, it is, on the other hand, impossible to retrieve a myth that reproduces original violence in every detail, because misrecognition constitutes a fundamental dimension of the religious (victimization can have beneficial effects only if all believe that it does). Every demystification of the system is already its dismantling. The abundance of fraternal conflicts that feature in Greek tragedies, for example, confirms the presence of a sacrificial crisis, which generally involves brothers brought together and then divided by something that both desire.

The disintegration of the sacrificial system appears as a fall back into reciprocal violence. Sacrificial crisis means first of all the loss of differences—that is, violent confusion. In the evolution from ritual to secular institutions, human beings distance themselves from essential violence, but never break away from it.[2]

The equivalent of myths for an epoch that may no longer be chronologically close to the birth of its culture is constituted by texts of persecution. Examples of texts of persecution are some medieval documents that refer to acts of collective violence that occurred during the Black Death, in the middle of the fifteenth century, and to ordeals of *auto-da-fé* imposed on Jews accused of spreading the plague. The only difference between these texts of persecution and myths is that here the sacralization of the victim is entirely absent or scarcely suggested. This difference derives from the fact that the demystification of persecution is an exclusive development of the modern Western world. Societies that possess texts of mystification do not possess properly defined myths; societies that possess myths do not possess texts of persecution. In primitive societies, it is the notion of persecution itself that is absent; violence always has an aura of sacredness. A society that produces texts of persecution is already a society on the path to desacralization. Our present situation represents an intermediate state between the sacralizing misapprehension of primitive societies and a practically accessible knowledge. This intermediate state consists of a limited recognition of mimetic victimage, which never fully comprehends its foundational role of the originary lynching for the establishment of human civilization.

Sacrificial crises, however, have not occurred only in the remote past. If in texts of persecution up to the fifteenth and sixteenth centuries the presence of innocent and, to a degree, arbitrary scapegoats is more apparent, it is only because today we face persecutors who are clever enough to leave no trace of their crimes.

If we are now able to analyze and to "dismantle" cultural mechanisms, that is because of the indirect and imperceptible but extraordinarily binding influence that Judeo-Christian Scripture exerts upon us. Although undoubtedly there are numerous resemblances between biblical myths and all other myths, what seems equally indubitable to Girard is the distinctiveness of biblical myths. In the Bible we witness an effort to trace a way back to origins and to return to the establishing *transfers*, to discredit and destroy them—to contradict and demystify myths. But the full revelation of foundational murder comes only in the Gospels. They present Jesus Christ as the innocent victim of a collective in crisis that rediscovers unity by scapegoating him.

The Gospels revolve around the Passion of Christ, or rather around the same drama that is present in every mythology in the world: the collective murder of a scapegoat. The Gospels are not, however, myths in the sense described above, because the Gospels direct responsibility for the violence to the persecutors and not to the victim. Such a "deconstruction" reveals the foundational mechanism and leaves human beings without sacrificial protection, prey to the ancient mimetic discord that is free to take its typically modern form: each person assigns to her or his neighbor the responsibility for persecutions and injustices, whose universality she or he begins to glimpse, but without being prepared to assume her or his own responsibility. The Gospels are no longer part of mythology, because with increasing eloquence they resist the sacred ambivalence and reveal the arbitrariness of the violence to which the victim is subjected.[3]

In an anthropological sense, then, the Gospels fulfill an essential role inasmuch as they shed light on the crisis that jeopardizes the whole representation of persecution when the mechanisms that support it begin to be revealed. The Gospels keep showing us what persecutors attempt to suppress—that is, the fact that their victim is a scapegoat. The Passion of Christ makes visible that which must remain invisible if such powers are to sustain themselves: mimetic victimage. The violent order of culture that is revealed in the Gospels, and primarily in the Passion, cannot survive its own disclosure.

It is necessary, however, to formulate a nonsacrificial reading of the Gospels. According to Girard, the Passion is presented in the Gospels as an act that does bring about the salvation of humanity, but that is not a sacrifice in the sense mentioned above. Jesus provides violence with the most perfect victim imaginable, the victim whom violence has most reason to choose: the most innocent. Jesus, in effect, stands as the expiatory victim par excellence, the most arbitrary because the least violent.

It is on these grounds that Girard draws an argument for Christ's divinity. To denounce the mechanism one must be outside it; someone is needed who owes nothing to violence, who does not think according to its norms, and who is entirely extraneous to it, when the whole of humanity is caught in its ambit. The fact that the Gospels enclose a genuine knowledge of violence and the way it works shows that such knowledge cannot be merely human in origin.

If the God of victims intervenes in the world in favor of victims, the outcome of that undertaking cannot be a victory: all that can happen to a victim is what happens to Jesus, to Job, and to all prophets. Rather than inflicting violence, Christ prefers to suffer it. Christ is the God of victims primarily in the sense that he shares their fate in its entirety. This seems to be a failure, but it transforms immediately into a victory.

In fact, the violent order of culture revealed in the Gospels and primarily in the Passion cannot survive its own revelation. Sooner or later, then, that which Christianity has fermented in culture must bring about the collapse of societies that it has penetrated, including those that are apparently grounded on Christian principles, so-called Christian societies, which effectively depend on the revelation of the Gospels, but do so in an ambiguous way because of a partial misunderstanding of the Christian principles, a misunderstanding that is necessarily sacrificial and rooted in the deceptive resemblance of the Gospels to mythological religious texts.

The Paraclete, the Spirit of truth as presented in the Gospel according to St. John, represents the knowledge that ever more progressively irrupts into the world, continuing the revelation of Christ. Even if the victory of Jesus is achieved immediately, from the beginning, in the moment of the Passion—the reality of the roles of victims and persecutors is clearly established—it is only made real for the majority of humanity at the end of a long history secretly governed by revelation and guided by the Spirit of truth.

2. "Religion" and "Philosophy"

Girard's theory explicitly asks to be considered in a scientific way and to acquire universal application. Such demands are, in fact, one and the same: a theory can only be scientific if it is valid for all observable phenomena—if, in other words, it is universally valid; only when this is the case is it possible to qualify a theory with the scientific label.

According to Girard, collective violence toward the originary victim constitutes not merely a fact, but the central event in the birth of civilizations. The applicability of mimetic victimage in all fields of cultural knowledge thus constitutes the conditio sine qua non of the validity of Girard's theory: either this is always valid, or it is never valid.

There have been numerous attempts to apply mimetic theory to various fields of knowledge: literary criticism, psychology, economics, and anthropology, just to mention a few. Contributions in the sphere of philosophy are rarer, probably because of Girard's unorthodox formation and his problematic affirmations of the "death of philosophy."

In the first part of the current volume, I apply mimetic theory to the philosophy of religion, to verify the cogency of Girard's hypothesis in this field, and to establish whether such an application can yield significant results. It is possible to attempt such an application thanks to the universal ambitions of Girard's theory in other fields: aesthetics, the philosophy of history, the philosophy of law, and political philosophy. My choice of the philosophy of religion is not arbitrary, however, and I believe the reason will become clear as the work proceeds.

The first step will be to clarify what Girard means by "religion" and "philosophy."

2.1. "Religion"

The expulsion of a scapegoat restores peace to a community. In order for such a miracle to happen again, thus preventing the community from sliding into the chaos of violence, two developments are necessary. The first is the conceptualization of the expulsion of the victim, with the aim of being able to repeat it; the second is the expression of that expulsion, with the aim of agreeing upon its details with other members of the community. Reason and language are generated in this way.

The expulsion is repeated by continually substituting new scapegoats for the original victim: it is this that generates rites. Sacrifice will become ever less gruesome, and rites will ever less recall the foundational event, the more chronologically distant we are removed from it. On the other hand, the memory of that experience will be preserved in narratives that are more or less explicit in recalling the foundational event: myths.

Rites and myths constitute the backbone of every religion—which thus is nothing but a complex of actions carried out to reiterate a victim's expulsion, so as to enjoy once again its beneficial effects—and of narratives whose purpose is to guarantee the good results of the sacrifice. Since rites and myths are no more than the perpetuation and mystification of mimetic victimage, the sacredness at the heart of every religion is nothing but the cloak of violence, which is the pivot of mimetic victimage itself.

The sacrificial nature of every religion, then, is beyond doubt. Since scapegoating can function only if human beings are unaware of it, it is evident that sacrifice as a particular act (expulsion) and the sacred more generally (everything surrounding the scapegoat) will always present themselves in the most dissimilar way possible from their actual nature: the community of persecutors may say that the scapegoat has been struck not by human violence but by divine vengeance, that he was a blasphemer (as Job's so-called friends declare, for instance). When the moment comes to invest the scapegoat with supernatural powers, it may be said that she has been pardoned, that divinity itself has chosen her for this role. In short, the facts will be presented in a light that, far from showing them in their violent nature, makes them appear as a divine rebuke. Only the desacralizing discourse that speaks of the scapegoat openly can reveal the lie that is hidden in the sacred discourse that is common to all religions.

Christianity, however, constitutes an exception. Inasmuch as it is based on a message of demystification, Christianity has nothing to do with the sacredness present in all religions. Indeed, Christ, in suffering a collective lynching but refusing the role of scapegoat, reveals the truth of mimetic victimage. However, even if the Christian message is safe from accusations of mystification—and indeed it constitutes the most perfect work of demystification—Christian *religion* is not safe from such accusations. If Christianity was capable of constituting itself as a religion, with a substantial sacred core, it is precisely because of a partial involution that led to the conceiving of the death of Christ as a sacrifice, to the conceiving of the Father as a bloodthirsty god who requires his Son's death in order to save humanity, and the conceiving of self-sacrifice as an act of holiness. Without entering into deeper analysis, these few indications are enough to establish beyond doubt the sacrificial nature of Christian religion in Girard's thought.

Religion is therefore one of the main instruments suitable for the perpetuation of mimetic victimage.

2.2. "Philosophy"

The positioning of philosophy within mimetic theory may seem problematic at first, but the problem is not as substantial as it appears. Girard takes almost for granted the identical nature of religion and philosophy in relation to sacrifice: "The processes of discrimination, exclusion, and conjunction are the products of the generative process. They are applied first to this same process, and this application gives rise to religious thought. But they do not confine themselves to religious thought alone; they are the mechanism for all orders of thought" (VS, 236).

First, philosophy, in the dominant tradition of Western thought from Plato onward, is the reasoned investigation of the nature, scope, and possibility of knowledge, and we have established earlier that reason is a faculty that arises in order to conceptualize the expulsion of victims. The sacrificial nature of philosophy thus seems to derive directly from its own definition.

There exists an even more cogent argument, however, that also demonstrates the sacrificial nature of philosophy, and it concerns the relation between philosophy and mythology. Girard considers myths to be essential in every culture (their presence wherever human communities exist is, in any case, a fact). They are narratives, created a posteriori, of past sacrificial crises. Once the last sacrificial crisis has become chronologically distant, the mythical-ritual system loses effectiveness and no longer functions, while in parallel certain truths of mimetic victimage begin to emerge (this is what we see represented, for example, in Greek tragedies). Mythical justifications of the expulsion of victims appear unpleasant, in that they portray events that recall too closely what the community is now reliving. Thus, myths are changed and made more harmonious with the new mentality. According to Girard, we may speak of a true "history of mythology" (see S, 76–79) whose first stage is the concealment that aims to erase the foundational murder from collective memory, and whose next stage is Plato's aversion to traditional myths. Plato believed that myths should be forbidden because the truths that they express had become intolerable and the society in which he lived did not have the energy to conceal them. Girard writes: "The Platonic stage, as opposed to the preceding one, does not culminate in an actual re-creation of myth, though it is just as fundamental. Another culture is founded, no longer truly mythological but 'rational' and 'philosophical'" (S, 77).

The expulsion of myths is therefore nothing less than the intellectualized version of original violence—and it is with this expulsion that, significantly, Western culture is born. Cultures seek new justifications of the expulsion of victims, and find them in philosophy.[4]

As myths are misapprehended and conceal the presence of the victim—the mediator loved and hated at the same time—so philosophies also conceal the presence of the mediator. And this concealment is even more deceitful, for while religions connect violence to sacredness and attribute it to a divinity that alone rules the destinies of all human beings, philosophies are generally inclined to defend an illusory autonomy of humanity: "Subjectivisms and objectivisms, romanticisms and idealisms, individualisms and scientisms, idealisms and positivisms appear to be in opposition but are secretly in agreement to conceal the presence of the mediator. . . . They all depend directly or indirectly on the lie of spontaneous desire. They all defend the same illusion of autonomy to which modern man is passionately devoted" (DDN, 16).

What is more, history itself demonstrates a link between metaphysical systems and violence. Such *intellectual* violence is expressed in the very nature of metaphysics, which suppresses and rejects any other perspective and point of view. However, intellectual violence is also the real and concrete violence that stems from philosophical systems when they find expression in the cultural configurations each society incarnates. As such it is a violence that is often not exclusively intellectual, but which is also transmitted practically into the societies in which those philosophical messages rule.

Philosophy therefore hides not only a mythical aspect—the narrative of a past sacrificial crisis and at the same time a justification for the expulsion of victims—but also a ritual aspect: it perpetuates the expulsion of a substitute victim on an intellectual plane. Philosophy incorporates within itself the two pillars of the sacrificial mechanism, which in religion are separate: myth and ritual.

It is clear, then, that philosophy performs the same *function* as religion. Philosophy also has the same *origin* as religion: "Philosophy stands in the same relation to the primitive sacralizing features of violence as 'metaphysical' desire does to the mimetic frenzy induced by the gods of violence" (TH, 296).

One objection that could be made against such arguments is that, if philosophy truly did fulfill the same role as religion, philosophy should also have the sacred at the center of its reflections, where violence lies hidden; but this does not always occur, and in any case it does not occur in modern philosophy, which in fact comes into being as a move away from religion. We may respond to this objection by underlining the paradoxical nature of the process of desacralization that modern philosophy undertakes. In fact it is quite easy to recognize how even the most desacralizing philosophies end up making reference to a new sacred. In overthrowing old transcendences, they designate new ones. The sacred is everything that belongs to the scapegoat, to the loved and hated rival, and it is precisely this love-hatred that creates the sacred. At the moment when the subject abandons a model that has led to disappointment, this ceases to be sacred, but sacredness itself does not disappear: it reappears very quickly as an attribute of a new model that—the subject is self-deludingly sure—will not disappoint in the way the previous one did. It is here that the paradox of the desacralization process lies.[5]

This conclusion may be confirmed with the illustration of two cases; their distinctiveness derives from the fundamental role they perform in philosophy. These cases concern two thinkers who might be considered alien to any suspicion of positing the sacred at the center of their reflections. The first of these philosophers is Descartes, universally regarded as the founder of modern philosophy. The second is Nietzsche, whom many credit with having brought that tradition to a close. From the point of view of mimetic theory, it is evident that both are situated historically in moments of transition; they are at once narrators and protagonists of sacrificial crises. Now, there is one phenomenon that may be perceived at the paroxysm of mimetic crises: the monstrous double.[6] This is the name Girard applies to every phenomenon of hallucination provoked, in the paroxysm of crisis, by monstrous reciprocity. The monster substitutes everything that each subject wishes simultaneously to absorb and destroy—that is, the monster substitutes the rival. Because during the crisis each subject is a rival to every other subject, each is also the double of every other, which in fact precipitates hallucinatory experiences of doubling. Let us consider the passage in which Girard examines the words of Georges Poulet on Baillet's biography of Descartes:

> We turn to the biography of Baillet, as does Georges Poulet in his *Etudes sur le temps humain*,[7] in order to set in relief all the self-divisions that the Cartesian experience involves. This critic shows us that "in the intoxication of Descartes, there is . . . a shadow side and there is a light side. . . . These two sides are . . . tragically dissociated." The mind of the philosopher is affected by a "pendulum movement"; it suffers from the alternate swings of "cyclothymia." Poulet speaks even of the "enemy brother" whom the philosopher harbors in his breast. He describes "the great misfortune of a time torn between a mind which is situated in nontemporal reality and the remainder who live only an obscure and indistinct duration." Beside the "dominating" Descartes here is a Descartes "swept off his route by a power that dominates him and transcends him." This is to say that "we enter into that dark country of anxiety . . . which subsists subterraneously in us and whose action upon us never ceases." It should be understood that this experience of the underground division is strictly bound to what is most fundamental in the philosopher's conduct. "One in its goal, his research was double in its method." (RU, 91)

By invoking the "self-divisions that the Cartesian experience involves," Girard here clearly refers to the emergence of the phenomenon of doubles. To detect the presence of the monstrous double not only in the biography of the founder of modern rationalism, but in the very act of founding that philosophy (in much the same way as Girard does when he underlines that the *method*, the most distinctive element of the Cartesian project, yields to a cyclothymic doubling), is a clear equivalent to implying it is sacrificial.

A similar argument can be made about Nietzsche:[8] his own madness may be said to have originated once again from the unsustainability of a doubling that had reached its limit. In particular, Girard's attention turns to an episode that occurred in January 1883—at least five years before signs of Nietzsche's madness appeared—and more precisely to the famous Rapallo vision, which provided Nietzsche with the character of Zarathustra: "On the route to Portofino the writer saw his hero appear and pass him without saying a word to him. Nietzsche evoked this strange event in a poem that lets no doubt exist concerning the nature of the experience: 'Then, suddenly friend! one became two!— / And Zarathustra passed by me'" (RU, 92).

For Girard, this episode indicates the extent to which Nietzsche's philosophy is filled with images of the monstrous double. Nietzsche's work corresponds to a moment of crisis within philosophy itself—which is hence revealed once more as a sacrificial cultural form. What is more, this assertion is a clear pleonasm, since, given the presuppositions discussed above, to say "cultural" is the equivalent of saying "sacrificial": to define philosophy as a cultural form means immediately linking it back to mimetic victimage.

As a form of mystification, philosophy will never arrive at revealing the truth of the scapegoat, exactly as we cannot expect a ceremonial ritual, whose only purpose is to perpetuate the original expulsion of a victim, to unveil the mechanisms that have produced it: "Ritual thought can never fully grasp its own origin, which is perpetuated in philosophical thought and, today, in the social sciences that have inherited the powers of rite as well as its basic importance" (J, 97).

Philosophy is structurally incapable of leading back to the mechanism that produced it. Philosophy represents the move from an ostensive to a declarative attitude; accordingly, philosophy dematerializes the desired object. This seems to solve the problem of mimetic rivalry; considered as an object of desire, truth is something that all competing subjects can have access to. However, the mythical aspect does not disappear, because it is constitutive of philosophy; and the solution that philosophy presents is only a temporary one.

The structural incapacity of philosophy to lead back to the mechanism that produced it does not, however, preclude the possibility that subversive flashes of truth may emerge from within it. This may happen in two ways.

First, truth may be brought to light by means of a work that we may define as textual archaeology, which is carried out on mystificatory texts. Just as a crude or clumsy lie unconsciously indicates the truth that it wishes to hide, and just as accounts of the medieval Inquisition appear to our eyes to be narratives of sacrificial persecution, so a philosophy may reveal, almost as a photographic *negative*, the workings of its own mechanism, precisely while it seeks to conceal them in every possible way. In other words, philosophy plays the same role as texts of persecution: a purely conceptual operation might well point to something that is intended to be hidden, precisely because it does not address it. It is clear, however, that this is possible only if the analyzing subject has grasped at least a grain of truth, on the basis of which it is possible to follow the traces of mystification. (It is evident to us today that witches were not responsible for epidemics of the plague, but this was not evident for a person living in the eleventh century.)

Second, demystificatory truth may appear *positively* where we assume the point of view of the victim, rather than that of the persecutors; we know that this occurs in some books of the Old Testament and in a complete and revelatory way in the Gospels. But we also know that for Girard this revelation is not complete once and for all: the promise that Christ makes, in the Gospel according to St. John, to send the Paraclete, the "Spirit of truth," is kept. Thanks to the unceasing combined and indissoluble action of the text of the Gospels and of the Spirit, human beings increasingly come to understand truth, reject falsehood and assume the point of view of the victim; the very evolution of the social sciences may be traced back to the action of the Paraclete. Therefore we should not be surprised that philosophy increasingly does lead to greater comprehension of certain phenomena, without, however, entirely grasping their common roots in mimetic victimage, just as the ministers of a rite may fleetingly comprehend the reasons behind certain gestures but will never comprehend the global sense of what they are doing, insofar as they cannot grasp its sacrificial nature.

3. A Philosophy of Religion?

3.1. Intellectual Symbolism

There is an interpretative approach to Girard's anthropological findings that has not yet been sufficiently explored. This is the examination of the workings of mimesis, not in their configuration in sociological terms (or at least not only in that), but in their articulation on the intellectual plane—that is, in addressing the violence stemming from the endless debates between disciplines and intellectual adversaries. One perspective does not exclude another, but rather one integrates the other. And as far as our inquiry is concerned, this reciprocal integration neatly defines the search for those elements of the philosophy of religion that are mystificatory, and those elements that, in the end, are revelatory.

In this sense, the aspect of Girard's thesis that is most productive and open to development is the substantial homogeneity of philosophy and religion: mimesis constitutes a basis on which religion and philosophy must stand to be significant in relation to the system of which they are an integral part and to the establishment of which, at the same time, they have contributed. Mimesis, therefore, plays an important role in the relationship between religion and philosophy, which is also to say that every philosophy of religion, insofar as it is *symbolic*, is also mimetic. By "symbolic" here I mean those forms of communication and signification that are characteristic of the human in its uniqueness, and through which humans are able to transmute something concrete in the realm of abstract thought—as they do by transmuting victimary violence in religion and in philosophy.

To consider the philosophy of religion is to consider the relationship that exists between religion and philosophy. The problem is therefore the nature of that relationship, the determination of what kind of relationship could exist between these two symbolic-cultural forms.

To address this problem it is essential to clarify that, for Girard, violence does not necessarily mean force. If force is the most evident form of violence, indeed chronologically the first to become manifest, violence nonetheless transmits itself in a multiplicity of channels:

> Force is only the crudest weapon available to consciousnesses drawn up against each other and consumed by their own nothingness. Deprive them of this weapon . . . and they will make others such as past centuries were not able to foresee. They will choose new areas of combat, like impenitent gamblers whom paternal legislation cannot protect from themselves, for with every restriction they invent new ways of losing their money. . . . They will always get on together just enough to enable them never to agree. They will adapt themselves to the circumstances which seem least propitious to discord and they will never tire of inventing new forms of conflict. (DDN, 110–11)

In all of Girard's work, the only form of relationship that exists in the world is (more or less) violent mimeticism,[9] but the subjects of such a relationship always appear as individuals or as assemblages of individuals, not as intellectual forms. Might not this objection disqualify my argument before it even begins?

To this objection it is possible to reply that if it is true that subjects are always individuals, their relationship, once it is ritualized, and insofar as they are violently mimetic, is always intellectual (at least at a very elementary level), because such a relationship needs to be thought in order to be perpetuated; furthermore, even the expulsion of the scapegoat may sometimes be achieved in an intellectual mode. Girard remarks: "The generative principle cannot be subverted. As soon as anything appears that might uproot it or make it seem illusory . . . the mechanism of elimination is set in motion, either in a primitive physical form . . . or in a derived, attenuated and intellectualized form" (J, 123).

The mimetic-scapegoating relationship is therefore always intellectual in nature and sometimes also in its conclusion. However, to apply mimetic victimage to the philosophy of religion we must consider religion and philosophy as subjects by the same standards as individuals or groups of individuals. Is this permissible?

The response to this hypothetical but legitimate objection is as follows: behind every philosophy (but also, for Girard, behind every religion)[10] there is always an individual or a group of individuals. Now, human beings enact their mimetic relationships by means of the particular sociocultural forms of their milieu: this is true of religion and is therefore equally true of philosophy. Cultural and intellectual forms are therefore instruments for humanity's use; in particular, we have seen how religion and philosophy serve to perpetuate mimetic victimage. In following the development of Girard's thought, we have also seen how the coming of Christ made sacrificial expulsion more difficult: indeed, the demystification of the Gospels showed the real truth of the victim, making the role of persecutor far less popular.

My hypothesis is that after the coming of Christ, religion and philosophy, which are sacrificial instruments from their moment of origin, serve to channel mimetic conflicts together with their violent resolutions—conflicts that, actualized by force, would appear too evident to a consciousnesses no longer blind to the truth of victims. In this process, *the mechanism perpetuates itself, in less evident forms*, in what one may define as an *intellectual symbolism.*[11] Sacrificial symbolism designates the totality of signs that is the expression of mimetic victimage: by intellectual symbolism, I mean the same totality of signs as they present themselves in a particular age of human history—that which we usually refer to as "Western civilization" (from ancient Greek culture onward). In this age, in fact, mimetic victimage uses religion and philosophy not only as instruments for perpetuating the beneficial effects of sacrifice, but also as substitute subjects in the victimage relationship itself—and in so doing, it camouflages itself. In other words, *the "being" that is the only sign of victory is incarnated in religion and philosophy to such a degree that mimetic conflicts determine the genesis of an intellectual symbolism, which thus also remains sacrificial.* What is more, Girard himself underlines that victims substitute an original scapegoat: hence, we should recognize *the possibility of substituting the original victim with intellectual scapegoats*, such as ideas, disciplines, or texts.[12]

In addition, it should be kept in mind that, after the Christian revelation, it is more and more difficult for sacrificial crises to find a proper resolution. Specific crises can, of course, still be resolved according to the usual pattern of scapegoating (the victim expelled and then sacralized); at a more general level, however, there is a massive sacrificial crisis, in which the emptying or even the scapegoating of the Christian revelation itself is at stake. From this point of view, the entire history of Western civilization after the Christian revelation is the history of a (seemingly endless) succession of sacrificial crises that never find a proper resolution. And since these crises cannot find a proper resolution, they follow one another, becoming more intense as we approach modernity, each time escalating the violence involved in them— because each time they get closer and closer to the truth of mimetic violence. Such sacrificial crises express themselves through concrete individuals, but insofar as truth is what is at stake, they also express themselves on the level of intellectual symbolism.

It is possible to show the consistency of this hypothesis with Girard's mimetic theory through a consideration of those parts of his work where he focuses on the climax of this process of intellectual symbolization of mimetic victimage, which is constituted by the sacrificial expulsion of, not so much a symbolic-ritual form such as religion or philosophy elevated to the status of a subject, but truth itself: "The monster is always expelled in sacrificial rituals, first in person, and later *in purely intellectual operations*; for it is a waste of time, we are told, to think what is contrary to the laws of thought" (TH, 60; emphasis added).

Therefore, the expulsion of a victim can be an intellectual operation and the victim can be truth itself elevated to the status of a subject. But if truth can be considered by the same standards as a victim, to the point of being expelled during a purely intellectual sacrificial crisis, there is no reason why religion and philosophy may not assume the same role, as subjects and victims, in a mimetic process.

Religion and philosophy, each time they come into relationship, repeat, in a more or less conscious and evident way, the same game of circular mimesis. The scapegoat that was once expelled physically is now expelled from a text; and while this expulsion is an intellectual one, it nonetheless attains real effects. Such a reading of mimetic theory thus leads us to consider *intellectual expulsion as the foundational event of philosophy itself.*[13] From Thales of Miletus onward, the entire history of philosophy can be read as a succession of such intellectual expulsions, with every philosopher grounding her or his thought on the expulsion, or scapegoating, of some if not of all of her or his predecessors. Plato's famous "parricide" of Parmenides can be regarded as the paradigmatic instance of such a dynamic.

With the confirmation that symbolic-cultural forms may be considered parts of an intellectual symbolism that is still (and indeed in large part) sacrificial, we arrive at the following hypothesis for reading Girard's work: *it is possible to demonstrate the role of mimetic victimage in the historical unfolding of philosophical doctrines.* The clarification and verification of this hypothesis will be the main concern of the rest of the first part of the current volume, which will be devoted, in the following two chapters, to the chosen sphere of development, that is, the philosophy of religion.

In this sense, the philosophy of religion becomes a sort of privileged category, thanks to the intrinsic possibility of a content that simultaneously hides and reveals itself. In other words, for reasons that I will try to illuminate, it becomes the privileged field of mystification for mimesis, but, for that very reason, also the privileged field of its revelation, in the problematic identity of its two terms. The project on which we are embarking may be considered successful if it demonstrates the relevance of these hypotheses.

3.2. Hessen's Scheme

Thus far, we have remained in the sphere of the results obtained from Girard's mimetic theory, partially radicalizing them, perhaps emphasizing certain aspects more than others, but without ever venturing outside the horizons of Girard's work itself—which is what I am now going to do. This undertaking still hinges on the principle of coherence with the fundamental framework of mimetic theory as it has been outlined by Girard. However, I have chosen to explore the relevance of Girard's thought in relation to the philosophy of religion, which again raises the question of whether Girard can legitimately be considered to be a philosopher of religion—or even a philosopher *tout court*.

We may avoid answering that question by arguing that Girard's thought is remarkably fruitful independently of the disciplinary label that one might use to define it. Beyond any labels that could be applied to Girard's thought, and beyond its claim of scientific truthfulness, I think that the way in which it draws attention to the sacrificial nature of symbolic-cultural forms undoubtedly constitutes the result of a philosophical endeavor, to the point that it is now almost impossible to conceive of the categories of "religious" and "philosophical" without referring to the conclusions that Girard has reached. From the religious point of view, he has outlined the process of the demystification of the sacred, a demystification that has led him to recognize in Christianity the only nonsacrificial faith, and also the only one that is truly demystifying. From the philosophical point of view, Girard has argued that philosophy, as an intellectual-sacrificial form, is destined to disappear (the "death of philosophy"; see TH, 438); but in doing so he has also opened *the possibility, at least as a hypothesis, of a nonsacrificial knowledge* that does not, so to speak, enter into the semantic area of sacrifice-rite-mystification, but into that of secularization-revelation-unveiling.

That Girard may not be a philosopher of religion in the strict sense, or that the expression "philosophy of religion" is not found in his work, for me counts less than the fact that his work still lends itself to a reading that leads precisely in that direction. The most general reason why I feel authorized to make this claim lies in the substantial homogeneity that Girard perceives and claims to exist between religion and philosophy, and that I am about to examine in the field that supposedly embraces both: the philosophy of religion.

Surrounding the notion of "philosophy of religion" there is some troubling uncertainty, and it will therefore be useful to seek a point of view that on the one hand is the most general possible, and that on the other takes into account the mimetic setting in which we are working. I propose to use, as a general framework for the application of mimetic theory to the philosophy of religion, the scheme provided by Johannes Hessen.[14] Hessen argues that historically either religion or philosophy has been dominant in the philosophy of religion.

Religion can assume logical precedence: in this case it may take either of two typologies, according to whether the religious is presented as a historically or psychologically grounded given (philosophy of religious experience), or whether it proceeds intuitively, seeking its legitimation phenomenologically (the intuitive typology).

Logical precedence, however, may also shift to philosophy, which in its own turn may be defined in a speculative or critical sense. Thus this will lead to either a philosophy that subjects religion to the norms of its own system (the speculative sense), or to a philosophy that aims at the discovery of the origins of religion, the clarification of its essence and the explication of its functions (the critical sense).

Beyond these rigorous distinctions indicated by Hessen, I will use his scheme only as a perspective from which to observe the role of mimetic victimage in the context of the philosophy of religion. Reworking this scheme in light of Girard's thought, I will attempt to indicate certain examples of what we may now call "intellectual sacrifice" (resolutions of sacrificial crises in which the role of the victim is assigned to a symbolic-cultural form). When religion assumes logical precedence, we will recognize in the corresponding philosophy of religion the traces of an expulsion carried out at the expense of philosophy; equally, when philosophy assumes precedence, we will recognize traces of an expulsion carried out at the expense of religion. Naturally, we should expect that such expulsions would be mystified in philosophical texts, in the same way as in myths the presence of an expelled victim is signaled by the persecutors' more or less clumsy attempts to conceal it.

NOTES

1. Jean-Pierre Dupuy has called this mechanism "passive collaboration." He has dedicated some very interesting writings to this notion, and to its connection to the theme of the "self-fulfilling

prophecy." See Jean-Pierre Dupuy, *Ordres et désordres: Enquête sur un nouveau paradigme* (Paris: Seuil, 1982), 125–85.

2. In relation to what has been said thus far, see TH, 19–30, as well as René Girard, "Vers une définition systématique du sacré," *Liberté* (Montreal) 15, nos. 3–4 (1973): 58–74; Alfred Simon, ed., "Discussion avec René Girard," *Esprit* 429 (1973): 528–63; René Girard, "Rite, Travail, Science," *Critique* 380 (1979): 20–34; René Girard, "La violence et le religieux," interview by L. Schneiter, *Construire*, September 30, 1981, 20–21. See also Alexandre Doutreloux, "Violence et religion d'après René Girard," *Revue Théologique de Louvain* 7 (1976): 182–95; Carlo Formenti, "La guerra e il sacro," *Alfabeta* 60 (1980): 23–24.

3. For a comprehensive commentary on Girard's reading of the Bible, see Raymund Schwager, *Brauchen wir einen Sündenbock? Gewalt und Erlösung in den biblischen Schriften* (Munich: Kosel, 1978), trans. Maria L. Assad, *Violence and Redemption in the Bible* (San Francisco: Harper and Row, 1987). See also René Girard and Raymund Schwager, *Correspondence, 1974–1991*, ed. Scott Cowdell, Chris Fleming, Joel Hodge, and Mathias Moosbrugger, trans. Chris Fleming and Sheelah Treflé Hidden (New York: Bloomsbury Academic, 2016).

4. Troisfontaines has written: "In Girard's view, in reality all our sciences do no more than prolong the 'bad conscience' inherent in the victimage process." Claude Troisfontaines, "L'identité du social et du religieux selon René Girard," *Revue Philosophique de Louvain* 78 (1980): 72.

5. This objection was considered by Dupuy, *Ordres et désordres*, 163–64: "The progressive process of desacralization in the Western world is a paradoxical movement. . . . Each step in desacralization, by its own violence, has created a new sacred. Successive demystifications, purporting to be universal in nature or transcendent beyond the reigning order, have succeeded only in installing new false universals and new false transcendences."

6. On the phenomenon of the monstrous double, see Cesareo Bandera, "The Double Reconciled," *MLN* 93, no. 5 (1978): 1007–14; Jean-Michel Oughourlian and Guy Lefort, "Psychotic Structure and Girard's Doubles," *Diacritics* 8, no. 1 (1978): 72–74.

7. Georges Poulet, "Le songe de Descartes," in *Extudes sur le temps humain* (Paris: Plon, 1950), 16–47.

8. On this topic, see the following writings by Girard: "Superman in the Underground: Strategies of Madness; Nietzsche, Wagner and Dostoevskij," *MLN* 92, no. 6 (1976): 1161–85 (now DBB, 61–83); and "La meurtre fondateur dans la pensée de Nietzsche," in *Violence et vérité: Autour de René Girard*, ed. Paul Dumouchel (Paris: Grasset, 1985), 597–613.

9. There is one other form of relationship, about which Girard speaks often, which is Christian love. However, given that the terms of the relationship that we are examining are two symbolic-cultural forms that are, for the most part, of a sacrificial nature, this alternative automatically excludes itself.

10. Christianity is the exception; to avoid always having to make qualifications like this every time the term "religion" is used, we should reserve for Christianity, insofar as it is a demystifying and antisacrificial truth, the designation of "faith."

11. Girard almost never speaks of "symbolism," and if he does, he never associates it with the term "intellectual." However, it seems that the term expresses correctly what Girard's discourse implies, even if it does not say so openly.

12. Girard agreed on this in a letter to me, June 14, 1997, a copy and translation of which can be found in this volume.

13. "Intellectual expulsion as the foundational event of philosophy itself" is my own expression; however, it is coherent, I think, with Girard's method of analyzing cultural forms, but Girard has not offered a complete formulation for it.

14. See Johannes Hessen, *Religionsphilosophie*, 2 vols. (Munich: Ernst Reinhardt, 1955), 1:17–22. Hessen's scheme, as it is presented in this text, offers first, the possibility of the logical precedence of philosophy and, following this, the possibility of the logical precedence of religion. I have chosen to reverse the order of exposition (without, I believe, damaging the substance of the discourse) because this better serves the order followed in the next chapter.

CHAPTER 2

Historical Forms of Mystification

1. Philosophy as the Scapegoat of Religion

In the previous chapter, we saw that for Girard the Gospels are not mythical texts, but the greatest form of demystification of mimetic victimage. In the Gospels there is no kind of confrontation with philosophy, understood as a discipline based on rational investigation. That confrontation rather takes place in the Pauline texts, where "knowledge of God" (σοφία τοῦ Θεοῦ) is contrasted with "worldly knowledge" (σοφία τοῦ κόσμου) (1 Corinthians 1:20). The former is the knowledge of God that was revealed first in the Old Testament and then by means of Christ; this must be the object of *faith*, as Paul often remarks with his frequent use of the expression "faith [πίστις] in God" (1 Thessalonians 1:8, for instance). The latter, that is, worldly knowledge, is the wisdom that the Greeks knew as philosophy.[1]

Paul excludes the possibility of presenting the Gospels as texts supported by philosophical argumentation. This should not surprise someone who endorses the basic principles of mimetic theory. Paul refutes pagan religion as much as pagan philosophy; both, as we have seen, are forms of sacrifice. This, then, is Paul's attitude toward the religion and philosophy of the pagan world: total renunciation of the former, and refusal to use the latter.

Such an attitude is easily identifiable in the texts: in Paul's epistles, just as in any part of the New Testament, not a single philosophical interpretation may be found.[2] Paul is aware of the wisdom of the Greek philosophers, but condemns it in favor of a form of wisdom that, to reason, is madness: faith in Christ.[3] It is important to emphasize, however, that this denunciation of Greek wisdom is not a condemnation of reason. As long as it is made subordinate to faith, Paul does not exclude rational knowledge.

The argument becomes slightly different in the case of the Gospel according to St. John. Attempts have been made to read in this Gospel a clear resumption of the terminology and categories of Greek philosophy. Do we find ourselves, then, facing the paradox of a philosophical and therefore sacrificial Gospel? There is another possibility, which is the presence, in such a Gospel, of a radical and uncompromising leap from a violent *Logos*, such as that of the Greeks, to the *Logos* of peace, such as that of the Gospel of John. For the time being, let us set aside the close comparison of the two *Logoi*,[4] and limit ourselves to considering how, beginning from the concrete persona of Jesus, which is the object of Christian faith, John turns to philosophers in order to tell them that what they call *Logos* is Christ himself; that *Logos* has been made flesh and has lived among us, to the point that—in a scandal intolerable for those who seek a purely speculative explanation of the world—we actually saw it.[5]

The distinctive attitudes of Paul and John do not change with the Apostolic Fathers. They spread further a critique of philosophy based on the notion of its uselessness as a guide to truth. It is important, however, to note that this critique of philosophy remains, at least in this first phase, adherent to the spirit of the Gospels—that is, it never develops into persecution of pagan philosophers and the doctrines preached by them. It is a hard and radical critique that brands as lies the discoveries of truth that philosophy attempts, a critique that is therefore quite distant from an idea of "tolerance," but certainly never a violent critique.

As Wolfson remarks in *The Philosophy of the Church Fathers*, the irreconcilability of Pauline doctrine with "the polytheism and idolatry of the pagan world remained unchanged" throughout the history of the Patristics. The Apostolic Fathers attacked polytheism "when they were the spokesmen for a persecuted minority in a pagan world; they attacked it also when, as the favorites of the powers that be, they could, whenever their Christian conscience allowed them, turn persecutor; they continued to attack it even after they had succeeded in destroying it as a living religion and nothing of it was left but a memory" (11). The Apostolic Fathers, therefore, followed in the footsteps of Paul and preached a "faith" based on the power of God without relying on "the persuasive words of wisdom" (1 Corinthians 2:4).

For the Apostolic Fathers, Christianity was different from philosophy. The fundamental difference lay in both the degree and the origin of their truth: one, being of divine origin, can be nothing other than truth; the other, being of human origin, results from a composition of truths, but also of falsehoods. This is like saying, much as Girard does, that the truth of the victim can only derive from a superhuman reality, given that all human civilizations and cultures are based on mimetic victimage.

From the second half of the second century, with the so-called Apologetic Fathers, we find a new, altered outlook. Great heresies abounded, and many Christian theologians reached the conclusion that philosophical thought was in large part responsible for such departures from orthodoxy. Some thinkers asserted that the most effective way to halt the propagation of heresy would be to eliminate philosophy from Christianity entirely, but as this seemed impossible, they restricted themselves to discouraging its study.

While some fathers came to regard philosophy with suspicion, others began to present Christianity as a doctrine that did not necessarily clash with it. Let us take as examples the divergent attitudes of Justin Martyr and Tatian the Assyrian.

For Justin, those who lived according to the *Logos*, like Socrates and even Heraclitus, were Christians *ante litteram*.[6] Thus we witness, from the point of view of a mimetic reading, an attempt to include the violent and not yet demystified *Logos* into the *Logos* of John. Such ambiguity could even be regarded as one of the sources of the progressive transformation of Christianity into "Christian religion," that is, a mythical-ritual system, in which the demystifying message of Christianity is gradually lost.

On the other hand, for Tatian it is entirely pointless to criticize in miniscule detail the systems of the philosophers; they have taken on that task themselves, as they spend their time refuting one another's ideas. Tatian's attitude toward philosophy is extremely critical, and one might be tempted to describe it as *violent*.[7]

Let us analyze these events from a mimetic point of view. Almost simultaneously, two Christian theologians make opposing choices: one (Justin) seems to seek conciliation, indeed almost an identification with philosophy, while the other (Tatian) rejects it, or, it may be said, *expels* it, almost claiming that it is responsible for the spread of heresies. In short, Tatian turns philosophy into an intellectual scapegoat. How do we explain two such divergent attitudes?

We should now recall that a victim, to be capable of liberating the community from violence through her or his own expulsion, must first belong to that community. Only once philosophy has been already assimilated by religion—that is, when philosophy is sufficiently similar to religion to undergo the *transfer*—can religion then expel philosophy. It is for this reason that there is alternation between doctrines that assimilate philosophy and doctrines that expel it. If sacrifice is to have any effect, the victim must first be part of the community.

It might be objected that Tatian's attitude is nothing but the radicalization of the Pauline critique of "worldly knowledge." And indeed it is impossible to deny the ambiguity between having an attitude (such as Paul's) that rejects philosophy, because it is sacrificial, and argues that the Gospel shares nothing at all with it, and the scapegoating of philosophy by religion; yet this is only an apparent ambiguity, because in the latter case the expelling subject is not the Gospels but "Christian religion." This is, in other words, the ambiguity between the choosing of a scapegoat and the singling out of the persecutors—subtle and insidious, but necessary. We moderns know very well that the best way to victimize someone is to present that person as a persecutor, and that often the persecutors of today, once they are singled out, become the persecuted of tomorrow.

From the point of view of intellectual symbolism, then, we are witnessing the first great *intellectual sacrifice*, that is, the scapegoating of philosophy by religion, an expulsion that founded the cultural order of the Middle Ages.

It might be objected that while these examples could correspond to one of the hypotheses of Hessen's scheme, specifically the case in which religion dominates philosophy, the "religion" discussed here neither completely coincides with nor may be reduced to the concept of religion as mythical ritualization (as presented in Girard's theory). In short, for Girard, religion is above all a mythical-ritual organization, while Hessen uses the same term to mean a form of "religious philosophy." That is not mistaken: the "religion" discussed here is no longer religion as a mere system of mythical ritualization (in the sense used in the previous chapter), because it is religion itself that changes, and becomes more "intellectual." This change is not mere chance either: that is, it is not mere chance that in the West, after the advent of Christianity, no religious development has been entirely alien to philosophy. It may be objected, then, that the same movement of progressive intellectualization of religious forms could also be identified in pre-Christian religious formations, and this might well be true. After all, myths and texts of persecution also combine true elements and false elements, but this does not detract from the fact that the texts of persecution are closer to the truth because, paradoxically, they are significantly more mystificatory. Similarly, the intellectualization of religion takes a new form after Christianity, and produces intellectual conflicts that are much more evident. Before the coming of Christ, philosophy and religion were no more than superstructures of the mimetic victimage that acted as a unified mechanism; after the advent of Christianity, it has become increasingly difficult to be spectators or—worse—players of a performance whose backstage workings have been exposed. And yet mimetic violence always needs to perpetuate itself: the birth of the intellectual symbolism responds to such a need, insofar as it allows different, more intellectualized, and more sophisticated forms of mimetic violence. Such movement also has had the consequence of breaking the unity of the mechanism, thus favoring the transformation of philosophy and religion into subjects of a mimetic relation.

The Apologetic Fathers, followed by the whole body of Thomistic scholasticism, reject pagan religion but substitute it with a new religion, the Christian one, invigorated by as much philosophy as will make the *transfer* possible, and thus the intellectual expulsion of philosophy itself: it is an *intellectual* sacrifice, a sacrifice adapted to the new conditions of progressive revelation heralded by the revelation of Christ. The proof that Christian religion substitutes itself, functionally, for pagan religion lies in the lynchings, both physical and intellectual, to which non-Christians have been increasingly subjected.

The Middle Ages, then, were an era of innumerable victim expulsions: crusades, persecutions of heretics and witches, purges against Jews are all examples of sacrifices.[8] As has already been stressed, only a fine line distinguishes the individuation of persecutors—an individuation that is, so to speak, "participatory," because only those who assume the point of view of the victim can understand the dynamics of expulsion—and the restoration of difference, which always signals a new act of lynching.[9]

We are now in a better position to understand why Girard maintains, in *The Scapegoat*, that Christian "religion" has its roots in a sacrificial reading of the Gospels, a reading according to which Christ comes into the world in order to restore Difference, to divide once and for all persecutors and victims, pagans and Christians, evil and just.[10]

This sacrificial reading of the Gospels is shared by the author of the Epistle to the Hebrews,[11] St. Anselm, and most of the thinkers in medieval scholasticism. All of these authors, according to Girard, posit a God who needs to avenge his honor, and for this purpose demands a precious and beloved victim, his own Son. The emergence of the sacrificial reading of the Gospels shows that the mimetic vortex of intellectual symbolism is already at work.

As always happens in the mechanisms of mimetic rivalry, while religion declares verbally the victories it has achieved over its rival (philosophy), in reality it offers philosophy all the instruments necessary to transform these presumed victories into patent defeats. Religion and philosophy thus anticipate their role of "doubles." In other words, scholasticism so sharpens its dialectical weapons that they end up being used against it, turning the situation on its head and achieving a new and different intellectual sacrifice. Girard remarks: "Agreeing with Dostoevsky, Simone Weil saw in the inquisition the archetype of all totalitarian solutions. The end of the Middle Ages is an essential moment in Christian history; the heir, having reached the age of an adult, lays claim to his heritage. His guardians are not wrong to mistrust his maturity, but they are wrong to want to prolong indefinitely their tutelage" (RU, 123).

Consider once again the distinction between "Christian religion"—which in its sacrificial nature is similar to every other religion in all times and places—and the core of the demystifying message of the Gospels. It is necessary to restate this distinction because, with the twilight of the Middle Ages, Christian religion begins to die. This happens because, paradoxically, the effects of the ongoing work of the Paraclete (the Spirit of truth) become more and more visible in history.

The "death of God," as a cultural modern phenomenon, is therefore the death of the image of a cruel, violent god (as he is still sometimes pictured in the Old Testament); that death is an effect of the self-affirmation of the demystifying spirit. It is indeed the return of the authentic Christian message, which can often be retrieved—paradoxically—in the fiercest so-called antireligious criticism, such as that of Voltaire, which aims at demystifying the sacrificial intent of any religion, including Christian religion: "A formidable revolution is about to take place. Men, or at least certain men, will not allow themselves to be seduced by the persecutions that are claimed by their own beliefs and especially by 'Christianity' itself" (S, 201).

2. Religion as the Scapegoat of Philosophy

Between the fourteenth and fifteenth centuries, Western civilization finds itself prey to a gigantic sacrificial crisis—perhaps the first crucial moment in that succession of sacrificial crises that characterizes modernity. The decades bridging these two centuries were the pinnacle of witch trials,[12] purges of heretics, and pogroms against Jews. The "autumn of the Middle Ages"[13] saw the twilight of its two great institutions: the papacy and the empire. From a mimetic perspective, the collapse of sociopolitical institutions signals the emergence of a massive sacrificial crisis. From this point of view, the frantic search for scapegoats that is typical of that age should not come as a surprise.

Because of the importance that intellectual symbolism has acquired, scapegoats are looked for not only among physical individuals, but also among cultural forms. The progressive decadence of scholasticism shows how the ritual sacrifice of philosophy, which had characterized the previous period, could no longer be repeated. This might be taken as constituting the cultural side of this new sacrificial crisis. Accordingly, a new intellectual scapegoat had to be found. Religion, as an intellectual subject, is necessarily involved in this crisis, which means that it possesses the fundamental stereotype of persecution.

In all crises, each subject views others as absolute difference. This dynamic is also reproduced at the intellectual level. Duns Scotus, for example, affirms the heterogeneity of theology with respect to speculative science and does not accept the dogmatic character of self-legitimizing religious positions—which is equal to refusing to perpetuate an expulsion that, because it is perceived as arbitrary, no longer has any beneficial effects. We may identify the other two stereotypes of persecution as follows: religion now appears entirely different from philosophy (stereotype of abnormality), while the demands of philosophy are still carried out in a religious context (stereotype of undifferentiation). We should not forget that the victim must be abnormal, so as not to be too easily identified with the community; but if the *transfer* of violence is to occur and the expulsion of the victim is to lead to a truly positive result, the scapegoat and the persecutor must still be undifferentiated.

Renaissance humanism is the cultural context where the new intellectual sacrifice is prepared. The phenomenon that makes this sacrifice possible is the emergence of the philological method and its application to texts.[14] It is the philosophical text itself that becomes the site of a victim-expulsion: "Philosophy, like tragedy, can at certain levels serve as an attempt at expulsion, an attempt perpetually renewed because never wholly successful" (VS, 296).

It is *in* the text that philosophy points to religion as a scapegoat. This is a fundamental movement in the history of Western civilization: up to this moment, the sacred has been considered everything that surrounds humanity, while having with it only the rarest points of contact, constituted by rituals (indeed, what allows the sacred to function is the idea that it is external to the community). With humanism, the idea of the externality of the sacred is progressively rejected and brought back down to earth (consider Marsilio Ficino's idea of the human being as *copula mundi*, middle term between the divine and the earthly). Thus begins the process of the worsening of ontological evil: we shift from a moment in which all human beings are equally sinful beneath a heaven populated by the sacred, to a moment in which, while it is said that the sacred is within us, each person feels deprived of it and sees others gifted with it. As heaven is gradually depopulated, so the sacred flows back down to earth (see DDN, 62).

What would seem to be the most advanced point of humanism—its skepticism toward everything to do with religion—in Girard's opinion is in fact the most distinctive legacy of religion: indeed, humanism assumes religion's persecuting role, thus perpetuating the whole mechanism. It is the moment in which the greatest benefits of a perfectly achieved expulsion are reaped: the more the victim is held responsible for evil and violence, the more it is respected and adored. Girard remarks: "The humanists' scepticism seems to be the ultimate criticism of religion yet, in reality, it is its heir and, like all heirs, is only too interested in the perpetuation of the capital to be inherited not to respect it secretly" (J, 38).

Interestingly, Girard indicates, as a constant in all modernity, the repeated expulsion (we may go so far as to say the *ritualized* expulsion) of religion, upon which is cast the blame for all violence in civilization:

> The modern mind still cannot bring itself to acknowledge the basic prin-
> ciple behind that mechanism which, in a single decisive movement, cur-
> tails reciprocal violence and imposes structure on the community. Because
> of this willful blindness, modern thinkers continue to *see religion as an
> isolated, wholly fictitious phenomenon* cherished only by a few backward
> peoples or milieus. And these same thinkers can now project upon religion
> alone *the responsibility for a violent projection of violence* that truly pertains
> to all societies including our own. (VS, 317; emphasis added)

There is, notably, some truth in what philosophy says about religion: religion is not innocent, but actually responsible (as a symbolic-cultural and there-fore sacrificial form) for past violence; but—and this is the mystification that philosophy enacts—it is not solely responsible. Like Oedipus, religion is no more responsible than the other members of the community (in this case, other symbolic-cultural forms). Like Job, religion simply had a preeminent role in the past, and this distinction constituted a sign of victimage that, in the undifferentiation of a sacrificial crisis, was enough to see it selected as a scapegoat.

Additionally, a certain display of indifference toward the expelled scape-goat (religion) in fact indicates the attempt, which is typical of all persecutors across time, to conceal the sacrifice. Once again, the mechanism repeats itself with no major differences. Whether it is the banishment of a cripple from a tribal village or the intellectual expulsion of religion, to stop and reconsider the event is always a risk. It is enough to think about such an expulsion so far as to ritualize it and enjoy its benefits. Indeed, it is these that deserve the greatest share of attention: the community has been pacified, newly unified in an unexpected and miraculous harmony. It is thus no mere chance that modern philosophy begins with Descartes and his "moral theory of generos-ity," on which Girard comments as follows:

> We can no longer fail to recognize the effects of this metaphysical poison-
> ing, for they unceasingly grow worse. These effects have made themselves
> felt, in a concealed but recognizable fashion, well before the twentieth and
> even the nineteenth centuries. Perhaps it is most suitable to seek the first
> traces of our malaise in the very origin of the era of the individualist, in
> that morality of *generosity* that Descartes, the first philosopher of indi-
> vidualism, and Corneille, its first dramatist, developed at the same time. As
> Lucien Goldmann has quite rightly remarked in his *Mediations*, Descartes
> cannot strictly justify his principle of generosity, because he cannot deduce
> it from the *cogito*. (RU, 94)

One of the prominent aspects of modern individualism, as a philosophical
tenet, is a violent attitude toward religion, suggesting a belief that by expelling religion and placing the human being, the I or Self, at the center, violence
and evil can be eliminated from the earth once and for all. And indeed, the I
is the new protagonist of this phase, the I that believes it has eliminated the
element of discord, that is, religion; the I that believes in its own divinity and
lives by congratulating itself on having restored peace, but which, in order
to do so, must continue to confirm its identity by comparing itself to the
religious element it has expelled.

> In the early stages of the dynamic, the Self feels itself strong enough to tri-
> umph over its rivals. But still it must prove to itself its superiority. In order
> that the proof sought may be satisfying in its own eyes, the rivalry must
> be honest. The solution asserted is evidently generosity. It is necessary to
> respect the rules of "fair play," and to gain agreement from the Other that it
> respects them equally, so that victor and vanquished may be cleanly judged
> and distinguished. "The general interest" is always alleged to be the goal, as
> it is necessary to dissimulate the egotistic object of this maneuver.
>
> The morality of generosity is much less 'underground' than the morali-
> ties that succeed it, but it is already underground in the sense that the Self
> imposes on the regime of *proof*. It actually believes in its own divinity, i.e. in
> its superiority over others, but it does not believe in it sufficiently to dispense
> with a concrete demonstration. It needs to reassure itself. (RU, 95)

Actually, the religion evoked as an enemy to be defeated no longer represents a danger to philosophy. However, as international politics teaches us, it

might be very useful to keep alive an enemy who could be easily defeated, and that may even already be defeated, for the purpose of reinforcing the home front. Philosophy does exactly the same. First, it denounces the persistence of religion and intensifies declarations of war on it; second, it tastes the effects of this sacrifice and preaches generosity; when at last religion shows itself to be manifestly too weak to keep up the role of the skulking enemy, philosophy, to keep it alive, discovers sensibility and romanticism. Attacks then give way to concessions, to admissions of rights, to the discovery of the "place due to religion":

> The transition from Cartesian "generosity" to pre-romantic "sensibility" is connected with a serious worsening of the conflict between the selves. The Self is incapable of reducing the Other, all the others, to slavery. The "divinity" that remained more or less solidly anchored in the Self during the first century of individualism tends henceforth to become displaced toward the Other. In order to avoid this catastrophe, which is otherwise imminent, the Self tries an arrangement with its rivals. It does not renounce individualism, but it seeks to neutralize its consequences. It endeavors to sign a non-aggression pact with the Other . . . but this cushioning of the effects is purely tactical and has nothing to do with true love. (RU, 95–96)

It is the moment of romanticism, the moment of the Romantic "lie" that Girard contrasts with romanesque "truth." Actually, romanticism is no more truthless or mystificatory than the modes of thought that preceded it, but its peculiarity consists in considering as sublime certain passions that in fact are terribly mundane.

What is distinctive in the Romantic attitude is the fascination for a mediator who increasingly appears as a rival, as well as the denial of that mediation.[15] Romanticism detects the presence of the mediator but does not make it explicit. It is in a literary rather than a philosophical context that the truth begins to emerge. Girard considers romanticism as the philosophy of metaphysical desire, that is, a thought advancing a conception of the human as constituted by a spontaneous desire of its own being, without realizing that this desire derives from a sense of deeply lacking a *being* that others do seem to possess: "Romantics and symbolists want a transfiguring desire which is completely spontaneous; they do not want to hear any talk about the Other" (DDN, 39).

The passage "from Cartesian generosity to the pre-romantic sensibility" is crucial: it is the shift from a form of philosophy that still respects religion as an "other," as different from itself, to a philosophy that, while it apparently defends religion against the attacks of the Enlightenment, is actually focused on the I, and considers religion as a subjective expression of the I—here one can think of Romantic thinkers such as Schleiermacher, who grounded the relationship to God in *feeling*. This emphasis on the I is an instance of a serious aggravation of ontological sickness. In this shift of focus, something must have happened to have brought about such an aggravation.

The problem is that the sacrificial expulsion of religion has worked too well. Soon the moment arrives when it is recognized that the expiatory victim is not coming back, in consciousness or in history, to begin the mimetic conflict over again. Once the beneficial effects of expulsion have been discovered, the victim should offer itself to the adoration of its former persecutors; but in this case this does not happen, because it *cannot* happen. All efforts in this direction—for example, those of Joseph de Maistre, who declares himself sure that the passing "madness" of the Enlightenment would soon end and that religion would become an even greater pillar of society than it had been in the past—in reality result in ever greater demystification of the mechanism, whose dynamics become ever more obvious. Why does this happen?

We should not forget that the sacrificial crisis we are talking about is situated historically after the revelation of the Gospels. I have introduced the notion of the "intellectual symbolic," justifying it, in the footsteps of Girard, as an attempt by mimetic victimage to mystify truth once more, camouflaging itself in intellectual conflicts. Yet, we should note that this escamotage of the mechanism is achieved to the detriment of the mechanism itself: indeed, if on the individual plane the possibility of substituting the original victim with ritual victims is potentially infinite, on the intellectual plane this turns out to be more difficult, precisely because of the textual memory that philosophy preserves of itself. No one adores religion any longer, because all remember the role that it fulfilled, and in part still does fulfill.

Considered from this point of view, then, the very affirmation of intellectual symbolism could be rightfully considered as an important event in the history of salvation, insofar as it facilitates the emergence of truth. The whole dynamic could be considered the work of the Paraclete.

The history of the sacrificial expulsion of religion by philosophy, in fact, has a destiny different from the (otherwise similar) history of the sacrificial expulsion of philosophy by religion. Gradually, the beneficial effects of the expulsion fade away, and religion (as a cultural form) no longer returns as a god of harmony to be adored and ritually sacrificed. So here emerges the terrible truth: God is dead. It is evident for Girard, and he confirms it often (see, e.g., RU, 93), that the God who dies is the jealous, violently religious God of the Old Testament, the God of revenge against whom Job rebelled in the name of all victims. From now on—Girard is extremely clear on this point—all of philosophy's efforts will be dedicated to seeking a "substitute for God": "For two or three centuries this has been the underlying principle of every 'new' Western doctrine: God is dead, man must take his place. Pride has always been a temptation; but in modern times it has become irresistible because it is organized and amplified in an unheard-of way. The modern 'glad tidings' are heard by everyone. The more deeply it is engraved in our hearts the more violent is the contrast between this marvellous promise and the brutal disappointment inflicted by experience" (DDN, 56).

Thus philosophy finds in the human being a substitute for God. And yet, this *pharmakon* produced by philosophy to cure itself of metaphysical sickness turns out to be, consistently with its ambiguous nature, a potent poison rather than a miraculous remedy: "the human being" is an abstract notion, the invention of a symbolic-cultural product such as philosophy, while in reality there is only the "I" and the "Other," neither of which is capable of filling the void left behind by religion.

> Here the question really is *who* will be the heir, the only son of the dead God. The idealist philosophers believe that it is enough to respond in terms of the self or subject to resolve the problem. But the Self is not an *object* alongside other selves, for it is constituted by its relation to the Other and cannot be considered outside of this relation. It is this relation which the effort to substitute oneself for the God of the Bible always corrupts. Divinity cannot become identified either with the Self or with the Other; it is perpetually part of the struggle *between* the Self and the Other. Sexuality, ambition, literature—all intersubjective relations—become burdened with this underground battle. (RU, 94–95)

Idealism is characterized by the attempt to substitute the human for the religious, an attempt destined from the beginning to fail. The human, Girard remarks, always splits into the I and the Other:[16] it is therefore already a double; the recourse to it denotes the beginning of a new sacrificial-intellectual crisis. The temporary sign of victory begins to settle cyclically, first on one and then on the other, without stopping, thus impeding at this stage the choice of a scapegoat. For Girard, Hegel's philosophy clearly demonstrates this ambivalence: "Hegel's unhappy consciousness," Girard argues, "and Sartre's *projet* to be God are the outcome of a stubborn orientation toward the transcendent, of an inability to relinquish religious patterns of desire when history has outgrown them. . . . Promethean philosophy sees in the Christian religion only a humanism which is still too timid for complete self-assertion" (DDN, 158–59).

Girard seems to consider Hegel's philosophy on one hand as an attempt to come to terms with religious forms of desire, with religion in its sacrificial sense; on the other hand, Hegel's conception of religion as a humanism still in development means reversing the terms of the relationship and hoping that humanism itself may one day fulfill the same role as religion and bring even greater benefits, in terms of pacification and harmony. Such an effort, however, is destined to have no curative effect on metaphysical sickness.[17]

It is the worsening of this metaphysical sickness that produces nihilism. In fact, the vertical transcendence between God and the human being is deviated and turns into the horizontal transcendence between the subject and the model. It is this deviated transcendence that represents the foundation of radical nihilism: God is dead, and there is no longer room for any vertical transcendence.[18]

It is not by chance, Girard believes, that Nietzsche's thought arises from a meditation on Christ and the destiny of Christianity. In the sacrificial crisis of modernity that Girard delineates—another crucial step in the history of sacrificial crises following one another without being resolved, which characterizes Western civilization from the Christian revelation onward— Nietzsche is a central figure precisely insofar as his thought is located at the intellectual center of that crisis. His reflections capture fundamental aspects of the process that is under way, even if they flow away in directions that cannot be followed.[19]

Girard applies mimetic theory to Nietzsche's biography first, and interprets Nietzsche's relationship to Richard Wagner as a relationship of doubles.

To Nietzsche, Wagner stood as the mediator, the model at once adored and hated. Girard writes: "What about the *ideas* of Nietzsche? Even if mediated desire has a bearing on the writings about Wagner, one might still argue that his philosophy remains unaffected. It can be shown, I believe, that such is not the case. In the opinion of many scholars, the 'will to power' is one of the most important ideas of Nietzsche. An objective examination clearly reveals that the will to power provides an intellectual justification for the most self-defeating behavior demanded by the acute stages of the mediation process" (DBB, 68).

According to Girard, the notion of the will to power cannot be separated from Nietzsche's biography: once again we are dealing with sublime thoughts that hide terribly mundane passions, and with mimesis camouflaged in an intellectual form. What is hidden under this form will only appear once any kind of mystification has been eliminated. Girard interprets Nietzsche's thought as follows: Christ set humanity on the trail of God and gave it a glimpse of eternity. Humanity's impotent attempt to grasp that eternity falls back on humanity itself and engenders the horrendous universe of deviant transcendence, built on the belief in the insufficiency of the I and the superiority of the Other. It is therefore necessary to reject the folly of Christ and renounce the infinite. Nietzsche proposes a *pharmakon* that is meant to cure the ontological sickness that derives from the idolatry of the other; this *pharmakon* is the inversion of desire from the Other to the I. In this sense, Nietzsche's philosophy is not far from Cartesian generosity and Romantic sensibility, for which the substitute for religion must be not the Other, but the I. Nietzsche's great discovery, however, is to realize that all the previous attempts to divert the desire away from the Other toward the I have been too weak, as they were still trying to preserve religion in one way or another; hence, Nietzsche represents the extreme radicalization of that tradition, which consists in a full divinization of the I. Girard claims: "The Christian's desires are transfigured by his thirst for immortality. Neither science nor humanism can quench that thirst. Neither philosophical atheism nor social utopias can stop this mad pursuit in which each one tries to steal a phantasmal divinity from his neighbor. To annul Christianity the current of desire must be reversed, it must be deflected from the Other to the Self" (DDN, 275).

Although Nietzsche's attribution of divinity to the I rather than to the Other constitutes a novelty, it still follows coherently from the individualistic premises that have characterized philosophy from its earliest origins. As Girard argues, "The Nietzschean meditation takes place in the . . . dimension of individualism. . . . Superhumanity will be based on a double renunciation of both vertical and deviated transcendence. Zarathustra tries to enter into the sanctuary of his own existence through a purifying *askesis* analogous to religious *askesis* but differently oriented. This analogy is continually underscored by style and Biblical images. *Thus Spoke Zarathustra* is a new gospel which should mark the end of the Christian era" (DDN, 274).

From this point of view, Nietzsche is the unconscious prophet of a huge sacrificial crisis. He tries to put an end to Christianity because, in a mimetic perspective, the Christian message is now more unacceptable than ever, and it is unacceptable insofar as it is becoming more and more intelligible, thus threatening mimetic victimage to its very foundations. The true novelty of Nietzsche's thought, according to Girard, lies in the attempt to contrast the demystification of Christ with a new Gospel, the Gospel of the I, without, for that matter, realizing that many of his own demystifications have been made possible by the very evangelical message that he wishes to substitute.

Girard does not, therefore, deny that there is a revelatory dimension to Nietzsche's thought, determined by a certain "fullness of time" in which the action of the Paraclete is gradually becoming more evident. Girard discerns this revelatory dimension even in Nietzsche's acute criticism of sacrificial Christianity, that is, of Christian religion as a sacrifice of the self—in a word, as resentment. What, then, is ressentiment in the Girardian reading? Girard answers as follows: "Many features of ressentiment, as Nietzsche describes them, resemble the consequences of the mimetic process. Ressentiment is really a thwarted and traumatized desire" (DBB, 73).

Resentment is really a disease, or rather one of the signs of the propagation of metaphysical sickness. Nietzsche's error lies in believing that only the weakest are infected with it, and in thinking that the spread of the disease can be stopped by divine transformation of the I. For the same reason, he commits another error by confusing resentment with the Christian message itself. Nietzsche became "obsessed by mimetic *resentment*" at the point of looking on it "as the legitimate heir to the Bible and even as its earliest inspiration"; however, "Resentment is merely an illegitimate heir, certainly not the father of Judaeo-Christian Scripture" (J, 108).

To shift divinity from the Other to the I is nothing but another sign of the gravity of the sacrificial crisis in which we find ourselves: it signifies that we have reached the moment in which every human being, every single "I" holds the illusory belief of having victory in its grasp, when the only consequence of such a belief is a new and bloodier return of violence. Neither does the illusory nature of the promise spare the one who makes it first: in Nietzschean terms "being divine" means exercising the will to power to the greatest degree possible, overcoming all obstacles. But then, Girard asks, "What happens if we start judging Nietzsche according to his own criteria? Where are his *victories*? Was not his life an almost continuous defeat? Is not defeat *the worst bacillus for the soul*?" (DBB, 70). Elsewhere, Girard does not hold back harsh words for Nietzsche: "Interiorized vengeance, the 'reversed' vengeance of sinful Christians, is certainly a terrible evil, but one would have to be the spoilt child of the Bible . . . and have truly forgotten the taste of black blood in the dust, to look for a new *great remedy* for resentment in a return to real vengeance, as Nietzsche does, both consciously and unconsciously. . . . Nietzsche is truly mad, but no one notices it in a world where every effort is made to catch up with him in respect of this madness" (J, 151).

In a sense, Nietzsche truly marks the end of an era, the era in which truth could still be mystified because unity had once again been renewed by the sacrificial expulsion of religion. His was the last attempt that could be fulfilled—and it failed. The proud I that wishes to occupy the role fulfilled in the past by religion finds itself confronting the Other, which continually reminds the I of its humanity. Girard maintains that this path cannot lead to anything but violence and madness.

The place left vacant by religion cannot be taken by the I. Moreover— and in the context of mimetic theory this has the value of a final proof—the entire mimetic-victimary process is based on the original sense of inferiority in every individual (for Girard, even a narcissist is fundamentally insecure) (see DDN, 161–63). It is therefore absurd to think that the I can convince itself of its own divinity.

Yet neither can the place of religion pass to the Other, and not only for the reason that is a constant in the realm of mimeticism: that the master-mediator often disappoints the subject-disciple (what counts is that the place occupied by religion should be occupied by a substitute—it matters little how quickly the substitutes follow one another). What prevents the full substitution of religion by the Other is the level of awareness attained by the demystifying truth of the Gospels, which remains continually active in history. Following Girard's lead, let us take a backward step in our narrative: "It is at the end of the eighteenth century that Christianity, simply repudiated by the French philosophers, reappeared in inverted form in the underground. . . . Literature becomes 'subjective' and 'objective' and the underground self-divisions multiply. A little later the Double itself, whose presence corresponds to a paroxysm of tearing apart between Self and Other, makes its appearance among the most agonizing and anguished of the writers" (RU, 96).

In the hypothesis that has been outlined so far, philosophy has kept alive an imaginary enemy, religion, so as to sacrifice it ritually and enjoy the benefits of such a sacrifice. Once religion is found to be absent, philosophy seeks some kind of substitute for it, but never leaves off expelling religion, in order to secure the more and more scarce beneficial effects that ritual sacrifice would bring. However, in the context of mimetic psychology, a bluff can easily become reality. To keep an enemy alive still carries the risk that it will regain the strength it has lost. But this is not simply another reversal: across all these centuries, the Christian message has continued to insinuate itself into the consciousness of humanity, and the religion that philosophy has begun to fear is no longer the one defeated by Renaissance humanism and the early Enlightenment. It is still a *religion*—that is, a symbolic form that is still sacrificial in nature—that, however, carries within it, albeit in an embryonic form, the demystifying "faith" that cannot be dissolved in mimetic victimage. In other words, the Christianity that begins to emerge at the end of the eighteenth century is no longer the same symbolic-cultural form that played the role of persecutor in the Middle Ages. Its nature is no longer sacrificial because the Christian truth now emerges not as *religion* (a sacrificial system) but as *faith* (that is, a demystifying and antisacrificial truth). Modern thought, then, begins to discover its own past as a persecutor and to reveal itself as a dissembler: it is, in other words, approaching its end. This also implies that philosophy turns its critical weapons against itself, to demonstrate that even its own basic principles must be subjected to an effort at demystification.

Therefore, if the demystifying truth of the Gospels, which we have called faith, reveals the mimetic victimage that is expressed in religion as a symbolic-cultural system, then the breaking down of that system is part of the progressive unveiling of faith, and can therefore be incorporated unreservedly as a central event into the history of salvation. Put differently, secularization, or rather the process of the progressive loss of the sense of the sacred in the wake of a trend of "scientific" transparency, is not in the least an event that is hostile to faith but a condition for its development and, simultaneously, one of its consequences. What secularization overthrows is the violent sacred, the religion that has been expelled by philosophy and now cannot return.[20]

In the context of mimetic theory, all that contributes to the progressive fulfillment of Christian prophecies is part of the history of salvation. Following our hypothesis, then, we may affirm that the genesis of the intellectual symbolic and the consequent sacrificial expulsions—first, of religion by philosophy, and then, of philosophy by religion—are phenomena that can be read in two ways. On the one hand, they constitute a matter of expedience that mimesis enacts in order to "camouflage" itself and continue to perpetuate itself; on the other, they are steps that must be taken so that the mechanism does not repeat itself and truth may flourish.

The final stage in this process is also the decisive moment, in which humanity may autonomously choose its own destiny. It is the paroxysm of the sacrificial intellectual crisis, the moment in which all idols are rejected in the name of the supreme idol, that is, of that which remains unknown, the absolute Other—in a word, the pure sacred.

To sum up: after the medieval (presumed) "faithfulness to religious principles" that sacrifices philosophy, there is the furious agitation of all the philosophers who sacrifice religion; and after this furious agitation there is the immobility determined by the fact that every cultural element can be exchanged for any other, because all attempt to grasp the mystery of the sacred, but none succeed. If no contemporary philosophy is able to grasp such mystery, this happens not because we are extraneous to it, but because, in spite of everything, we still remain *in* the sacred. To paraphrase Girard, it is "behind modern phantasmagoria, behind the whirlwind of events and ideas" (DDN, 286), at the end of the increasingly rapid evolution of inner mediation, that there lies the purely sacred. Thus we have arrived at the paroxysm of crisis. It is contemporary philosophical hermeneutics that incarnates this ambiguous and decisive "point of death," constituted by concentric circles that draw ever nearer to each other and to the mystery that they may reveal once and for all.

3. Hermeneutics and Sacrificial Thought

3.1. Cultural Sacrificial Crisis

Human beings become one another's gods, and this, far from signifying the fulfilment of humanistic-Enlightenment promises, aggravates humanity's ontological insecurity. Furthermore, the shortage of scapegoats—or rather, the ever growing difficulty of exercising the role of the persecutor without being recognized as such, by oneself, even before others do—renders this crisis, which we may rightfully describe as sacrificial-cultural, tendentially irreversible. It is worth underlining a point that should be taken as central in mimetic theory and that, even if it has been one of the reference points of our argument thus far, has not yet been clarified. Secularization, for Girard, is indeed an irreversible process—it is, after all, an aspect of the history of salvation, which is by its very nature irreversible—but it is such sub specie aeternitatis, and not from the point of view of the phenomena that it embraces. For example, the progress of science constitutes an important step in the process of secularization, but that does not preclude that within science itself a central role, even if a misconstrued one, may be attributed to the sacred, which is supposed to have been defeated once and for all. Nevertheless, and in an endlessly repeating circularity, even the centrality of the sacred within science holds considerable importance in the process of secularization, because it can be said to be consistent with Popper's method of falsifiability: that is, it constitutes an error that, once it is understood as such, levels out the path to truth.[21]

What I have said about science also goes for contemporary philosophy and particularly for hermeneutic thought, insofar as both are symbolic-cultural forms. I am now going to draw a comparison between Girard and some themes and thinkers of the hermeneutic tradition, not only because of the weight that such thought has acquired in contemporary philosophy but also, and more importantly, because of the fruitfulness that, I believe, such a comparison may offer to the philosophy of religion.

The birth of modern hermeneutics can be traced to the Protestant Reformation. It is in that historical context, in fact, that a consciousness arises of the hermeneutic problem, which had been substantially extraneous to all previous conceptions of interpretation. The first field of application for the hermeneutic method was constituted by the Judeo-Christian Scriptures:

Matthias Flacius Illyricus, the sixteenth-century Lutheran reformer, even went so far as to assert that interpretation is effective only when the interpreter him- or herself approaches the text not in an abstractly neutral way but animated by a living religious sensibility, by a sort of precomprehension of the truth of the text that seeks and finds in the text itself its own confirmation.[22] Such an assertion fits rightfully into mimetic theory: texts must indeed be interpreted in the light of the demystifying principles that only Judeo-Christian Scripture presents.

However, it is interesting to note that Johann Heinrich Ernesti,[23] the seventeenth-century philosopher and Lutheran theologian, distinguished between a "theological" hermeneutics and a "profane" hermeneutics: a distinction that, from a mimetic perspective, is not only meaningless, but creates the illusion (and for Girard that is what it is) that a text can express its truth—the truth of the victim rather than the lies of the persecutors—without being contingent on the demystifying principles that Judeo-Christian Scripture makes available.

Since then, hermeneutics has retained this fundamental ambiguity, which I have already mentioned and which I will now seek to clarify by considering a literary form that, prima facie, might not seem to have much to do with hermeneutic thought: tragedy.

I contend that on the grounds of the fundamental principles of mimetic theory it is possible to deduce that in the context of Western culture, philosophical hermeneutics fulfills a role similar to that of tragedy in ancient Greek society. At issue in both cases is the knowledge of violence, which emerges because the effects of the last victimary expulsion have begun to disappear: a new sacrificial crisis announces itself—or rather, what is announced is another crucial step in that history of seemingly endless sacrificial crises that follow one another without finding a proper resolution. Furthermore, just as the truth of Greek tragedy is limited by its being only a partial demystification of myth, likewise limited is the deconstruction of the sacred character of difference in hermeneutic thought. Indeed, what is at stake in philosophical hermeneutics is the loss of specificities: thought is now closer to the pure sacred; but an implication of such proximity is that the sacred can exercise more effectively its power to disintegrate that thought which is trying to demystify the sacred. All interpretations risk appearing equally valid. The sacred, even in the process of being revealed in its ultimate reality, continues to exercise its power, and it is fragmented in a universe that is no longer the monolithic world of myth, but rather the atomized world of doubles. That is, the sacred, in hermeneutic thought, does not disappear, but changes its context of application: it no longer exercises its power directly in the form of religious beliefs, that is, in terms of a theological transcendence, but rather in its purest form, that is, as a force that keeps "sacred conflictual differences" in an endless fight among interpretations.

The loss of specificity in fact signifies the emergence of the phenomenon of doubles. Philosophy and religion increasingly tend to resemble one another: each becomes the other's double, and, at the same time, their rivalry becomes increasingly fierce; or, which is the same, they increasingly resemble each other because their relationship is still dependent on the sacred.

Philosophy, in short, is prey to this purest mimetic mechanism, and the two paths that it takes only confirm this conclusion. On the one hand, philosophy, like one of Dostoyevsky's characters,[24] meditates on fusing with its own double, on being entirely *one* with him—on recovering, in short, the lost unity. Thus, everything becomes more and more conformed to the undifferentiating logic of mimetic desire. Naturally, this does not prevent doubles from misapprehending this indifferentiation and, sometimes, to mistake one another for absolute Difference; and this is the second path. They are two phenomenological epochés, because they both suspend judgment on the evidence of violence that flows from the encounter of philosophy with religious experience.[25]

Whether a hermeneutics that proceeds toward demystification in light of the Judeo-Christian Scriptures and comes to culturally express this victory over desire exists or not, and what form it may eventually take, is a problem that will be addressed later. Now, however, I will attempt to verify the hypothesis proposed for reading hermeneutic thought on the basis of mimetic principles, examining first of all what Girard himself argues concerning the work of one philosopher indispensable to the consideration of hermeneutics: Martin Heidegger.

3.2. Heidegger's Two *Logoi*

In *Things Hidden since the Foundation of the World*, Girard takes into consideration the distinction drawn by Heidegger between the *Logos* of Heraclitus and the *Logos* of the Gospel of John.[26] According to Girard, Heidegger recognizes that the entities united in the Heraclitean *Logos* are opposites, and that the *Logos* unifies such opposites not without violence. Furthermore, Heidegger defines the Heraclitean *Logos* in a way that Girard would consider correct, that is, as the violence—the sacred, in the mimetic reading—that holds doubles together and prevents them from destroying one another. However, Heidegger does not achieve a real distinction between the Heraclitean *Logos* and the *Logos* of St. John, and rather insists on perceiving in the latter a divine authoritarianism that, in his view, is characteristic of the Bible.

> The illusion that there is difference within the heart of violence is the key to the sacrificial way of thinking . . . [Heidegger] wishes to differentiate the two types of Logos, but by inserting violence into both of them, he deprives himself of the means of doing so! . . . The warring doubles have been installed in the very heart of European thought—and it is a fact that, for Heidegger, the two types of Logos are indeed *doubles*. Heidegger claims to differentiate them, but in reality, they are becoming increasingly undifferentiated. The more attempts are made to remedy this state of affairs, the more incurable it becomes. . . . If we define Western philosophy as the assimilation of the two types of Logos, Heidegger undoubtedly belongs to its tradition; he is incapable of *concluding* the philosophical tradition because he cannot show the genuine difference between the Heraclitean Logos and the Johannine Logos. (TH, 266–67)

Girard emphasizes that Heidegger, although he may have grasped some aspects of the violent sacred, remains inside mimetic victimage, which, as we have seen, characterizes the history of philosophy as of that of religion.[27] If, as Heidegger argued, Heraclitus's *Logos* is the site of a reunification of opposites that is not achieved without violence, then that *Logos* is, in mimetic terms, the violence of the sacred. Quite different (and this, Girard believes, Heidegger did not recognize) is the *Logos* of St. John, in whose definition the moment of the expulsion ("the world did not recognize it," John 1:10) is essential: the Johannine *Logos* is expelled precisely because it is extraneous to violence.[28]

For the purpose of our work, what is most significant is that the Johannine *Logos* implies the meaning of the Heraclitean *Logos* (the Johannine

Logos is expelled because it does not submit to the logic of violent unification that the Heraclitean *Logos* represents), but not vice versa; in other words, the Johannine *Logos* "reads" the *Logos* of Heraclitus, but the *Logos* of Heraclitus cannot "read" the *Logos* of St. John. This means that only on the grounds of the Christian message of demystification is it possible to recognize the truth of violence and the sacred, and possibly to develop a knowledge out of it. Conversely, disregarding the Christian message would inevitably preclude the possibility of any interpretative development; the results that such a "hermeneutics" can lead to—and it can only be called "hermeneutics" improperly—are none other than the new proposition, *mutatis verbis*, of the false truths of persecutors; this without accounting for the fact that if we do seek to interpret the *Logos* of John from the point of view of the *Logos* of Heraclitus, we inevitably fail, and the only consequence would be that Judeo-Christian Scripture would appear to be—as indeed it often has appeared to be—a merely mythical text.

Heidegger seeks every possible way to reach the genetic core of every symbolicity, that is, the scapegoat, and to an extent he succeeds, if only because he recognizes in the *Logos* of Heraclitus "the Logos of expulsion, the Logos of violence, which, if it is not recognized, can provide the foundation of a culture" (TH, 271). However, Heidegger's perspective remains "mythical," insofar as the point of view from which he speaks is philosophical—or rather symbolically sacrificial. If Heidegger is examined in light of the "truth of the victim," we see that, behind his mediation on "being," the question is always, in the final analysis, the sacred. The sacralized victim is the "being" of Western tradition, the same one of which Heidegger laments its consignment to oblivion on the part of the philosophical inquiry.

> The discovery of the scapegoat as the mechanism of symbolic thought, human thought itself, justifies a deconstructive discourse and at the same time completes it. It can also explain the characteristic aspects of this contemporary discourse. Because much of contemporary thought is still without an anthropological basis, it remains given to verbal acrobatics that will ultimately prove to be sterile. The master tropes are not what it lacks; it is only too well endowed with words, but the mechanisms behind the word are still not sufficiently apparent....
>
> Everything that [Heidegger] says concerning being can also be said

of the sacred, but philosophers will hardly admit this since they have no desire to go back beyond Plato and the pre-Socratics to consider Greek religion. (TH, 63–64)

It is highly significant for our hypothesis that Girard brings Heidegger's thought into comparison with the perspective of the tragedian Aeschylus, as though to indicate that the function that both fulfill in relation to mimetic victimage is the same. Girard argues: "In a movement that might well be termed pre-totalitarian, as in certain dialogues of Plato, Aeschylus becomes the *shepherd* of that violence. This is Heidegger's profound and violent meaning when he speaks of the *shepherd of being*. The latter, for some reason, has always made me think of the wolf in disguise of the fable. Beneath the pure white coat of the sacrificial lamb, one black paw is showing" (J, 151).

When a society finds itself in the grip of a sacrificial crisis, knowledge about violence becomes more transparent to those able to grasp its implications. Aeschylus and Heidegger are indeed the "shepherds" of the violent sacred. There is a difference, however, between them: Heidegger, as Girard points out in an ironic (although not merely ironic) fashion, "disguises" himself as a victim, and his thought should therefore be demystified in its own right. Girard has often recalled that ever since the Christian revelation the role in which every person has wished to appear, at least publicly, is that of the victim. Even persecutors present themselves as scapegoats. However, Girard maintains, Heidegger's "game" does not entirely succeed, and his thought still appears linked to the violent sacred, which he cannot seem to give up. For Heidegger it is a question not so much of bad faith as of the fear of returning to the origins of cultural order, of discovering the sacrificial nature of every symbolic form and the elementary disorder upon which every successive order is founded. The nature of Heidegger's thought thus appears fundamentally ambiguous. If on the one hand he misconstrues the role of the violent sacred, on the other hand he has sought, as Girard himself remarks, to clarify and resolve the separation of the two *Logoi*:[29] "Insofar as he remains a philosopher and, unwittingly, turns philosophy into the last, final refuge of the sacred, Heidegger is constrained within the limits of philosophy. . . . Heidegger, like all the rest, is really helping to produce the decisive break he talks about. But his work also operates as a powerful obstacle to this break" (TH, 267–68).

As I have already emphasized, every expediency that the sacrificial mechanism enacts on the cultural plane to perpetuate itself is a step toward the unveiling of truth, because it prevents that expedient from being used again in the future. From this point of view, Heidegger's thought can be incorporated into the history of salvation as Girard understands it, inasmuch as it prepares the end of Western metaphysics, which is a violent thought insofar as it does not allow for dissident viewpoints on the alleged dogmatic "truth," which is nothing but the hidden sacred. Girard argues: "What goes for Heidegger also goes for the other thinkers of modern times. His philosophy is not a fantasy. It serves its purpose. It may not bring about the separation it proposes, but it prepares for the decisive discrimination. It does genuinely presage the end of Western metaphysics which is its constant pre-occupation" (TH, 267).

Our next goal is to establish how the double legacy of Heidegger's thought—its refusal of original knowledge and the partial revelation of the sacred—has been received, and what sort of cultural mileage such legacy has generated.

3.3. The Refusal of Knowledge

Girard adopts extremely critical positions in relation to those whom he calls "Heidegger's epigones" and more generally toward philosophical hermeneutics, which sometimes Girard addresses, admittedly, without the attention and rigor that such a tradition would deserve. Naturally this critical position is not unrelated to the fact that mimetic theory, especially in Girard's formulation, has often been criticized because it proceeds by analogy, whereas—it is objected—one text should not be compared to another if they do not share at least some cultural context. Notwithstanding the generalizations and approximations into which he often falls, Girard delineates well the sacrificial-cultural crisis to which our culture is prey, and of which philosophical hermeneutics is one of the most interesting expressions.

It seems that the aspect of Heidegger's legacy that has had the greatest impact is the refusal of knowledge, the renunciation of truth. The condemnation of the arrogance of eighteenth-century positivism has not permeated our culture with an attitude of humility, but rather it has led to a refusal of the possibility that history has a *meaning* or that it is possible to achieve true *knowledge*, and thus it has led to a rejection of any instrument that, like Judeo-Christian Scripture, allows us to orient ourselves on such a search. In an interesting passage of the French edition of *The Scapegoat*, Girard argues:

> Our contemporaries . . . arrogantly condemn the pride of the modern West, but they fall into a worse form of pride. In order not to acknowledge our responsibilities in the bad use of the prodigious advantages that have been given to us, we deny their reality. We give up the myth of progress to fall into the far worse myth of the eternal recurrence. If we assess all this from the viewpoint of our men of wisdom, we are no longer moved by any principle of truth: our history has no meaning, the very notion of history means nothing. There are no signs of the times. We are not living the peculiar adventure that we believe we are living. Science does not exist, knowledge does not exist.[30]

This is a position that, to use an expression that Girard employs elsewhere, we may call "cognitive nihilism" (TH, 257). Once again, we are witnessing the expulsion—all the more underhanded, because silent and, perhaps, unconscious—of the Judeo-Christian Scriptures, that is, of the only instrument that is truly useful for breaking out of the interpretative circle to which contemporary philosophy seems condemned. "What is really frightening today," Girard remarks, "is not the challenge of this new meaning, but the Kafkaesque rejection of all meaning. What is frightening is the conjunction of massive technical power and the spiritual surrender of nihilism. A panic-stricken refusal to glance, even furtively, in the only direction where meaning could still be found dominates our intellectual life" (TH, 261).

It is this refusal of knowledge that generates the conviction, which is typical of certain extreme forms of hermeneutics and deconstruction, that interpretations are infinite and all equivalent: they therefore find themselves in a condition of perennial rivalry, thus guaranteeing the perpetuation of violence in a rite—the rite, indeed, of interpretation—that can continue to fulfill itself. Girard remarks:

> In the faster and faster vortex of "methods" and "theories," in the waltz of interpretations that benefit for a short time from the favor of the public

before falling into an oblivion from which they will probably never emerge again, it seems that there is no stability whatsoever, no truth that can *hold*. The last mandate of fashion even claims that interpretations are infinite and all equivalent, because one is never more true or false than another. Of a text there can be, it seems, as many interpretations as readers. They are therefore forever destined to come one after another in the general euphoria of a freedom finally achieved, in such a way that none of them will ever prevail over its rivals.[31]

At this point we may understand more clearly the historical weight of the divergence between a "profane" hermeneutics and a "religious" hermeneutics. According to the former there can be infinite interpretations that all respond to the demands of persecutors, from whose point of view—which is the point of view of the violent sacred—the only important thing is that the role of the scapegoat be mystified. The nature of the latter, conversely, is a search whose objective is to unveil the only valid interpretation, that is, the only one that lays bare the truth of the victim. Girard reiterates this idea in *Job: The Victim of His People* as follows: "The current desire to 'respect differences' reaches the point of putting all 'truths' on the same level. It basically eliminates the very idea of truth, seeing it only as a source of conflict. But if we put the 'truth of the persecutors' on the same level as the 'truth of the victim,' there will very quickly be no difference or truth for anyone" (J, 107).

Those who maintain they wish only "to respect differences" are perfectly sincere: they "know not what they do" in the literal sense that Girard attributes to the words of Jesus, as reported in the Gospels —that is, they do not "understand." Nevertheless, this "respect for differences" legitimates the lynching of innocents. The truth that the Gospels enunciate is quite different: it is unconditional, absolute truth. It is not sufficient to recognize the object of the debate, which is violence: "We must also recognize the two perspectives on this violence and, more importantly, choose between them. Avoiding participation is a deception. Any pretence at *impassiveness*, whether stoic, philosophic, or scientific, perpetuates the *status quo*, prolongs the occulting of the scapegoat, and makes us effective accomplices of the persecutors" (J, 107).

Girard does not hesitate to satirize ferociously the attitude of those who, in the name of a presumed objectivity, avoid taking up any position: if certitude is not acceptable, he argues, "if we hold absolutely to the great democracy of a never-true-never-false interpretation that is so popular these days for anything nonquantifiable, then that [renouncing the demystification of texts] is inevitably the result. We must condemn in retrospect all those who brought an end to the witch trials. They were even more dogmatic than the witch-hunters and, like them, they believed they possessed the truth. . . . If our ancestors had thought in the same mode as do today's masters, they would never have put an end to the witch trials" (S, 98–99).

At this point it becomes necessary to consider a further hypothesis: that the figure of the contemporary philosopher (the hermeneutic thinker or deconstructionist, as Girard presents such figure in the various citations reproduced here) is substantially comparable to the figure of the writer ana-lyzed in *Deceit, Desire, and the Novel*. Such a hypothesis appears legitimate not only because in both cases it concerns intellectual figures who, in Girard's reading, oscillate between the mystification of the truth and the possibility of an (inevitably partial) access to it, but also because, as we have seen, it is Girard himself who places on the same level the figures of the tragedian and the philosopher; and tragedy is for the ancient world what the novel is for the modern world.

Now, consider what Girard argues concerning the comparison of the contemporary writer to the writer of times past:

> Never before has so much been written but it is all to prove that commu-nication is neither possible nor desirable. The aesthetics of "silence" with which we are overwhelmed are quite obviously an outcome of the under-ground dialectic. . . . The author still publishes his works, but to cover up this crime he does everything he can to avoid being read. For a long time he has claimed to be speaking without anything to say.
>
> But he is not telling the truth. The writer talks in order to seduce us just as he did in the past. He constantly watches our eyes to see in them the admiration aroused by his talent. It is objected that he does everything to make us loathe him. This may be true, but the reason is that he is no longer able to pay court to us openly. First he has to convince himself that he is not trying to flatter us. Thus he courts us negatively like Dostoevsky's tortured characters. (DDN, 263–64)

The philosopher of the idealistic-romantic era also sought for a long time to convince human beings that he could set before their eyes the truth that they had never seen, that is, that the sacred was not transcendent but immanent, that it was effectively possible to replace the divine with the human—a deformed version of the incarnation. Today, however, evidence of the truth has given way to the presumed evidence of its absence: it is a position that is not limited to the existence of the sacred, but that actually affirms that the sacred may allow infinite interpretations. This is the "cognitive nihilism" mentioned above, a form of thought that is dominated by the terror (which we could rightly define as "sacred") of saying anything at all, and that therefore could be embraced by what we may define as a "philosophy of silence." And yet the philosopher still always says *something*, as in the past: she or he does all she or he can to ensure that what she or he says is not "the Truth"; and this attitude responds to a precise logic. After Heidegger, every position that holds the ambition of being true risks being taken for metaphysical truth, that is, the truth of the persecutors. The philosopher prefers not to take risks: she or he suspends judgment through a very real epoché. She or he does not realize that, in this way, she or he makes her- or himself complicit with the entire persecuting tradition, which continues to carry out the expulsion of the only text that could resolve this vicious circularity, that is, the Judeo-Christian Scriptures.

We are witnessing the perfect expulsion, that is, the sacrifice that leaves behind no document that can lead back to the truth of the victim. This occurs because this form of thought makes itself *simia Dei*, by presuming that it emulates God in defending the "truths" of all those clamoring to be victims. It does not realize that in this way it makes itself an accomplice of all those persecutors who pretend to be victims. Thus this form of thought arrives at the refusal of all knowledge and all truth, because it bases itself on the false principle, which is distinctive of what we called the profane hermeneutics, that believing in anything whatsoever equates to being violent. As Girard puts it: "Present-day thought is the worst form of castration, since it is the castration of the signified. People are always on the look-out to catch their neighbours red-handed in believing in something or other" (TH, 442).

The philosopher of modernity sought to prove the greatness of her or his own subjectivity, that is, the divinity of humankind, by coming closer to truth than *others* ever could.[32] The philosopher of postmodernity seeks to prove the same thing, but via the opposite method: she or he claims to be closer to Truth because he or she suspends judgment on any truth. No one, in our times, believes in *one* truth more than in *another*. This is the reason why truth is, for the new philosophy, the absence of any truth. This is an intuition that Girard developed as early as in *Deceit, Desire, and the Novel*: "Contemporary reflection discovers 'myths' and 'mythology' in every one of our desires. The eighteenth century demystified religion, the nineteenth century demystified history and philology, our era demystifies daily life. Not a single desire escapes the demystifier who is patiently occupied in constructing on top of all the dead myths the greatest myth of all, that of his own detachment. He alone, it seems, never desires. In short it is a question of convincing Others and especially of convincing oneself that one is completely and divinely autonomous" (DDN, 270–71).

When two subjects find themselves immersed in a full mimetic crisis, they become increasingly violent and, at the same time, increasingly attractive to one another. Even philosophy and religion, like all other rivals, block one another's path "just enough" to prevent, mutually, access to truth; it is this that produces cognitive nihilism, the "castration of meaning." The spider's web of difference and the outlandish acrobatics that have fascinated intellectuals in the last few decades serve above all to conceal the lack of a solution to all the essential questions.

Like the fourth tormentor of Job (J, 17), "profane" hermeneutics believes itself more capable only because it is young. It does no more than reiterate what the philosophy and the religion of the past have already said and repeated. It represents an advanced state in the decay of an ancient tradition. Moreover, the things that it says make more evident than ever what lies concealed within it: sacrificial violence.

> This still partial deconstruction confounds our present philosophical and cultural crisis with a radical impotence of thought and language. One no longer believes in philosophy but one keeps rehearsing the same old philosophical texts. And yet beyond the current crisis there are possibilities of a rational but no longer philosophical knowledge of culture. Instead, deconstruction seems content with a pure mirroring of the sacred that amounts to nothing, at this stage, but a purely literary effect; it risks degenerating into pure verbalism. And what the literary critics and academic disciples of

deconstruction do not realize is that as soon as one seeks nothing but the essence of literature it disappears. (TH, 64)

3.4. Interpretation and the History of Salvation

History, for Girard, far from being meaningless, has a distinct orientation. The conception of time that best reflects the principles of mimetic theory is a linear one. History, it should be remembered, is the history of salvation, which is achieved, after the coming of Christ, by means of the Paraclete and the progressive demystification made possible via the action of the Scriptures; it is the "Spirit of truth" itself that acts by means of the Christian texts.

Now, all this has a great deal to do with the conception of hermeneutics. Girard maintains that the Gospels themselves are susceptible to diverse interpretations, which may be classified into two distinct currents: one current that still reads the Gospels in a sacrificial way, and another that instead takes them for what they are, that is, the major instrument of demystification. If interpretation has always had a decisive weight in the process of demystification, to the point of functioning as the privileged key for escaping from the prison of violence, it is plausible that the advent of hermeneutic thought may hold some relation to the history of salvation. Only after the Christian revelation can a "history of interpretation" be possible, that is, a progressive disclosure of the truth of violence; moreover, a "history of salvation" is possible only insofar as the texts of the Judeo-Christian tradition are interpreted beyond their merely sacrificial reading.[33] In this sense, hermeneutic thought is the child of Christianity. It is nothing but the response to the final crisis to which the Christian message has led.

Therefore, Girard's harsh criticisms of hermeneutic thought should not be read as a refusal of the methods used by that mode of thought (not least because Girard often makes use of them himself), but rather as an exposure of the limits within which hermeneutic thought is constrained. We have seen how the refusal to accept the Gospels as the key to demystification turns into a radical misapprehension of the truth of the violent sacred. But there is more to this: in the historical moment in which we find ourselves, intellectual symbolism has reached its peak. The truth of violence is so close to us that we seek every possible way to avoid it: the hunt is on to find any intellectual scapegoat that can still be expelled, without leaving us identified as persecutors. In the mimetic-sacrificial vortex in which we find ourselves, even the very concept of sacrifice can be, in turn, sacrificed:

> This refusal [of all distinctions between legitimate and illegitimate violence] is in itself quite reasonable and commendable, but it is sacrificial all the same because it takes no account of history. At the present moment, sacrifice is being sacrificed; culture in its entirety, especially our own culture, historic Christianity, is playing the role of the scapegoat. We attempt to wash our hands of any complicity with the violence that lies at our origins, and this very attempt perpetuates the complicity. We all say: "If we had lived at the time of our forefathers, we would not have joined ourselves with them to spill the blood of artists and philosophers." (TH, 399)

Hermeneutic thought, despite being the child of Christianity, runs the risk of remaining entangled in a sacrificial reading of the Gospels, assuming the position that is typical of unconscious accomplices of persecutors throughout time. Medieval theologians were horrified by the killing of Jesus and maintained that, if they had been in the position of the Jews and the Romans, they would never have committed that "deicide"; modern philosophers were not much different in reproaching their fathers for the expulsion of philosophy at the hands of religion. Now, we can say, paraphrasing Girard, postmodern thinkers proclaim aloud: "If we had lived in our fathers' time, we would not have been complicit in their spilling the blood of religion and philosophy." They do not realize that this rejection of all violence is still sacrificial, because it derives from that epoché, from that suspension of judgment which is the ultimate attempt by the mimetic-sacrificial mechanism to conceal a truth that has come too close to the surface. As Girard confirms, the rejection of all violence is in itself a positive point and can be traced back, in the last analysis, to the Christian message; but the fact that, within intellectual symbolism, the concept of sacrifice becomes the new expiatory victim shows the level that the sacrificial crisis has in fact reached. Hermeneutic thought, in short, is the response to the *final* crisis to which our knowledge of violence has led us all—a response that on the one hand derives from the Christian message, and on the other from our incapacity to absorb that message immediately and wholly. Yet it is still a response: hermeneutic thought still pauses to listen to the sirens of mimetic victimage and, unlike Odysseus, allows them to bewitch it. In the first analysis, then, it seems that any response to the enchanting song of mimetic victimage will be destined to fall once again into the vortex of the violent sacred. Yet in a more attentive analysis, we understand that the question is more complex and not resolvable with the judgment that has just been expressed here. Let us be guided, for a deeper analysis, by the interpretation that Girard offers of the parable of the Grand Inquisitor, which Dostoyevsky narrates in *The Brothers Karamazov*. The Inquisitor defies Christ with the accusation that he wished to found his kingdom on freedom, to which humanity will invariably still prefer some kind of idolatry: freedom does nothing but multiply idols and conflicts between idols, so that in the last analysis humanity is thrown once again into violence. What is described here is the scenario into which Western civilization falls after the coming of Christ and precisely because of the action of his message—action that leads to only partial demystification, because humankind has refused to embrace the message in its totality: "The Inquisitor predicts that a new Tower of Babel will be raised up, more dreadful than the former one and dedicated, like it, to destruction. The grand Promethean enterprise, fruit of Christian freedom, will end in 'cannibalism'" (RU, 122).

In the context of intellectual symbolism that we have postulated above, hermeneutic thought can be regarded as representing one of the highest levels of that "tower of Babel," that is, one of the final stages of the "grand Promethean enterprise." Christ's error, in the eyes of the Inquisitor, is even less excusable because, he says, "there was no lack of warnings." In the course of the "temptations in the desert" the Devil revealed to the Redeemer and placed at his disposal the three instruments that could, so he said, assure the well-being and happiness of humanity. These three instruments were the miracle, authority, and mystery. Christ refused them, but the Inquisitor and all like him took them up, and now work, still in the name of Christ but in a spirit contrary to his, for the coming of an earthly kingdom that more closely reflects the limits of human nature.

Now, what are, in the light of intellectual symbolism, the three instruments that the devil offers to Christ, if not the pillars on which the entire sacrificial mechanism rests? The victimary expulsion of philosophy stands on the miraculous appearance of a Christ who is seen as an idol; the ensuing expulsion, of religion at the hands of philosophy, stands on the authority of reason, which sought to construct paradise on earth; lastly, postmodern thought, a prisoner of its own struggle between doubles, those multiple never-true, never-false interpretations, can do nothing better than appeal to mystery.

Violence and the sacred are the same thing: when one is silent it is because the other is raging. As long as postmodern thought remains imprisoned in a struggle between interpretations aimed at gaining an ephemeral sign of victory that immediately passes to the enemy in continual alternation, Western culture will never emerge from the underground into which its mimeticism has led it. For the sacred to be recognized as such, it is necessary to "rise again to the surface of the earth," to reappropriate that freedom which overcomes every suspension of judgment, every hesitation, and in the last analysis, every sacrifice.

This, then, is the first and necessary step on the journey of salvation, which goes through freedom. To choose freedom not only means the active renunciation of mimeticism and of the comfortable implications of the sacrificial mechanism, but also, and perhaps above all, means devoting oneself to an arduous interpretative (that is, hermeneutic) labor: to discern between the *Logos* that is definitively falling into ruin, that of sacrificial violence, and the *Logos* that continues to be sacrificed and whose pressure upon us increases day by day.

Now is the time to outline a distinction, within hermeneutic thought, that may allow us to understand the concrete expression of the fundamental ambiguity that we have theorized and traced back to the *Logos* of Heraclitus and the *Logos* of John, which have already been central to our brief reflection on Heidegger. Let us return here to a hypothesis[34]—one whose character we might call terminological, but whose meaning extends beyond that—relating to the distinction between the truth of the content of hermeneutic thought, which we might call the *revelation of the sacred*, and the truth that hermeneutics derives from the juxtaposition of partial truths extracted from the interpretation of various philosophical and religious myths, which we might call the *revelation of the lie of the sacred*. Regarding the first point, the content of hermeneutic thought falls within the lie of philosophy and religion, reveals its metaphysical and violent pretenses, but *reproduces its structures at the level of interpretation*: the sacred does not disappear, but enters the sphere of immanence, which is constituted by what we might call the *ritual of interpretation*, the stakes of any interpretative dispute. For this reason, in hermeneutic thought, the lie continues to exert its power of misapprehension. To reveal the sacred, concealed in philosophy as much as in religion, that sacred which is a total lie, does not yet mean revealing the truthfulness of the lie, but reproducing the lie itself at the level of interpretation.

The hermeneutics that we have designated as "profane," then, may be, in its content, the revelation of the sacred, but certainly not the revelation of its lie. What is more, even the hermeneutics that we have designated as "theological" runs the risk of being only the revelation of the sacred, a risk to which it succumbs whenever the interpretative criteria on which it relies become part of an intellectual symbolism that is still sacrificial.

Regarding the second point, that is, the revelation of the lie of the sacred, before the decay of truth in hermeneutics, there exists interpretation itself. Beyond the various philosophical-religious points of view, which witness to only partial truths, we deal with the sacrificial-intellectual crisis in its entirety. In other words, interpretative truth is not the truth of hermeneutics, or at least it is not the truth of hermeneutics without the "external" contribution constituted by the Gospels.

I will now proceed to analyze briefly a few instances of hermeneutic thought that, for reasons that will become clear as the analysis proceeds, may be considered representative of the hypothesis proposed above.

3.5. The Revelation of the Sacred: Jacques Derrida

Consider the work of Jacques Derrida. Girard expresses succinct but clear opinions on Derrida's thought. For instance, in a 1978 interview, he claims that Derrida's work "Plato's Pharmacy"[35] shows that mimetic crisis and the victimary mechanism still function, in an evolved but still observable form, in culture and philosophy.[36]

Intellectual symbolism, we might argue, constitutes a derivative form of mimetic victimage, in which the mechanism is not merely at work, but actually represents the sacrificial-intellectual crisis typical of postmodernity—a crisis of which Derrida's work cited above is an example. Girard unpacks the intuition mentioned above in the *Violence and the Sacred*, where he contends: "Philosophy, like tragedy, can at certain levels serve as an attempt at expulsion, an attempt perpetually renewed because never wholly successful. This point, I think, has been brilliantly demonstrated by Jacques Derrida in his essay *La Pharmacie de Platon"* (VS, 296).

The importance of intellectual symbolism in the context of our work is becoming increasingly clear as we proceed in the analysis. Far from being merely a different plane for the action of mimetic victimage, intellectual symbolism is itself the very nature of every philosophical text, the place where victimary expulsion is continually repeated and thus ritualized; however, Girard maintains, it never reaches a conclusion, which is why it is possible to repeat it again and again. Following up on Girard's hints above, it might be argued that this is precisely what "Plato's Pharmacy" exemplifies: in Derrida's work, victimary expulsion would be constantly repeated and ritualized. Therefore, it is worth looking at this text more closely—but first, it is useful to consider another remark by Girard, this time from *Things Hidden*, where he contends: "If you examine the pivotal terms in the finest analyses of Derrida, you will see that beyond the deconstruction of philosophical concepts, it is always a question of the paradoxes of the sacred, and although there is no question of deconstructing these they are all the more apparent to the reader" (TH, 64).[37]

Beyond any act of deconstruction in Derrida's work, then, there is the sacred, and it is far from being demystified; such work, therefore, constitutes a revelation of the sacred, because here the sacred is reproposed, at the level of interpretation, in its lie. Moreover, this is a "profane" form of hermeneutics insofar as it makes no use of the demystifying principles offered by the Gospel.

Let us verify these assertions. Derrida's reflections have their origins in Plato's *Phaedrus*, whose core is represented by a "mythology . . . of a logos recounting its origin,"[38] represented by the twofold and ambiguous use of the term *pharmakon*. In relation to the Sophists, it acquires the meaning of "poison," but when Plato applies it to Socrates its meaning as "remedy" takes precedence. Plato, in other words, institutes an arbitrary difference, expelling the Sophist from the philosophical city with a violence of which the use of the *pharmakon* is proof.[39]

Derrida's thesis is that the Platonic condemnation of writing in the *Phaedrus* is not unambiguous. On the one hand, Plato maintains that *grammé*, substituting "viva voce," that is, the presentness of *phoné*, falsifies philosophical discourse; but on the other hand, Plato underlines the duplicity of writing (which is *pharmakon*—that is, not only poison, but also medicine) and writes the dialogues.[40]

For the classification of Derrida within our scheme to be appropriate, we should search his work for signs of a partial comprehension of mimetic victimage, in tandem with a not-yet-demystified violent sacred. Regarding the former, we may indeed effectively perceive hints of the central aspects of mimetic theory, particularly the relationship of attraction and rivalry that a disciple feels simultaneously for a model. For example, in addressing the relation between Thamus (the supreme god) and Thoth (god of invention) in the Egyptian myth from which Socrates's discourse is developed in the *Phaedrus*, Derrida writes: "In distinguishing himself from his opposite, Thoth also imitates it, becomes its sign and representative, obeys it and *conforms* to it, replaces it, by violence if need be."[41] But it is in the conception of the scapegoat that we may identify a partial comprehension of the role of violence—partial because it is based upon a sacred that, in turn, is unsusceptible to demystification. Consider the following passage:

> The city's body *proper* thus constitutes its unity, closes around the security of its inner courts, gives back to itself the word that links it with itself within the confines of the agora, by violently excluding from its territory the representative of an external threat or aggression. . . . Yet the representative of the outside is nonetheless *constituted*, regularly granted its place by the community, chosen, kept, fed, etc. . . . Beneficial insofar as he cures— and for that, venerated and cared for—harmful insofar as he incarnates the powers of evil—and for that, feared and treated with caution. Alarming and calming. Sacred and accursed. The conjunction, the *coincidentia oppositorum*, ceaselessly undoes itself in the passage to decision or crisis. The expulsion of the evil or madness restores sōphrosunē.
>
> These exclusions took place at critical moments (drought, plague, famine). *Decision* was then repeated.[42]

And if this is not enough, we should consider how Derrida finds in that expulsion the fundamental meaning of the figure of the *pharmakos*, which is identified with the scapegoat: "The character of the *pharmakos* has been compared to a scapegoat. The *evil* and the *outside*, the expulsion of evil, its exclusion out of the body (and out) of the city—these are the two major senses of the character and of the ritual."[43]

Being an interpretative text that discusses the sacred without revealing it, and hence a text that reflects a sacrificial-cultural crisis, "Plato's Pharmacy" should present, we might expect, some form of double, that is, a certain conflictuality transferred onto the plane of intellectual symbolism. And the reference to this phenomenon is quite explicit. Derrida writes: "As soon as the supplementary outside is opened, its structure implies that the supplement itself can be 'typed,' replaced by its double, and that a supplement to the supplement, a surrogate for the surrogate, is possible and necessary. . . . And writing appears to Plato (and after him to all of philosophy, which is as such constituted in this gesture) as that process of redoubling in which we are fatally (en)trained: the supplement of a supplement."[44]

Writing represents the prototype of every intellectual symbolism; indeed, it is its founding event. Writing is a substitute for the discourse, the *logos*, which is already in its own turn a substitute for thought. From the point of view of mimetic theory, first comes expulsion (thought), then the original victim is substituted by an intellectual symbol (writing). Derrida is not mistaken when he argues that philosophy establishes itself as such in this gesture. It might be objected that so far we have posited intellectual symbolism as a characteristic trait of history following the Christian revelation: but that does not mean that such symbolism was not already at work, albeit in the underground and in a less evident way, before the Christian era. *Intellectual symbolism is as old as the history of philosophy: it is indeed the essential instrument of philosophy*; however, it becomes the site to which mimetic-victimary conflicts gradually shift only after divine revelation has made persecutors' attempts at concealment more difficult. More appropriately, the question is whether the introduction of intellectual symbolism does in fact placate violence. Derrida's answer is a negative one: "Writing—or, if you will, the *pharmakon*—can only *displace* or even *aggravate* the ill. . . . what is supposed to produce the positive and eliminate the negative does nothing but *displace* and at the same time *multiply* the effects of the negative, leading the lack that was its cause to proliferate."[45]

Derrida's response to our hypothetical question matches what we expected. *To expel a scapegoat, indeed an intellectual scapegoat, means only shifting violence from the concrete into the abstract, multiplying the effects that fall from the abstract back into the concrete*, and vastly magnifying the ontological sickness that the expulsion itself has stimulated. Violence always invokes further violence: "In choosing violence—and that is what it's all about from the beginning—and violence against the father, the son—or patricidal writing—cannot fail to expose himself, too."[46] The destiny of writing is indicative of such dynamics: qua the prototype of every intellectual scapegoat, it is expelled only to be readmitted into intellectual symbolism with full honors, as an essential component.

Derrida seems somehow to be reproaching Plato for this ambiguous attitude—first the expulsion of writing, and then its readmission. When seen in a demystifying light, all becomes clearer: philosophy is born with an act of expulsion, directed at writing, but, like all victims, writing returns, and indeed it becomes the cornerstone around which a new culture—Western culture, and therefore also philosophical culture—is founded. The sacrificial origin of society is therefore replicated, at an intellectual level, in the origin of philosophy. Indeed, every culture is founded on this sacred violence against the victim: it is this absent-present sacred that Derrida's work implies. Absent in that it is misapprehended, indeed the sacred is the only thing that is not deconstructed; present in that everything involved in such deconstructions leads back to a foundation that in fact is never reached.

Derrida's analyses are fundamentally correct. However, from the point of view of mimetic theory, it is only through its own expulsion that writing could become *pharmakon*—and not *before* or *without* that expulsion. Derrida does not grasp that, and therefore he blames Plato. Derrida, and some other postmodern thinkers with him, desires the sacred without expulsion, its benefits without sacrifice—which is impossible. In this sense, it is true that, as Derrida concludes, in the pharmacy it is not possible to distinguish the poison from the remedy.

Or, at least, it is impossible to do that without the "litmus test" offered by the Judeo-Christian Scriptures.

3.6. Revealing the Lie of the Sacred: Paul Ricoeur

The next thinker we are going to consider is Paul Ricoeur. Girard himself offers some orientation in this direction in *Things Hidden*, where he writes: "Traditional Christian thinkers could proclaim the cleavage between

Christianity and everything else, but they were incapable of demonstrating it. Anti-Christian thinkers can note the continuity but they are unable to come to terms with its true nature. Among our contemporaries, only Paul Ricoeur, particularly in his fine work *La Symbolique du Mal*, is willing to argue with determination that both positions are necessary" (TH, 445).[47]

It is to *The Symbolism of Evil*, then, that we will turn in order to place Ricoeur in the scheme of our hypothesis. In this work, Ricoeur sets himself the task of analyzing those myths that concern the problem of evil. But what does Ricoeur mean by "myth"?

> Myth will here be taken to mean . . . a traditional narration which relates to events that happened at the beginning of time and which has the purpose of providing grounds for the ritual actions of men of today and, in a general manner, establishing all the forms of action and thought by which man understands himself in his world. . . . myth reveals . . . its power of discovering and revealing the bond between man and what he considers sacred. Paradoxical as it may seem, the myth, when it is thus demythologized through contact with scientific history and elevated to the dignity of a symbol, is a dimension of modern thought.[48]

This passage contains all the elements that constitute Girard's theory of the sacred. "Myth" is taken to mean a narrative of events that possibly took place in reality, even if they are now transfigured; in it, we recognize the establishment of rites; Ricoeur then emphasizes its role in revealing the relation between the human being and the sacred; finally, Ricoeur identifies in the myth a "dimension of modern thought" in the moment when it is "elevated to the dignity of a symbol." Myth therefore becomes a symbol, that is, a revelatory text, that may in turn be interpreted in the light of principles of demystification.[49]

Aside from this clarification, it is nonetheless beyond doubt that, given the degree of attention that Ricoeur reserves for myths, it is fair to expect to find in his work other intuitions of mimetic victimage. First of all, there should be some suggestions of the role of mimesis. In fact, Ricoeur claims: "It is always in the sight of other people who excite the feeling of shame and under the influence of the word which says what is pure and impure that a stain is defilement."[50]

Ricoeur brings to light the connection that unites the sacred to mimesis: what is impurity if not the condition that arises from a dangerous encounter with the violent sacred? And is the object of mimetic desire not the sacred object par excellence? Ricoeur continues: "Our own desire projects itself into the desirable object, reveals itself through the object; and so, when he *binds himself*—and that is the evil thing—a man accuses the object in order to exculpate himself."[51]

Evil, then, arises from being a prisoner of desire, in which one also imprisons oneself. This wish to remain within the universe of mediation is the sin that generates all other sins, and that, in the final analysis, leads to self-destruction. Ricoeur argues: "Such is the sin of sins: no longer transgression, but a despairing and desperate will to shut oneself up in the circle of interdiction and desire. It is in this sense that it is a desire for death."[52]

The destiny of the human being, tormented by the weight of her or his own desires, unfolds via the fluctuations of ontological evil: desire no longer has an object, but has become metaphysical. Ricoeur addresses this question in a longer passage, which is worth quoting in full:

> Desire is evil only because it is no longer strictly corporeal; it must be seized by a frenzy of immoderation; and immoderation comes to desire only through "falsehood." The *tyrant* is the living proof of the madness that takes possession of desire. The tyrant, indeed, is for philosophy a magnitude that is more than political and is, properly speaking, metaphysical, because he is the symbol of the man who has the power to satisfy all his desires; he is the myth of unlimited desire—unlimited because it is ministered to by a power that is itself not limited by law. Now the tyrant gives evidence that this body of desire undergoes a sort of mutation from the fact that of the unjust soul which inhabits it, that desire is a creation of injustice and not vice versa.[53]

Note that, from the point of view of mimetic theory, Ricoeur here falls into a subtle error of comprehension, in pointing out a consequentiality that is the reverse of the mimetic mechanism (as Girard understands it). Every form of violence is caused by desire, and therefore includes injustice. To reverse these terms, that is, to maintain that desires originate from a violent and unjust "nature," means falling once again into subtle confusion about the role of the violent sacred. This does not mean, however, that Ricoeur does not grasp the real importance of a desire that makes itself romantically infinite, and that indeed he designates as the true essence of humanity: "Henceforth the evil infinite of human desire—always something else, always something more—which animates the movement of civilizations, the appetite for pleasure, for possessions, for power, for knowledge—*seems* to constitute the reality of man. The restlessness that makes us discontented with the present *seems* to be our true nature, or rather the absence of a nature."[54]

As mentioned before, Ricoeur combines with this strong understanding of the mimetic aspect of the mechanism an equally sound understanding of the role that violence has played "since the foundation of the world." Ricoeur claims: "The invincible bond between Vengeance and defilement . . . is so primitive that it is anterior even to the representation of an avenging god"; and later on, he remarks: "Thus Violence is inscribed in the origin of things, in the principle that establishes while it destroys."[55]

Violence, then, is primary in this world, preceding any order, which indeed is founded on originary disorder by violence and through violence, and precedes all representations of a violent god, who is no more than the abstraction of violence, at a level that is even more primitive than intellectual symbolism. Order is maintained through the ritualization of violence, that is, through the expulsion of victims. As Ricoeur puts it: "Last Judgment, expiatory sacrifice, juridical penalty, internal penance. Their mere enumeration sufficiently attests that the demand implicit in the law of retribution is not exhausted in the archaic explanation of all human ills by the evil of fault."[56]

The choice of a victim is based on certain criteria that we have already considered. Job, for example, is a perfect scapegoat because he is the focus of every possible misfortune. What occurs in his case is a "self-fulfilling prophecy": Job is already the predetermined, designated victim, but his persecutors will never admit it and will emphasize how the misfortunes of which he is the object all derive from a divine anger, directed at him: he is therefore a threat and deserves to be expelled. As Ricoeur puts it: "Punishment falls on man in the guise of misfortune and transforms all possible sufferings, all diseases, all death, all failure into a sign of defilement."[57]

In Ricoeur's work, we also find a position on secularization that is quite original among the thinkers we have considered thus far. Such conception stems from the equivalence that he establishes between science and ritual:

"Thus the ritualization of ethics is a corollary of its heteronymy: the scrupulous conscience desires to be exact in its accepted dependence, and the rite is the instrument of that exactness, which is the ethical equivalent of scientific exactness."[58] Thus, Ricoeur sees a continuity between the ideal of scientific exactness and ancient ritualistic systems in the field of ethics.

What is most interesting to note is that Ricoeur distinguishes between the set of myths and the narratives contained in Judeo-Christian texts: he distinguishes, in the terms of mimetic theory, between the Heraclitean *Logos* and the Johannine *Logos*. This distinction may be found in Ricoeur's contrast between cosmogonic myths, in which violence is central, and the book of Genesis, in which the word is central: "Creation is no longer conflict but 'word': God says, and it is so."[59]

The distinction between the mythic element and the Christian element becomes clearer where Ricoeur addresses the figure of Christ. Central for Ricoeur, in a spirit of pure demystification, is the shift away from the *transfer* of violence to which the protagonist of myths is subjected, to the lucidity with which Jesus allows violence to destroy himself, but only in order to unmask its true role: "This alliance supposes that the substitutive suffering is not the simple transfer of defilement to a passive object, such as the scapegoat . . . but the voluntary 'gift' of a suffering taken upon himself and offered to others."[60]

For Ricoeur, as for Girard, the figure of Jesus appears irreconcilable with the legacy of myth, untranslatable into any symbol. Ricoeur correctly notes that while all myths may be read through the hermeneutical method, the evangelical narrative turns out to be unreadable. As we noted above, hermeneutic thought may read myth, but only evangelical demystification can read hermeneutic thought: "That Jesus could be the point of convergence of all the figures without himself being a 'figure' is an Event that exceeds the resources of our phenomenology of images. All the images we have examined are subject to our hermeneutic method insofar as they are scattered images, but their temporal and personal unity is not; the event announced in the Gospel, the 'fulfilment,' is properly the content of the Christian Kerygma."[61]

Ricoeur's hermeneutics represents, therefore, a demystification of myths, made possible by the direct action of the interpretative principles provided by Christian texts. In this sense, Ricoeur confirms that only the modern human being can recognize the myth as myth, because he alone has reached the point where history and myth become separate. This "crisis," this decision, after which myth and history are dissociated, may signify the loss of the mythical dimension . . . : we are tempted to give ourselves up to a radical demythization of all our thinking. But another possibility offers itself to us: precisely because we are living and thinking after the separation of myth and history, the demythization of our history can become the other side of an understanding of myth as myth, and the conquest, for the first time in the history of culture, of the mythical dimension. That is why we never speak here of demythization, but strictly of demythologization, it being well understood that what is lost is the pseudo-knowledge, the false *logos* of the myth, such as we find expressed, for example, in the etiological function of myths. But when we lose the myth as immediate *logos*, we rediscover it as myth. Only at the price and by the roundabout way of philosophical exegesis and understanding, can the myth create a new *peripeteia* of the *logos*.[62]

The interpretation of myths, then, opens the way to a form of knowledge that omits what is false in them and retains what is true. Ricoeur's thought, therefore, can be considered a "theological" hermeneutics, and since his interpretation of Christian texts does not risk falling into sacrificial symbolism, he reveals the lie of the sacred. Ricoeur's hermeneutics is therefore the overcoming of the oblivion of the sacred. He even states that explicitly: "Hermeneutics, an acquisition of 'modernity,' is one of the modes by which that 'modernity' transcends itself, insofar as it is forgetfulness of the sacred."[63]

Our knowledge of the sacred has become gradually more precise, less ambiguous, but for this very reason we have had to face the eclipse of the signs of the sacred, and even of humanity, insofar as it is a reflection of the sacred. In the context of a radical confrontation with modern consciousness, Ricoeur has shown the persistence of a residual mythicality, which is never entirely reconcilable with rational reflection.[64]

Ricoeur recalls elsewhere that symbology of the sacred is, at its height, the aporia of representation, but at the same time it is also the representation of aporia, on the fringes of absolute knowledge.[65] We are standing on the fringes of absolute knowledge, and therefore on one hand we are still standing within *logos* and within philosophy; yet, on the other hand, precisely this *logos* gives us access to authentic transcendence, to a faith that is not blind or unfounded abandonment.

3.7. Between Knowledge and Ritual Interpretation

We have reached the end of this brief excursus into hermeneutic thought, and therefore we may now draw some conclusions.

What emerges from the analysis carried out so far is that the strength of the founding movement of hermeneutics (as well as its extreme paradoxicality) consists precisely in the establishment of a meaning, that is, in the separation of good from bad reciprocity, which we have seen to be common to all hermeneutic thought, and in the genesis of any symbology.[66]

Hermeneutic thought is therefore revelatory thought, but it runs the risk of ritualizing its own act of interpretation and thus of perpetuating the mimetic victimage once again on the intellectual level. Thus, we might consider the following hypothesis: if hermeneutics reads philosophical-religious myths, then the total revelation of originary truth can read hermeneutics. It is only retrospectively upon reaching this conclusion that we can recognize the stages of mystification in their entirety.

We find ourselves at an epochal turning point, even at the level of intellectual symbolism. The "virulence" of which Girard speaks (DBB, 139) heralds the apocalypse, self-destruction. To avoid this path, it is necessary to follow the idea of freedom that Dostoyevsky's Grand Inquisitor refuses to follow because it seems to pose a risk that he considers too great: to abandon "the historical paths of mystification" and to take "the path of demystification." Girard calls the abandonment of the paths of mystification the "death of philosophy": such death means recognizing the truth of philosophy (as well as of religion) and therefore the lies it has built around the sacred. But if the truth of philosophy is death, death is not the truth of "knowledge," or the truth of that philosophy from which any trace of demystification has been stripped away: "Out of supreme disorder is born supernatural order. . . . The apocalypse would not be complete without a positive side" (DDN, 290–91).

NOTES

1. On this subject, see Harry Austryn Wolfson, *The Philosophy of the Church Fathers* (Cambridge, MA: Harvard University Press, 1964).

2. Compare Wolfson, *The Philosophy of the Church Fathers*, 72.

3. See Étienne Gilson, *History of Christian Philosophy in the Middle Ages* (London: Sheed and Ward, 1955): "When Saint Paul speaks of Christ as the 'power' (*energeia*) or the wisdom (*sophia*) of God (I Cor. I, 24) he certainly was making use of two Greek philosophical notions" (5); however, "there is no trace of any systematic use of philosophy in canonical writings," and "when Saint Paul wrote that Christ was 'wisdom,' he was not intending to reduce the person of Christ to the abstract notion of *sophia*; rather, he was saying that what the philosophers had vainly expected from their so-called wisdom, the Christians had just received from Christ, and again, this was not a philosophical statement; it was a religious one" (6).

4. We might say that the intellectual symbolism is the expression of the *Logos* that has its origins with Heraclitus, just as Christian symbology is the expression of the *Logos* that has its origins with John.

5. See Gilson, *History of Christian Philosophy*, 6.

6. Justin Martyr, *First Apology*, chap. 46.

7. Gilson writes on these two theologians: "It is significant for the history of Christian thought that this arch-enemy of Greek philosophy [Tatian] died out of the communion of the Church, whereas he who had claimed for Christianity the benefit of all that was good and true in Greek culture [Justin] had died a martyr and a saint." Gilson, *History of Christian Philosophy*, 16.

8. Formenti writes: "When read formulaically as a sacrifice, with the intention of expiating human sin, the death of Christ functions as the archetype of scandalous injustice; outraged by this monstrous crime, we prepare to hunt down the killers; we attempt to excuse all future notions of 'just' punishments, sentences, executions, wars, and so on." Carlo Formenti, *Prometeo e Hermes* (Naples: Liguori, 1986), 115.

9. "The indignation caused by scandal is invariably a feverish desire to differentiate between the guilty and the innocent, to allot responsibilities, to unmask the guilty secret without fear or favour and to distribute punishment." TH, 426.

10. "We cling to the sacrificial reading for some sign of our own right to salvation and of the just damnation of others; we beg for purification from violence while committing violence against others—the enemy, the impure, the murderer—in the delirious belief that we are extirpating evil." Formenti, *Prometeo e Hermes*, 115.

11. Girard later changed his mind on the sacrificial reading of the Epistle to the Hebrews. See the essay "Transition: Corrections and Paradoxes," in this volume, for more details on this issue.

12. The first witch trials were held in 1250 (other sources claim 1258), and the first witch was condemned to the stake in 1275 in Toulouse, but the period of the greatest persecutions can be traced to the beginning of the fifteenth century, for which calculations have shown that no fewer than a million people were condemned and burned alive. It should be noted that very early there emerged some texts that denounced abuses in trials against witches: Johann Weyer, *De praestigiis daemonum* (1563) and Reginald Scott, *Discovery of Witchcraft* (1584).

13. See Johan Huizinga, *The Autumn of the Middle Ages* (Chicago: University of Chicago Press, 1997).

14. See Eugenio Garin, *Medioevo e rinascimento* (Rome: Laterza, 1954).

15. Chris Fleming and John O'Carroll, "On Romanticism," *Anthropoetics* 11, no. 1 (2005).

16. Consistently—I believe—with Girard's thought, we should use this expression to distinguish the

subject from whose visual stance the process is observed (the I) from otherness constituted by the rival-mediator (the Other).

17. Here I am addressing Hegel's philosophy from a strictly Girardian point of view; however, I believe that Hegel's philosophy can be interpreted in a much more sympathetic light, in the context of mimetic theory. See the last two essays in this volume.

18. See Livio Bottani, "La mimesi, la violenza e il sacro: Nota sul pensiero di René Girard," *Filosofia* 38, no. 1 (1987): 53–56, 55.

19. See DBB, "Chapter 4: Strategies of Madness: Nietzsche, Wagner and Dostoevski," 61–83. This chapter is absolutely central to understanding Girard's position in the context of modern philosophical thought.

20. Vattimo comments: "If the natural sacred is the violent mechanism that Jesus came to unveil and undermine, it is possible that secularization—which also constitutes the Church's loss of temporal authority and human reason's increasing autonomy from its dependence upon an absolute God, a fearful Judge who so transcends our ideas about good and evil as to appear as a capricious or bizarre sovereign—is precisely a positive effect of Jesus' teaching, and not a way of moving away from it. It may be that Voltaire himself is a positive effect of the Christianization of mankind, and not a blasphemous enemy of Christ." Gianni Vattimo, *Belief*, trans. Luca D'Isanto and David Webb (Stanford, CA: Stanford University Press, 1999), 41.

21. This has been well outlined by Serres: "Scientific crisis is a crisis of closure, that is, a sacrificial crisis. . . . Comte was not wrong to link fetishism and positivism: even—perhaps above all—among those who repudiate positive philosophy, or believe they have banished it forever, fetishes are reviving en masse, invisible, where they are least expected. It is the return of religion, the return of the sacred, as one would say of a returning exile." Michel Serres, *Hermès V: Le passage du Nord-Ouest* (Paris: Minuit, 1980), 147.

22. Compare Maurizio Ferraris, *Storia dell'ermeneutica* (Milan: Bompiani, 1988), 42–45; Marco Ravera, ed., *Il pensiero ermeneutico* (Genoa: Marietti, 1986), 8.

23. Compare Ferraris, *Storia dell'ermeneutica*, 53; Ravera, *Il pensiero ermeneutico*, 9.

24. One can think here of Golyadkin, the protagonist of Dostoyevsky's *The Double*. See RU, 34–35.

25. "But the only authentic *epochē* is never mentioned by modern philosophers; it is always victory over desire, victory over Promethean pride" (DDN, 300).

26. See Martin Heidegger, *An Introduction to Metaphysics*, trans. Ralph Manheim (New Haven: Yale University Press, 1968), 134; originally published as *Einfuehrung in die Metaphysik* (Tübingen: Max Niemeyer, 1953).

27. Gianni Vattimo has commented: "Girard . . . insists upon the fact that Heidegger, although he did recognize a deep difference between the Greek *logos* of Heraclitus and the *logos* of the gospel of St. John, remained completely within the victimary logic that dominates the main line of modern thought. In particular, Heidegger offers emblematic evidence of the 'expulsion' the Judeo-Christian Scriptures have undergone in modernity." Gianni Vattimo, "Heidegger and Girard: *Kénosis* and the End of Metaphysics," in *Christianity, Truth, and Weakening Faith: A Dialogue*, by Gianni Vattimo and René Girard, ed. Pierpaolo Antonello, trans. William McCuaig (New York: Columbia University Press, 2010), 79.

28. For more on the interpretative possibilities of the two *Logoi*, see TH, 263–64; for Girard's discussion of Heidegger's *Logoi*, see TH, 264–70. The texts by Heidegger that Girard considers are *Einfuehrung in die Metaphysik* and *Vorträge und Aufsätze* (Pfullingen: Günther Neske, 1954),

in their respective French translations: *Introduction à la métaphysique*, trans. Gilbert Kahn (Paris: Gallimard, 1958) and *Essais et conférences*, trans. André Préau (Paris: Gallimard, 1958).

29. See Alfred Simon, ed., "Discussion avec René Girard," *Esprit* 429 (1973): 528–63.

30. *Le bouc émissaire*, 285–86, my translation. This passage is oddly missing from the English translation; it should follow the paragraph ending "Instead of breaking through the circle of violence and the sacred as they imagined they were doing, our predecessors re-created weakened variations of myths and rituals" and precede the paragraph beginning "In reality these myths have little importance" (205).

31. *Le bouc émissaire*, 138, my translation. This passage is also missing from the English translation; it is included in a portion of text that, in the French edition, follows the paragraph ending "The discovery of their secret would provide what must be called a *scientific* solution to man's greatest enigma, the nature and origins of religion" and precedes the paragraph beginning "It is important not to confuse the reciprocal and ritualized extermination of 'methodologies' with the totality of actual intelligence" (95).

32. This is consistent with that process of "radicalization" typical of philosophy, as it is described in Chris Fleming and John O'Carroll, "Revolution, Rupture, Rhetoric," *Philosophy and Social Criticism* 38, no. 1 (2012): 39–57.

33. "The history of salvation is what makes the history of interpretation possible, but at the same time, the history of salvation occurs or presents itself only as a history of interpretation. . . . Interpretation—above all the interpretation of the Holy Scriptures—has obviously always been connected, in the Hebrew-Christian tradition, with salvation." Gianni Vattimo, "Storia della salvezza, storia dell'interpretazione," *Micromega* 3 (1992): 106–10, 106; repr. in Gianni Vattimo, *Dopo la cristianità: Per un cristianesimo non religioso* (Milan: Garzanti, 2002), 63–74.

34. It seems the only mimetic theory scholar to have made this distinction explicit is Piero Burzio, "Mito, tragedia, romanzo in René Girard," *Rivista di estetica* 34 (1994): 41–68.

35. Jacques Derrida, "Plato's Pharmacy," in *Dissemination*, trans. Barbara Johnson (London: Athlone Press, 1981), 61–172; originally published as "La Pharmacie de Platon," in *La Dissémination* (Paris: Seuil, 1972), 71–197.

36. Bruce Bassoff, "Interview with René Girard," *Denver Quarterly* 13, no. 2 (1978): 28–40.

37. On this subject, see Sylviane Agacinski et al., *Mimésis des articulations* (Paris: Aubier-Flammarion, 1975), 231–70.

38. Derrida, "Plato's Pharmacy," 128.

39. For an analysis of the problem of the *pharmakon* in Derrida, see VS, 296–97, and the article "Lévi-Strauss, Frye, Derrida and Shakespearean Criticism," *Diacritics* 3 (1973): 34–38. For wider critical discussion of Derrida's analysis of Plato's *pharmakon*, see James G. Williams, "On Job and Writing: Derrida, Girard, and the Remedy-Poison," *Scandinavian Journal of the Old Testament* 7 (1993): 34–39.

40. Compare Maurizio Ferraris, *Differenze: La filosofia francese dopo lo strutturalismo* (Milan: Multipla, 1981), 58.

41. Derrida, "Plato's Pharmacy," 93.

42. Derrida, "Plato's Pharmacy," 133.

43. Derrida, "Plato's Pharmacy," 130.

44. Derrida, "Plato's Pharmacy," 109.

45. Derrida, "Plato's Pharmacy," 100.

46. Derrida, "Plato's Pharmacy," 149.

47. Paul Ricoeur, *The Symbolism of Evil*, trans. Emerson Buchanan (New York: Harper and Row, 1967); originally published as "La symbolique du mal," in *Finitude et culpabilité* (Paris: Aubier, 1960).

48. Ricoeur, *The Symbolism of Evil*, 5.

49. Kearney draws on Ricoeur to oppose Girard, in arguing the necessity that myth should also have an "eschatological" dimension, recalling the notion of the "exploratory force of myth," and the "ethical approach" and the "symbolic" character of myth, which Ricoeur had investigated in *The Symbolism of Evil*. However, if we are to keep faith with the principles of mimetic theory, we should assign to myth, as Girard construes it, a purely archaeological validity. This is for the simple reason that in Girard the eschatological dimension of a reference to the future—inasmuch as it is a "force of exploration" and a "revelation of the link between man and the sacred" (in the sense that Ricoeur intends)—finds form in a discourse different from that of myth, that is, in an authentically Christian one. See Richard Kearney, "Le mythe chez René Girard: Un Nouveau Bouc Émissaire," in Dumouchel, *Violence et Vérité*, 35–49.

50. Ricoeur, *The Symbolism of Evil*, 40.

51. Ricoeur, *The Symbolism of Evil*, 257.

52. Ricoeur, *The Symbolism of Evil*, 146.

53. Ricoeur, *The Symbolism of Evil*, 341.

54. Ricoeur, *The Symbolism of Evil*, 254.

55. Ricoeur, *The Symbolism of Evil*, 30, 182–83.

56. Ricoeur, *The Symbolism of Evil*, 42–43.

57. Ricoeur, *The Symbolism of Evil*, 27.

58. Ricoeur, *The Symbolism of Evil*, 135–36.

59. Ricoeur, *The Symbolism of Evil*, 240.

60. Ricoeur, *The Symbolism of Evil*, 266.

61. Ricoeur, *The Symbolism of Evil*, 269.

62. Ricoeur, *The Symbolism of Evil*, 161–62.

63. Ricoeur, *The Symbolism of Evil*, 352.

64. See Ricoeur, *The Symbolism of Evil*, 349.

65. Compare Paul Ricoeur, "Philosopher après Kierkegaard," *Revue de théologie et de philosophie* 4 (1963): 315.

66. Compare Jean-Pierre Dupuy, *Ordres et désordres: Enquête sur un nouveau paradigme* (Paris: Seuil, 1982), 128: "What I wish to understand is what allows one single explicatory principle that capacity to generate such varied and contrasting forms. How can simplicity, apparently on its own, produce complexity? Is this not a logical impossibility? How, after all, can more arise from less?"

CHAPTER 3

The Path of Demystification

1. Enemy Siblings

Girard's reflections have led us to recognize sacred violence as the foundation of Western culture. Sacred violence, in turn, has its roots in mimetic conflicts: the rivals are brothers who are both brought closer and divided by something they both desire. I have also argued that mimetic rivalry is the engine that drives all intellectual symbolism. Thus, the "figure" that represents that symbolism better than any other is that of enemy brothers, who are brothers precisely because they are enemies (or made alike by their reciprocal violent rivalry) and enemies precisely because they are brothers (or rivals inasmuch as each imitates the other's desire).

Another "figure" that Girard often uses to represent mimetic rivalry is that of doubles. The phenomenon of the double manifests itself at the paroxysm of the conflict between enemy brothers: they increasingly come to resemble one another because they increasingly imitate one another's desires and therefore confront one another with greater and greater hostility.

The thesis that has led us to this point, and that I will now make explicit, is that we may interpret the history of the philosophy of religion as the scene of a duel between two enemy brothers—or, perhaps, between two enemy sisters. *The double mediation unique to the philosophy of religion within the realm of intellectual symbolism is the homologue of the tragic dispute between enemy siblings in the realm of transfiguring myth.*

Double mediation is the illusion of difference, which goes hand in hand with the illusion of an unbridgeable distance between subject and mediator and which determines the metaphysical value of the object—the same illusion that, in another context, all tragic characters intimately share, when they believes they have uttered the crucial word or committed the crucial violence that at last will make them masters of the game, the illusion that, from a point of view external to the conflict, brings them ever closer to the identity of their enemy-companion.

Religion and philosophy continually confront one another, and the aim of each is victory over the other. Every theology and every philosophical doctrine desires to be ultimate, the seal of truth, the last word—a violent word—in the dispute. There is always, however, another philosophical doctrine or another theology that responds in turn with another "last word."

These reflections lead us to consider more attentively the relationship in which philosophy and religion find themselves historically. *They are not sisters first, and then enemies: they are sisters in violence.*[1] Their sacrificial nature binds them indissolubly.

If it is a sacrificial nature that binds philosophy and religion together, then only a form of thought that is situated within the dimension of the revelation of the lie of the sacred can bring that bond to light without mystifying it. That means, as we know, only a form of thought that refers to or, better, allows itself to be guided by the Gospels. Girard emphasizes that the Gospels foresaw the victory of a still sacrificial "Christian religion," as much as the rejection of the Christian message by modern culture: or rather, *mutatis verbis*, the sacrificial expulsion of philosophy by religion, and then of religion by philosophy.

It is through this mirroring of the roles successively filled by religion and philosophy that we understand their nature as "enemy sisters." In this light, modern philosophical culture, when it recognizes in religion all the evils of humanity, makes a scapegoat of it, no more or less than religious culture did to philosophical reason in the Middle Ages; in doing so, such philosophical culture demonstrates its religious, or rather sacrificial, origins. All viewpoints that do not reveal mimetic victimage are merely mutually opposing errors, doubles that keep kicking the same ball around without ever "scoring a goal." In the paragraph opening the chapter entitled "The Beheading of St. John the Baptist" in the French edition of *The Scapegoat*, Girard claims: "This error [our common interpretation of the relation between the Bible and religion in general] is common to Christians and their adversaries: in substance, both behave in a rigorously symmetrical way, as the good enemy brothers they are and intend to remain. They really only care about their controversy, because they live only in it. Stay away from them; otherwise they will all attack you."[2]

If violent reciprocity is the characteristic element of the relationship between enemy sisters or brothers, and thus also between philosophy and religion, *misapprehension* is a necessary element in perpetuating that relationship. A true double is always unaware of the relationship that binds her to her enemy sister or him to his enemy brother. If she or he were aware of it, she or he would realize the illusory nature of her or his desire and the mimetic mechanism would be definitively broken. In order that this not happen, the subject must be able to continue seeing its double as a rival, because only among rivals can a scapegoat be chosen and blamed. Today, paradoxically, anti-Christianity is compelled to maintain the violent nature of Christianity in order to expel it ritually.[3] This mimetic struggle is not merely a symbolic battle between disciplines or disciplinary approaches: very often, it takes the form of a mimetic conflict between individual scholars and thinkers.[4]

We have reached a new central point of the hypothesis: the importance of the figure of the rival within intellectual symbolism. No one can be a "rival" on one's own, and to be a "double," it is necessary to be the "double" of someone else—that is, we must always be at least a pair. The entire mimetic victimage therefore necessitates an "other," individual or symbolic, likewise caught in the mechanism's web. The proof of this is the fact that, in cases in which this "other" refuses to assume first the role of the rival and then that of the scapegoat (e.g., Job, Christ), the entire mimetic-sacrificial edifice collapses.

Religion, then, needs a sacrificial philosophy in order to survive: in parallel, philosophy, too, needs a religion or a sacrificial reading of Christianity in order to perpetuate itself. Such a "sacrificial philosophy" would be nothing without this "sacrificial religion," and vice versa. At this point, their rivalry no longer derives from a dispute over any kind of object (in intellectual symbolism, this would be the possession of truth), but from the need to maintain a role in the mechanism of rivalry itself.

So, let us recapitulate the bases of our hypothesis and our progress to this point. Philosophy is a mystification, that is, a system of scapegoating. So is religion. When these symbolic forms encounter one another, in the systems of philosophy of religion, each system dedicates all its strength to pursuing scapegoats in the other. Doubtless, they do so to demonstrate their perfect innocence and detachment from any type of intellectual lynching. But their innocence is mutually denied: the only truth that we discover—and it has been honed by twenty centuries of rivalry between these two "doubles"—is their essence as systems of victimization. Religion and philosophy end up demystifying each other continually and in turn, following almost exactly the same scheme.

The phenomenon that appears at the paroxysm of a sacrificial crisis— and the intellectual nature of such a crisis allows no exception—is that of the double. From the outset, the subject doubles itself: reflective thought is no longer convincing, and philosophy (or religion) splits into two poles, one that is exposed to criticism and contempt, and another that criticizes and despises. This is the sign of failure, which generates a twofold movement. The criticizing observer, one of the split poles, comes closer and closer to her triumphant rival. As the scission of inner consciousness strengthens, the distinction between subject and rival narrows; the two movements converge to bring about the "hallucination" of the double.[5] The rivals become so similar, one the double of the other, that it is no longer possible to distinguish them. Even within intellectual symbolism, the enemy brothers become a "monstrous double."

Contemporary culture finds itself precisely in this situation, at the very heart of that (seemingly endless) intellectual sacrificial crisis which has characterized Western culture since the Christian revelation—and of which the late phase of modernity that we are living represents the culmination. This crisis, however, cannot be compared to those that have preceded it. The *perfect* mirroring of religion and philosophy, on which I have insisted in the last few sections, is observable from a functional point of view, that is, in relation to the roles those symbolic forms fulfill, but once observed from the historical point of view, it is no longer *that* perfect. I have already remarked several times about the importance of the action of the demystifying Christian message within intellectual symbolism. Furthermore, what has also come to light is how the encounter between religion and philosophy renders the act of expulsion increasingly more difficult in a culture that preserves memories of its own past. Our attention has focused on hermeneutic thought, which seems to constitute a privileged position for observing the unfolding of this crisis: a problematic place, simultaneously ambiguous and decisive, which may foretell the possibility of a "nonsacrificial philosophy."

2. The Cunning of Reason

In evaluating the possibility of a nonsacrificial form of knowledge, that is, a form of knowledge not conditioned by mimetic victimage, it seems appropriate to emphasize above all the ambiguities, games of perspective, and subtle schemes that mimesis invents to make us once again misapprehend its nature and allow it to perpetuate itself. Only once we have laid bare all the possible delusions into which we risk falling while seeking a nonsacrificial form of knowledge, and only once the field has been cleared of all major objections to the possibility that such knowledge exists, will it be legitimate to try to identify it.

Nonsacrificial knowledge is, by definition, knowledge that does not rest on the mystifying power of mimetic victimage; it refuses mimetic and victimizing dynamics and reveals them in full light—that is, it demystifies them. Nonsacrificial knowledge is "knowledge of the victim," an expression we should understand in both its subjective and its objective senses: it is knowledge that reveals the fundamental role of the victim over the course of history, and the knowledge that the victim has of itself as innocent.

Such knowledge, however, loses its demystifying power—or, rather, fails to acquire it—whenever the role of the victim is taken, falsely, by a persecutor. From the moment persecutors are deprived of any justification for their sacrifices, because the Christian message has had at least some partial effects, they disguise themselves as victims.[6]

We may therefore postulate a distinction between a superficial consciousness of the role of the victim—a consciousness that, in fact, still functions to perpetuate the mechanism as it conceals it—and the true knowledge of violence. In this respect, Girard argues: "If we want to rid ourselves of the system of action and representation based on the scapegoat, commemorating victims and indulging in loud lamentation over them, which we are so good at doing—all the while calling ourselves 'Nietzscheans'—is not enough. On the contrary, it is by the infinite play of substitutions, modifications, subtle transfigurations, and wily inversions that the scapegoat system has succeeded in enduring until now and still dominates our thought today, even as it convinces us that it is nonexistent" (J, 152).

Reason appears to be, from its very origins and even in its fundamental practices, a sacrificial instrument.[7] Whoever has experience of dealing with concepts, of how, during analysis, they tend to transform themselves into their opposites, or double themselves, or conceal other concepts within themselves; whoever is familiar with the explosion of combinations that can disrupt even the most disciplined thought, or the sudden void that opens in the soundest and most agile exercise of memory, will not find it difficult to agree with this assessment of the ambiguous nature of thought.

When reason, an intellectual form with sacrificial origins, born to repeat sacrifice, turns back and seeks to clarify its origin and demystify everything that is sacrificial, the genesis of a self-referential paradox is unavoidable.[8] On one hand, reason cannot help but explore the sacred in order to seek its true origin, but on the other hand, being itself generated by the sacred, reason cannot explain its nature completely.

The sacrificial nature of reason, the fact that within it there persists a residue of the will to mystify, emerges also as reason is held up as an idol, something that repeatedly occurred in modernity. Western civilization has done nothing more than substitute the religious myth with the myth of reason: but always it is a question of myth, that is, of narratives of sacrifice.[9]

Language, too, is generated—Girard argues—to replicate the miraculous event of reconciliation that always follows the expulsion of a victim. If it is extremely difficult, not to say impossible, for reason to attain the truth about violence, then it is equally dangerous to communicate such truth with an instrument, language, that is also destined to perpetuate sacrifice, while mystifying it.

History repeats itself. Every generation exercises reason and considers that exercise sufficient to demolish the sacrificial cathedral erected or maintained by the preceding generation. In reality, such conflict, which is not exempt from the mimetic violence that always arises between fathers and sons, has only one result: the demolition of the most obvious, annoying, and archaic spires of that cathedral, only to substitute them with others that are less evident, more harmonious with the new landscape and that carry the prestige of novelty, but keep the building's foundations intact. As Girard puts it: "Children curse their fathers and become their judges. Contemporary scholars discover traces of magic in all the classical forms of rationalism and science. Instead of breaking through the circle of violence and the sacred as they imagined they were doing, our predecessors re-created weakened variations of myths and rituals" (S, 205).

In instances when the foundations of the mimetic-victimary cathedral are effectively called into question through the action of a message that can only be considered superrational—namely, that conveyed by the Gospels— the bearers of that message will be immediately victimized. What better scapegoat, in fact, could there be but the person who threatens the intellectual and social order itself? It is Girard who leads us in this direction: "All this tends to set the *unconscious* mechanism in motion once again. In order to fill the cracks and holes in the system, we resort *more or less unconsciously* to the generative and regenerative mechanism of this same system" (S, 54).

Thus, we realize the consequences of the self-referential paradox of reason: *the more reason demystifies itself, the more it becomes suspicious of itself.* In order to carry out an act of demystification, reason should be *more* than what it wishes to demystify; but this cannot happen, because the subject of such demystification is "pure reason," that is, reason that is reliant on no external forces, and the object of such demystification is reason itself.

Reason, by questioning itself and attempting to demystify itself, in reality does nothing more than anticipate its own act of self-sacrifice. If on the one hand reason remains within mimetic victimage, as it still intends to perform a sacrifice, on the other, as it ponders the significance of that act, it conceptualizes it, and in so doing, it exempts itself from it. Thus, it achieves the greatest lie of all.

To summarize: we cannot escape from the prison of mimetic victimage by means of reason, and neither can we communicate the truth on the violent sacred though a language that is guided by reason. If we remain in the universe of the human, every effort to free ourselves from the chains of mimesis and violence coincides with the identification of an "other" (an individual, a group, a culture, a doctrine, a concept, or even reason itself—when reason tries to demystify itself) who is responsible for our confinement. We only draw tighter the chains from which we wish to free ourselves. Girard outlines this dynamic quite sharply: "All the efforts to free himself only repeat and bind more tightly the original cycle" (RU, 111–12).

This definitive statement of Girard's seems to exclude the possibility of a form of nonsacrificial knowledge that is purely rational. This raises a problem: what do we make of Girard's own mimetic theory? Is it not also founded on the exercise of reason, and does it not rely on logic and various social sciences, which in turn have their foundations in reason? Does Girard not use language to communicate his theory to his readers?

We may respond to these legitimate objections, as Girard does (sometimes explicitly, more often implicitly), with two arguments. The first, which we might have expected, is that what allows knowledge of sacred violence to emerge is the demystifying action of the Gospels, that is, an element that entirely evades the labyrinth of sacrificial acts. However, this argument does not solve the whole problem. Even if we admit that what is revelatory in Girard's work derives entirely from the Christian message, what can we say of its other, obviously equally present, component, the rational component?

The answer to this second objection can be retrieved in a few brief but significant—and even somehow surprising—passages of Girard's work, where he does not back down, as it were, but admits *claris verbis* the limits of his own theory (as of any theory). The first consideration we must make is that the very concepts we use to explain mimetic theory (desire according to another [*désir selon l'autre*], sacrifice, expulsion, and so forth) do not have a real consistency; that is, they constitute conventional expressions (and, what is more, they are produced by a sacrificial form, that is, reason) that are utilized to express the way the world appears (the "phenomenal world," we might say, borrowing an expression from Kant's philosophy) to those who let themselves be guided by Christian demystification. In other words, these concepts are instruments (that do not lack sacrificial violence) that we use to grasp, in a Kantian sense, the phenomenal aspect of a reality—which we still call, improperly, mimetic and victimizing—that remains "noumenal," beyond the confines of our rational comprehension.

"Desire," "sacrifice," "expulsion" may thus be improper terms,[10] and they may even impede the revelation of truth. If this discussion has relied on such terms thus far, it is because we too, in good faith and without fully realizing

it, have moved, throughout the course of this analysis, along the "phenomenal" periphery of the mechanism and not through its "noumenal" center.
Nor could we have done otherwise. To be candid, we cannot even be sure
that we are out of this circular line of thought in which human knowledge
seems to be trapped.

This does not invalidate what has been said up to this point (at least
because I have openly admitted the mythical quality of the terminology I
have used, and the limits of the line of reasoning that it has determined) and
it does not prevent me from continuing the analysis. Girard himself does
not stop here. Not only do every thought and every theory, as much as they
are illuminated by the Christian demystifying light, appear constitution-
ally insufficient to grasp the ultimate reality of the logic that dominates the
world, but we can and must also consider the possibility that even the theories that aim to comprehend the "logic of the world,"[11] far from constituting
a real victory over that logic, are nothing more than cunning stratagems that
our minds, guided by a sacrificial form of reason, employ so as to slow and
diminish the effectiveness of Christian demystification. At worst, every rational evaluation of the problem could be considered an obstacle to the only
true demystification, the Christian one. As Girard puts it: "In comparison
with the astonishing work of demystification effected by the Gospels, our
own exercises in demystification are only slight sketches, though they may
also be cunning obstacles that our minds erect against the gospel revelation"
(TH, 179).

If on the one hand such an argument denies legitimacy to all who see
Girard, and mimetic theory in general, as guilty of a form of rationalism
aimed at explaining through human knowledge the ultimate reality of the
human and divine world,[12] on the other it might also raise questions as to
the "usefulness" of Girard's work and mimetic theory itself. In short, if every
rational consideration of the problem can constitute a "cunning obstacle" to
the deployment of Christian demystification, has not Girard himself committed the ultimate and most cunning act of misapprehension, precisely
while he believed he was carrying on a work of demystification?

The response to this objection could be retrieved first of all in Girard's
tenet that he has not "invented" anything. Whatever is demystifying in his
works depends not so much on human reason and the social sciences (which,
at most, constitute supports that Girard uses in the spirit of what we might

call the "Christian cunning") as on an authentic reception of the Christian message by a converted heart.

Second, we have often seen that in the mimetic universe what may appear, in the moment, as a defeat reveals itself to be a victory when viewed from the point of view of the history of salvation, insofar as it prevents the repetition of the same error. Thus we may argue that, even if Girard's rational exposition of the "logic of the world" was the ultimate and subtlest example of the cunning of reason, it would still have its place in the history of salvation as a stage on a journey aimed at progressively unveiling a Christian message now completely cleansed of all sacrificial implications.

It is Girard himself who clarifies this point. Mimetic victimage (which we have now called the "logic of the world") is also—and my analysis of intellectual symbolism aimed to demonstrate exactly this point—a system of *thought*. That system entirely embraces reason, language, and every other intellectual, cultural, and social form in civilization. Therefore it can never, at least not without "external" contributions, generate a doctrine, a hypothesis, or a theory capable of demolishing it. Girard is absolutely clear on this point: "No system of thought is truly capable of creating the thought capable of destroying it. To confound the world, therefore, and show that it is reasonable and just to believe in Jesus as sent by the Father . . . (in other words as a divinity that shares nothing in common with those of violence), the Spirit is necessary in history to work to disintegrate the world and gradually discredit all the gods of violence" (S, 207).

In the face of the cognitive nihilism to which our reflections seemed to have led us, what emerges now is the idea of an "elsewhere" as the place where truth may be unveiled. This "elsewhere" is generated by the action of the Paraclete and by the demystifying activity enacted by the Christian message. Within such liminal space that, in Kantian terms, constitutes the border zone between the phenomenal and the noumenal, does reason still belong? On the grounds of the analysis so far, we would have to respond in the negative; nonetheless, we cannot exclude the possibility that from the ashes of the Heraclitean *Logos*, violent and sacrificial, there might rise, through the demystifying action of the Spirit in history, a new reason, whose model might be defined by the Johannine *Logos*.

With these latest reflections we are falling into the vortex of intellectual sacrifice, the labyrinth created by the self-referential paradox of reason. A simple "intellectual" decision is not sufficient to adopt the "victim's point of view," which constitutes the only possibility of a nonviolent *Logos*. At stake, in fact, is the capacity to overtake the kingdom that violence and its lies have built "since the foundation of the world"—and in that case no ordinary form of human "wisdom" will suffice. To oppose the cunning of reason, what is needed is a Christian form of cunning.

Nothing in the Gospels urges humanity to deny its mimetic nature. In any case, humans cannot do that, as that nature is what has differentiated them from animals and constituted them as humans. Even the Gospels urge human beings to imitate a model, though this is a model of a particular kind, and second—and here is distinctively at work that which we have called "Christian cunning"—the Gospels encourage them to imitate the desire to refuse any kind of imitation. In Girard's words: "In the universe structured by the Gospel revelation, individual existence remains basically imitative even, and above all, perhaps, when one rejects with horror any thought of imitation" (RU, 57–58).

The only model that the Gospels urge their readers to imitate is Christ, for he, being not imprisoned by the chains of desire or violence thanks to his divine nature, does not offer rivalry to those who imitate him, but in exchange for imitation offers love. That is, the true difference between the slavery generated by all other forms of imitation and the liberty generated by the imitation of Christ becomes the difference between fascinated imitation, and a humble imitation of a model that promises the greatest happiness and most enduring richness.

We can retrieve a metaphor for such evangelical cunning in the already cited parable of the Grand Inquisitor, as Girard presents it. Philosophy, or, if we prefer, human reason, like the Inquisitor, "sees all, knows all, understands all. He understands even the mute appeal of love but is incapable of responding to it. What to do in this case but to reaffirm the presence of this love? Such is the sense of the kiss that Christ gives, wordlessly, to the wretched old man" (RU, 130).

This kiss may be the image of the *Logos* of St. John, that "knowledge in faith" which, from the point of view of mimetic theory, represents the dawn of the philosophy of religion.

3. "Knowledge" and "Faith"

3.1. Faith in Knowledge

The arguments we have considered seem to discourage us from trying to legitimize, in the world interpreted according to the categories of mimetic theory, the existence of philosophy outside the circular confines of mimetic victimage and from delineating the possible structure of such philosophy. We should now ask if it is still correct to continue this inquiry. The problem is this: does Girard's thought lead inevitably to a "mystical" result, that is, one ending in an abandonment to faith beyond the limits of reason, or—as others have already suggested[13]—is there another possible way out, which may not even be in conflict with the first? There is no doubt that Girard's thought does lead, in its conclusions, toward the "death of philosophy"; but this is still a *Christian* death, as above all it implies a *resurrection*. What dies is the fascination with metaphysical desire; what is born is renunciation of that desire.

So we return to the heart of the problem. What could the structure be of a form of knowledge born from the renunciation of the dynamics of mimetic victimage, or rather from the concept that best combines its dynamics in intellectual symbolism, that is, religion?

If it is true that the space from which we need to distance ourselves is now essentially the "religious," we must not forget that, properly speaking, we have never left that space. What is important, then, is not so much to assume a "point of view" capable of renouncing the "religious" dimension, as to assume one capable of "reading" right to the heart the origins of religion itself. Girard is very much concerned, to an almost obsessive degree, with the underlining of the incredibly ambiguous nature of every attempt to place oneself beyond the religious. If, in fact, by "religious" we mean a process that aims once again to expel a victim in order to create a unanimity, however precarious, around itself, then there is no form of opposition to religion that is not in its own turn *religious*—particularly in the modern world.

It is for this reason that I have insisted so much on the impossibility of human reason overcoming itself and becoming a nonsacrificial philosophy. Now we have a few additional arguments in favor of this thesis. In fact, the knowledge of violence does not eliminate the violence of knowledge.

Even if knowledge is not sufficient, it is nonetheless an indispensable component in individual conversion and the redemption of humanity itself. It is true that what is essential is to access true knowledge in order to be saved from victimary violence. However, "true knowledge" for Girard is not a particular philosophy or a collection of notions whose mere possession will automatically ensure salvation. Above all, this knowledge must be illuminated by a transcendent light, whose guarantee will certainly not be some kind of orthodoxy that inevitably depends on heretics, or scapegoats, to impose itself, but a labor of interpretative inquiry, driven by a heart that is ready to accept the *caritas* of the Gospels and whose overall purpose is the progressive elucidation of truth. Second, this new form of knowledge carries within itself a strongly ethical dimension that expresses itself through the choice—radical and unforeseeable—of a model who is more than human (Jesus Christ), as well as through a personal journey of liberation. From this it becomes clear that the path of salvation is accessible to all people, independently of any particular notion or discipline—even mimetic theory itself. On the other hand, this does not mean that a form of knowledge such as the one we are considering here cannot contribute in its own way to the slow emergence of truth.

In contrast to intellectual symbolism, which is dominated by that desire, Christian symbolism (that is, a form of knowledge illuminated by the demystifying evangelical message) possesses its own internal dynamic, which, in the long term, turns it into a formidable instrument of antisacrificial revelation. In a universe dedicated, by vocation, to the intellectual sacrifice of meaning, it declares the radical possibility of rediscovering Meaning, having a Meaning, believing in Meaning.

3.2. Knowledge in Faith

If Christian symbolism alone has the capacity to found a nonsacrificial form of knowledge, then that means that all truly fruitful experiences, all the greatest discoveries in all fields—natural sciences, literature, human sciences—have always assumed and will always assume the immutable form of every radical transformation, that of religious conversion, because their precondition is always freedom from mimetic desire and the illusions it imposes. Within the nonsacrificial knowledge born from that freedom, every radically antimythical representation will find its model in the symbology that the Christian texts will be able to offer.

It is precisely this, Girard believes, that the culture born in the wake of revelation—that is, Western culture in its entirety following the Christian epiphany—has not been able to accomplish. Whether it has defined itself as Christian, anti-Christian, or atheist, the common foundation of such culture remains bound to the mechanisms of primitive religion.

"Knowledge in faith" therefore constitutes the *pars construens* of the "critical" principle of Christian revelation. It will consist in a recapitulation of every stage of intellectual symbolism, but always already read from the perspective of their revealing end.

Now, let us identify some characteristics of this form of knowledge. First and foremost, such a form of knowledge will not be exclusively philosophical, but it shall assume within itself the results obtained in all natural and human sciences. Thus, it will be an *interdisciplinary* knowledge.[14]

Second, knowledge in faith will not be violent, that is, it will not flaunt a presumption of full understanding of the world (an attitude that, from the point of view of intellectual symbolism, is typical of what we have termed the "logic of the world"), and neither will it organize its results into absolutely rational structures that run the risk—or face the certainty—of falling back into the "violence of knowledge." Knowledge in faith will rather present itself as a narrative,[15] capable, by its nature, of indicating the residual violence still present in the *Logos*—we should not forget that, even if the model to which we turn is the Johannine *Logos*, we are still moving in a human dimension. The second characteristic of knowledge in faith is therefore the renunciation of the pretense of absolute comprehension in a violent sense, which is what knowledge dependent on intellectual symbolism brings with it.

The two characteristics outlined above describe the form of the new knowledge but not its content. Now, if the *pars destruens* must take on the devices of the "logic of the world" in order to demolish it, then the content of the *pars construens* must originate from the questions appearing in the context of the message that gave rise to such thought: the Christian message. Therefore, the new knowledge is manifestly a *Christian symbolism*. This Christian symbolism shall consist principally of a hermeneutic application of Christian principles: indeed, we have already seen how the history of salvation is always, for Girard, a progressive history of interpretation. In nonsacrificial knowledge, then, there is also a *hermeneutic dimension*.

There remains one characteristic of knowledge in faith that has been left, in a deliberately asymmetrical way, for this movement toward our conclusion. The reason for this deferral is that in fact this characteristic opens a new field of inquiry, rich in possibility, that we must now mention only briefly: ethics.

We have often seen how demystifying knowledge always arises from the experience, or from the narration, of an episode of scapegoating in which the role of the victim is portrayed in a way that psychologically "moves" the observer out of the circle of persecutors and leads her or him to the victim's side, to take the victim's part. This ethical truth is not humanly conceivable, in a universe completely dominated by its violent and sacralized origins; that is why it is identified with the *Logos* of John. In its origins it is a religious-Christian truth, but its content is ethical. For this reason, another characteristic of knowledge in faith is its nature as *ethical* knowledge.

What kind of relationship can this knowledge have to philosophy? If we remove from philosophy the skeletal structure of intellectual symbolism and substitute it with Christian symbolism, and furthermore if we deny philosophy both a specific field of inquiry and the pretense of full comprehension of the world according to its self-appointed canons, can we still speak of philosophy in the demystified universe of mimetic theory?

The answer is yes. *We can still speak of philosophy as an opening to a form of knowledge that does narrate the difficulties of the search for truth. Hence, philosophy not as possession but as exploration. This form of knowledge in faith is precisely the nonsacrificial philosophy of religion that we have been seeking.* A philosophy of religion as knowledge in faith is not only a hermeneutics of authentic religious experience. It resolves within itself, eliminating all its violent effects, the intellectual symbolism that is external to it, and it resolves it by means of Christian symbolism, in which intellectual symbolism is absorbed and already demystified—which is to say (as already mentioned) that the Johannine *Logos* explains the Heraclitean *Logos* and, by demystifying it, resolves it in itself; but the Heraclitean *Logos* cannot in any way explain the Johannine *Logos*.

The ultimate significance of this philosophy of religion is "incarnation": the final point of mystified experience, and hence the point from which the

Logos of revelation can attain its full, radical strength, enacting a reversal that is not the reversal of madness but the reversal of truth, the center of the circle of violence in which humankind, particularly Western humankind in its intellectual history, has always moved. This philosophy of religion does not carry residual violence in itself because the center is not "the privileged point of view," but the gathering point of all points of view, their fulfillment and their explanation.

This does not mean that no possibility exists of understanding that center purely as a center, which would lead us to lapse once again into the supposedly "mystical" results of Girard's mimetic theory. If anything, it means that such a possibility is not a "way of seeing": that is, it is not an "idea," in the Greek sense of the term (*idein*); it is not a "point of view." Girard insists on the radical insufficiency of every purely philosophical and rational endeavor to grasp what, by anthropological definition, should elude the reach of the Greek *Logos*; to find itself, so to speak, "transfigured" into "another" form of knowledge, represented most importantly by philosophy of religion. As Girard puts it: "Contemporary thought is in chaos, as it must be when progress is real. Where it still survives, it displays pathological symptoms. . . . [I]t is not by breaking out of the circle that thought will ultimately free itself, but by penetrating to its very center, while somehow managing to avoid the pitfall of madness" (VS, 240). And in a paragraph that immediately follows this statement in the French edition of the *Violence and the Sacred*, he adds: "For the moment, thought maintains that there is no center, and tries to go out of the circle to dominate it from outside. . . . When it gets to the center, thought will perceive the vanity of these last sacrificial rites. It will realize that mythical thought is not essentially different from the thought that criticizes myths and reconstructs the origin of myths."[16]

The "death of philosophy" of which Girard speaks is therefore above all the death of metaphysics—the end of that violent knowledge which, as we have seen, does not disappear instantly with the emergence of a nonviolent counterknowledge, but actually ends up insinuating itself into that new knowledge. In order for nonsacrificial knowledge really to come into being, philosophy must renounce its unilateral presumption of full understanding of the world, and the violence that such a position expresses. The essence of the knowledge that rises from the ashes of metaphysics must be alien to violence, and it will be so only if it renounces the inflexible single-mindedness of its own "point of view" to include all points of view—not in an absolute relativism, but in an all-embracing hermeneutics of Meaning, which alone can resolve within itself, canceling out all violent consequences, the violence of knowledge.

NOTES

1. See TE, 274: "Claudius and Old Hamlet are not blood brothers first and enemies second; they are brothers in revenge." On this subject, see also Matthew Schneider, "Mimetic Polemicism: René Girard and Harold Bloom contra the 'School of Resentment.' A Review Essay," *Anthropoetics* 2, no. 1 (1996).

2. S, 181, my translation. In the English translation of the book, this corresponds to p. 125.

3. "This confusion has affected historical Christianity and, to a certain degree, determined it. Those who are opposed to Christianity today endeavour to perpetuate it by clinging desperately to the most sacrificial theology in order not to lose that which nourishes it and to be able always to say: Christianity is only one among many religions of violence, and possibly the worst of them." J, 159.

4. Michael White has shown the role of rivalry in science in his excellent *Rivals: Conflict as the Fuel of Science* (London: Secker and Warburg, 2001). From this point of view, philosophy is not different from science.

5. This mechanism is clearly described in RU, 59–61.

6. Psychology has showed that every aggressor tends to present her- or himself, even in her or his own eyes, as the victim, and to identify the other as the aggressor. Compare Grazia Attili, Francesca Farabollini, and Patrizia Messeri, eds., *Il nemico ha la coda* (Florence: Giunti, 1996). To understand this dynamic within intellectual symbolism, see the case of Heidegger in TH, 64–65.

7. For Michel Serres, doubt, a fundamental element of reason, is a symptom of the sacrificial nature of reason itself: "Doubt (*duo-habere*) is the double, double conduct, bifurcation." Michel Serres, *Hermès V: Le passage du Nord-Ouest* (Paris: Minuit, 1980), 41.

8. "This is the elusive entity that in logic is named the self-referential paradox. It expresses itself thus: if *x* is false, then it is true; if it is true, then it is false. The self-referential paradox, also known as the *double bind*, has a long history: its formulation can be traced back to Eubulides, in the fourth century B.C.E., who did nothing more than repropose in a more rigorous form the famous paradox of the liar discovered by Epimenides of Crete two centuries earlier. The sense of a threat that that paradox imposed on self-reference has always colored it as a dangerous construction, best avoided. It took until the twentieth century to perceive the omnipresence of this paradox, and its fundamental role in all domains of life and thought. Girard, who perceives it at the very source of the human world, at the roots of the sacred and of culture, is a participant in this fruitful rediscovery." Jean-Pierre Dupuy, *Ordres et désordres: Enquête sur un nouveau paradigme* (Paris: Seuil, 1982), 159–60. See also *Le signe et l'envie*, the first part of Paul Dumouchel and Jean-Pierre Dupuy, *L'enfer des choses: René Girard et la logique de l'economie* (Paris: Seuil, 1979).

9. "In the eighteenth and nineteenth centuries, Westerners made an idol of science and believed in an autonomous scientific spirit of which they were both the inventors and the product. They replaced the ancient myths with those of progress, which might be called the myth of perpetual modern superiority, the myth of a humanity that, through its own instrumentality, gradually became liberated and divine" (S, 204).

10. "Obviously, 'true' monarchy and sacrifice exist only in minds distorted by Platonic essentialism and its modern substitutes, the Cartesianism of clear and distinct ideas, of which the latest variant is structuralism." J, 95.

11. This "logic of the world" can be considered to be the philosophical equivalent of that "knowledge of the world" which Paul contrasts to the "knowledge of God."

12. See Louis Lochet, "René Girard: Une gnose?," *Cahiers Universitaires Catholiques*, May–June 1979, 46–47; and Paul Valadier, who argues: "But does the message delivered by the Bible and manifested in the life and resurrection of Christ not perhaps lose its greatness when it is interpreted as an anthropological and social message?" Paul Valadier, "Bouc émissaire et révélation chrétienne selon René Girard," *Etudes* 357 (1982): 256. In passing—given that a full treatment of this problem would take us too far from the problem on which we are concentrating (the intellectual symbolism of sacrifice) and even outside the discipline in which we are working—it is interesting to note that Girard never intends to explain Christianity entirely in terms of reason, eliminating the dimension of faith. Indeed, fundamental questions remain to which Girard does not respond (and neither could he, or would he wish to). Thus Jacques Guillet's criticisms of Girard's presumed "reductionism" of Christianity are not entirely fair. See Jacques Guillet, "René Girard et le sacrifice," *Etudes* 351 (July 1979): 101–2.

13. This is one of the questions that moved Eric Gans to elaborate, on the grounds of mimetic theory, its own generative anthropology. Already in 1982, Gans wrote: "Are there no possible solutions other than the leap of faith? Is it therefore necessary to think of historical revelation as wholly present in the New Testament, when the New Testament must also be a part of it? I believe there is another path, and that the idea of truth to which Girard is entirely right to remain faithful can be safeguarded in another way." Eric Gans, "Le Logos de René Girard," in Michel Deguy and Jean-Pierre Dupuy, eds., *René Girard et le problème du mal* (Paris: Grasset, 1982), 186.

14. This characteristic is often highlighted by a line of mimetic theory scholarship that often has an "epistemological" focus (Michel Serres, Carlo Formenti, and, at least to some extent, Jean-Pierre Dupuy). We should note, however, that while these critics' starting point is the demand for a new epistemology based on interdisciplinarity and this thesis finds support only later in Girard's mimetic theory, Girard realizes the same need by deducing it as the necessary consequence of the common matrix of all human consciousness: indeed, if mystificatory knowledge has a single origin (that is, the sacred), then, in parallel, demystificatory knowledge too has a single origin (that is, the action of the Gospels).

15. This is what Michel Serres sought to delineate in his much-discussed and interesting book, *Hermès V.*

16. René Girard, *La Violence et le sacré* (Paris: Grasset, 1972), 332. This paragraph is missing from the English translation.

Conclusion

1. Apocalypse or Palingenesis

In the preceding chapter we considered the possibility of a nonsacrificial knowledge and, even if with many caveats, we resolved that question in the affirmative. There is still one dimension of Girard's mimetic theory, however, that in our journey through the history of the relationship between philosophy and religion we have not yet adequately examined: the "apocalyptic" dimension.

In Girard's thought, this dimension arises from the consideration that, as a result of the demystifying action of the Gospels, the sacrificial crisis in which we are living can no longer be resolved by yet another victimary expulsion. Moreover, humanity's present military capacity could well lead it to destroy itself. There is, however, one other possibility: the renunciation of violence. This does not constitute, so to speak, an instinctive fact; it is necessarily prepared by the revelation of the lie of the sacred. We should note, then, that the renunciation of violence is far from being a purely ethical choice, but is inseparable from a gnoseological dimension, that is, from a form of knowledge that refuses all violence and every intellectual sacrifice:

surely a knowledge that holds within itself the ethical element, and that cannot do without it, but that does not reduce itself to only that element. Intellectual symbolism is resolved in Christian symbolism; intellectual sacrifice is resolved in the deconstruction of knowledge in faith.[1]

The choice between destruction (apocalypse) and rebirth (palingenesis), between violence and love, is therefore wholly entrusted into the hands of humanity, of every last human being. The paths that culture chooses to take not only have an influence upon this choice, but constitute its deepest essence.

Girard's position could therefore be defined as a form of *millenarianist rationalism*. It awaits the moment, for which he believes preparations have already begun, in which humanity will have to decide, through its own reason, whether to turn toward destruction or palingenesis. If reason remains a mere sacrificial instrument, humanity will choose destruction. If, by contrast, humanity accepts Christian revelation, the choice will be palingenesis.

For Girard, it is not God who destroys humanity (nor could he, as the Christian God is above all loving and nonviolent) but humanity that destroys itself. The human being is the absolute protagonist of the decisive and conclusive events of this period in world history. And, paradoxically, the developments we have surveyed in religion and philosophy, which we have watched become fixated on intellectual sacrifices and insidious and more or less occult idolatries, are ultimately part of the history of salvation: "The reappearance of Satan does not nullify his prior defeat. Everything must finally converge toward the good, even idolatry" (RU, 128).

I should stress once again that even in drawing conclusions such as this, Girard's discourse still does not lapse into some sort of contemplative mysticism. The ethical dimension in fact is present here more than in other parts of his theory. Rather, it is the pure contemplative who runs the risk of becoming an accomplice of the unconscious persecutors, those who are thoughtlessly pushing humanity toward the abyss.

Our age, the end of modernity, is therefore the most decisive in all history, and for this very reason it appears as a threshold, on which, in a Heideggerian sense, the gods of the past have disappeared and the new god is delaying. But for Girard, God's delay is entirely our own responsibility—although even this last, tragic cognitive escape may possibly be part of the history of redemption:

If the world flees Christ, he will be able to make this flight serve his redemptive plan. In division and contradiction he will accomplish what he wanted to accomplish in union and joy. In seeking to divinize itself without Christ, humankind places itself on the cross. . . . There is not a fragment of human nature that is not kneaded and pressed in the conflict between the Other and the Self. Satan, divided against himself, expels Satan. The idols destroy the idols. Humankind exhausts, little by little, all illusions, including inferior notions of God swept away by atheism. It is caught in a vortex more and more rapid as its always more frantic and mendacious universe strikingly reveals the absence and need of God. The prodigious series of historical catastrophes, the improbable cascade of empires and kingdoms, of social, philosophical, and political systems that we call Western civilization, the circle always greater which covers over an abyss whose heart history collapses ever more speedily—all this accomplishes the plan of divine redemption. It is not the plan that Christ would have chosen for human beings if he had not respected their freedom, but the one they have chosen for themselves in rejecting him. (RU, 128–29)

In other words, the history of salvation constitutes the history of the human being not only because she or he receives the grace of God's love, but also because the human being her- or himself has the possibility—or, we may prefer to say, the freedom—to activate such grace. This centrality of the human being is expressed on two overlapping planes. The first is the ethical plane: the choice is between loving the Other, or adoring it and becoming its rival. The second dimension is the cognitive one. If the history of salvation is, as we have seen, a history of interpretation, the duty that humanity must fulfill is also a hermeneutic duty, in the sense that humanity must exert all possible effort so that the Spirit reveals itself ever further in history, and makes possible the realization of knowledge in faith.[2]

Certainly, knowledge in faith is a liminal concept. In spite of all our attempts to single out some of its characteristic traits, it remains forever beyond our possibilities of description. In fact, we find ourselves in the time of both the *not anymore* (as the omnipotence of intellectual sacrifice is definitively in its twilight) and the *not yet* (as revelation is not complete), and for this very reason we need a philosophy, a form of knowledge, that sets its sights on the distance that separates us from the "end times." If and when humanity succeeds in reaching, or rather in constructing, the kingdom of God, that knowledge itself will have served its purpose, or it will undergo some sort of palingenesis. In any case, we are now venturing into hypotheses that are really unprovable, because they refer to "another" time and condition so distant from our own that it would be presumptuous (or, worse, superstitious, and therefore once again sacrificial) to attempt to imagine them.

2. A Path of Exploration

It is now possible, having followed the stages of the sacrificial history of the relationship between philosophy and religion, in search of an articulation of the discourse that might render such historical complexity significant and retrieve its general structure, to summarize the interpretative hypotheses that I have developed so far, in order to indicate the directions in which those premises lead us.

Let us revisit briefly the different stages of the discussion. We explored the value of mimetic theory for the philosophy of religion. In order to approach mimetic theory from the point of view of that discipline, I have argued for the establishment of an intellectual symbolism that followed the coming of Christ and gave rise to an alternating trial of strength between religion and philosophy. If the culture of the Middle Ages rested on the victimization and expulsion of philosophy—the first great intellectual sacrifice—with the coming of the modern era the relation was reversed, and it was religion that took the role of the scapegoat. In the contemporary world, hermeneutic thought represents an ambiguous and decisive point, at which philosophy and religion confront each other but are no longer able to sacrifice each other, thus demonstrating the possibility of a nonsacrificial form of knowledge—one whose borders, however, are still to be determined and whose domain is still to be researched.

Girard never went that far; and yet Girard indeed created the premises that make this discourse possible. This is, I believe, the direction in which Girard's richest lines of thought may be developed; however, it is not my purpose, for now, to take a direction, which would lead to an even deeper analysis of the concept of sacrifice. By way of conclusion to Part 1, I want to emphasize on the one hand the sacrificial dimension of Western thought and, on the other, the fruitful research in the field of philosophy of religion toward a form of knowledge in faith.

In reality, these two aspects are intimately connected. Girard's anthropology, linking events and thoughts separated by great distances, has laid the foundations for an interesting and valuable inquiry. It is hoped that the present work may have contributed to that inquiry, even only minimally, by pointing out one possible path of development for mimetic theory. It would be interesting to examine—using the interpretative devices afforded us by Girard's hypotheses—what degree of sacrifice philosophy has inhered throughout its own history, given that the sacrificial dimension has too often been obscured and passed over in silence. However, demystifying philosophy also means wondering which philosophy is *not* sacrificial. This is why this first, we might say, *critical* stage of the inquiry is closely linked to a second stage, which we may call *constructive*, which involves identifying a form of knowledge that reveals Meaning in the truest sense.

This point of view makes clear the close interdependence that binds the rational and philosophical dimension to the religious dimension in which demystification was first expressed with its full reconciliatory power. But here our discussion must end, for, in reality, the previous paragraph has taken us far beyond the original intentions of this work. To provide its argument with a final sense of continuity, it should be stated once again that the reciprocal and unresolvable circularity of philosophy and religion is the starting point for serious reflection not only on Girard's own work (inasmuch as it contains unresolved elements), but on the distinguishing spirit of the contemporary age. That, at least, is the preoccupation of anyone who—despite all forms of scientism and all philosophies of the finite, all forms of skepticism and cognitive nihilism, the specialist atmosphere of knowledge and resignation to a fragmentary universe—still does not give up envisaging, even in anxiety, the possibility of ultimate, unavoidable Meaning.

NOTES

1. "The crisis has no solution other than the acceptance of truth: Christ did not die for our sins, Christ died without sin, no violence can be born of sin. Once unmasked, the sacrificial device is broken; it can never work again, and to attempt to reactivate it in the atomic age means seeking the destruction of our species." Carlo Fomenti, *Prometeo e Hermes* (Naples: Liguori, 1986), 107.

2. Vattimo has written: "Even if salvation is essentially 'achieved' through the incarnation, passion,

death and resurrection of Jesus, it is still awaiting its ultimate completion, and the Paraclete, the spirit of truth sent to the faithful at Pentecost, has the task of assisting them in this further hermeneutic undertaking." Gianni Vattimo, "Storia della salvezza, storia dell'interpretazione," *Micromega* 3 (1992): 107.

A Letter from René Girard

14 juin 97

Cher Paolo Diego,

Je m'excuse de répondre très tardivement à votre lettre de Janvier. Vos réflexions sur religion et philosophie m'intéressent beaucoup et me paraissent très justes. Je suis d'accord: il est indispensable de considérer la philosophie et la religion comme sujets dans un processus mimétique, déplacé sur le plan intellectuel.

Mais la religion chrétienne ne figure dans ce processus que parce ceux qui parlent en son nom ne voient pas qu'elle révèle tout processus mimétique. Et le Moyen Age n'expulsait pas la philosophie, peut-être lui faisait il même la part trop belle . . .

A la fin juin (du 23 au 27) je serai a une réunion a Graz (Autriche) ou se trouveront beaucoup de gens qui s'intéressent aux problèmes mimétiques. C'est la réunion annuelle de COV&R (Colloquium on Violence and Religion). Si vous voulez des renseignements vous pouvez téléphoner a mon ami Giuseppe Fornari . . .

Mais cette lettre arrivera peut-être trop tard. Voici aussi l'adresse de l'organisation de la réunion a l'université de Graz. . . .

L'an prochain ca réunion aura lieu a St Denis, juste au dehors de Paris.

Avec mes meilleures souhaits pour votre examen et l'espoir de vous rencontrer un des ces jours,

René Girard

June 14, 1997

Dear Paolo Diego,

I am sorry to be late in answering your January letter. Your thoughts on religion and philosophy interest me a great deal and seem quite just to me. I agree: it is essential to consider philosophy and religion as being subjects engaged in a mimetic process, [but] situated at [lit. "moved to"] the intellectual level. But the Christian religion is only [engaged] in this process because those who speak for it do not see that it reveals any mimetic processes. And the Middle Ages did not expel philosophy; maybe it was even given too many favors . . .

At the end of June (23–27) I'll be at a meeting in Graz (Austria), where there will be a lot of people who are interested in mimetic problems/issues. This is the annual meeting of COV&R (Colloquium of Violence and Religion). If you want any information, you can call my friend Giuseppe Fornari . . .

But this letter may arrive too late. Here is also the address of the organization for the meeting at the University of Graz . . .

The next meeting will take place next year in Saint-Denis, just outside Paris. With my best wishes for your discussion—I'm looking forward to meeting you one of these days.

René Girard[1]

NOTE

1. I am grateful to Chris Fleming for his amicable assistance in the translation of this letter.

STANFORD UNIVERSITY, STANFORD, CALIFORNIA 94305

RENÉ GIRARD
ANDREW B. HAMMOND PROFESSOR
OF FRENCH LANGUAGE, LITERATURE AND CIVILIZATION

14 juin 97

Cher Paolo-Diego

Je m'excuse de répondre très tardivement à votre lettre de janvier. Vos réflexions sur religion et philosophie m'intéressent beaucoup et ne paraissent très justes. Je suis d'accord: il est indispensable de considérer la philosophie et la religion comme sujets dans un processus mimétique, déplacé sur le plan intellectuel.

Mais la religion chrétienne ne figure dans ce processus que parceque ceux qui parlent en son nom ne voient pas qu'elle révèle tout processus mimétique. Et le Moyen Age n'expliqait pas la philosophie, lui faisait-il même la part peut-être trop belle...

A la fin juin (du 23 au 27) je serai à une réunion à Graz (Autriche) où se trouveront beaucoup de gens qui

s'intéressent aux problèmes mimétiques
(c'est la réunion annuelle de COVER
(colloquium of violence and religion)
Si vous voulez des renseignements, vous
pouvez téléphoner à mon ami
Giuseppe Fornari

Mais cette lettre arrivera peut-être
trop tard. Voici aussi l'adresse de
l'organisation de la réunion à
l'université de graz:
      Prof. G. Larcher, Institut für Fundamental-
      der Universität graz   theologie

L'an prochain cette réunion aura
lieu à St. Denis, juste en dehors de Paris
    Avec mes meilleurs souhaits pour
votre examen et l'espoir de vous
rencontrer un de ces jours.
                René Girard.

PART 2

Other Mimetic Paradoxes

2004–2016

Transition: Corrections and Paradoxes

Translated from the Italian by Theodore Ell

1. Sacrifice and Kenosis

Since 1961, Girard's production has grown without interruption, to at least the same degree as his fame. Without doubt, the fascination with Girard's thought derives from the fact that he has constructed a true "speculative cathedral," a theory that proposes to explain everything from myths to rituals, Greek tragedies to modern novels, holocausts of historical magnitude to everyday customs. At first glance, it would seem that Girard has changed little or nothing of his speculative construction since then, but if we look closely, there are noticeable problems and corrections that threaten the very foundations of mimetic theory. Indeed, recent criticism has emphasized these instances a great deal.

One of the most relevant conclusions reached by Girard's mimetic theory is that the violent cultural order revealed in the Gospels cannot survive its own revelation. Sooner or later, then, that which Christianity has fermented in culture must bring about the collapse of the societies that it has penetrated, even societies that seem to depend on its revelation and promulgation, that is, so-called Christian societies. Their dependency is in fact ambiguous and is due to a partial misunderstanding, rooted in the deceptive

resemblance of the Gospels to other mythological texts. A sacrificial reading
of the Gospels reintroduces violence into divinity and endorses a search for
guilty parties capable of exonerating some part of humanity, when in fact all
humanity is equally guilty. In his major works, Girard has asserted that in the
Gospels the Passion is presented as an act of salvation for humanity but in
no case as a sacrifice, and has maintained that if Christianity was capable of
constituting itself as a religion, with a weight of sacred baggage at its core, it
is because of a partial involution that has led us to conceive of Christ's death
as a sacrifice, and the Father as a bloodthirsty god who requires the son's
death in order to save humanity, self-sacrifice as an act of sanctity (see TH,
182; see also TE, 282–83). On this basis, Girard has criticized every sacrificial
interpretation of Christianity, including the Epistle to the Hebrews and in
general any reading that leads to the conclusion that God *needs* his Son's
sacrifice in order to avenge God's honor, which has been compromised by
the sins of humanity: Girard has not hesitated to define this as "a most enor-
mous and paradoxical misunderstanding" (TH, 180), the demonstration of
humanity's total powerlessness to comprehend its own situation. The Father
of Christ, in fact, is a God who is a complete stranger to violence, who desires
reconciliation among human beings without sacrificial intermediaries (TH,
182–83). If some people still posit sacrifice as a cornerstone of Christianity, it
is only because they know no other way to signify the transcendental nature
of Christian revelation.

On these grounds, it seems that *sacrifice*, for Girard, means always and
only *suppressive* sacrifice. Any element of *oblation*—what we might call a
kenotic sacrifice, that is, sacrifice as a gift, as a "giving oneself up for others"
or as a "making room for others"—seems to be fundamentally excluded. In
support of this thesis are the many instances in which Girard argues force-
fully against what he calls the "masochism of self-sacrifice," which does not
correspond in the least to the spirit of the Christian text. For instance, in
Things Hidden, he claims: "'Masochism' can also find expression in self-
sacrifice. . . . What might be concealed here is the desire to sacralize *oneself*
and make *oneself* godlike—which quite clearly harks back to the illusion
traditionally produced by sacrifice" (TH, 236–37; see also MRVR, 176–92,
and RU, 51).

The exclusion of the possibility of an oblatory or kenotic value in sacrifice constitutes a position that many critics consider excessively reductive,[1]

and some have even harshly judged it as superficial, insofar as it does not recognize the semantic polyvalence of the concept of sacrifice, particularly in the Judeo-Christian tradition. Effectively, sacrifice as gift, sacrifice as oblation or kenosis, seems to be absent in Girard's thought. This appears even more extraordinary if we consider that the paradigm of sacrifice as gift is, in the Christian tradition to which Girard refers, the κένωσις of Christ. Critics of Girard's work have invoked this often, to lament its absence. In fact, as mentioned earlier, Girard does contemplate the notion of self-sacrifice, but he does not consider it substantially different from all the other forms of violent sacrifice and connotes it essentially as a "masochistic self-immolation" that does not elude the rules of mimeticism and victimization but in reality is one of the most impressive examples of their dynamics. Girard's form of Christianity would seem to be a *Christianity without sacrifice*,[2] not only in the sense that it excludes any form of sacrificial violence, but also in the sense that there seems to be no room for a positive meaning of sacrifice. Is it therefore truly impossible for a genuinely gratuitous or kenotic sacrifice to exist—that is, an act of free love in which, for example, one offers one's own life for another, spontaneously and without conforming to a unanimous act of sacrifice?[3]

The problem here is terminological, as Girard himself recognized in a fairly recent interview. If by "kenotic sacrifice" we mean suffering torture consciously and in a nonviolent manner, or a disposition to renounce one's own life in order to save that of another, then not only is the crucifixion of Christ a kenotic sacrifice, but it is the kenotic sacrifice par excellence, for there never has been a more innocent victim. Yet if by the same term we mean, in conformity with certain streams of the Catholic theological tradition, *the necessary will* of the sacrifice of Christ, who *had* to be sacrificed for the whole of humanity to be redeemed, then in Girard's work there exists no kenotic sacrifice of any kind. Rather, Christ came to spread truth, and if humanity refused it, making Christ himself a victim, and in turn the God of nonviolence accepted Christ's torment, then this means only "the inevitable abandonment of the direct and easy way, which would be for all to accept the principles of conduct that he [Christ] has stated. It is now necessary to turn to the indirect way, the one that has to by-pass the consent of all mankind and instead pass through the Crucifixion and the Apocalypse" (TH, 203). The perplexity arising from these considerations also has consequences for the very internal equilibrium of mimetic theory. As we know, Girard "deduces" the divinity of Jesus *on the basis* of the divine nature (as it cannot be human, given the context) of the message that he conveys. Yet, even if the message that Jesus brings is a divine message, *that does not make the messenger himself the Son of God*. In other words—exercising a reductio ad absurdum but still respecting the principles of Girard's mimetic theory—God could have given life to an entirely innocent man, a stranger to mimetic rivalry, in which all other human beings are involved, but this man did not necessarily have to be God's Son. The divinity of Christ, and consequently the whole concept of the Trinity, is thus put perilously at risk.[4]

What Girard seems not to consider, or what at least appears to be a highly problematic element of his thought, is that to emphasize only the epistemological-ethical aspect of salvation—Jesus saves because he speaks the truth of the victim and offers himself as the only model that cannot transform itself into a rival[5]—is to overlook its most essential aspect: in Christianity, Jesus not only *saves*, but *he himself is salvation*. The distance between those two statements is not inconsequential. In the case of the first, Christ's nonviolent response to sacrifice demystifies mimetic victimage, but it does not differ qualitatively from the response offered by many other victims (Job, for instance), from whom Christ is distinguished in that the presentation of the *truth of the victim*, and hence of the *lie of the persecutors*, is more lucid and less subject to psychological concessions. The difference is therefore purely *quantitative*. In the second case, however, Christ *is* salvation precisely because the one who is sacrificed—or rather, the one who *sacrifices himself*—is God godself, and sacrifice thus assumes an ultimate value. The difference between Jesus and other victims is now *qualitative*.[6]

The difficulty that Girard has in admitting the *necessity* of the sacrifice of Christ, and more generally the possibility that there may exist a sacrifice of love that can be at the same time *authentic* and *necessary*, is not a question of insufficient analysis, so much as an implication of the coherence of the method that Girard adopts. Indeed throughout his body of work there are several instances in which he warns of the necessity both of a scientific point of view and of keeping a distance from a form of contemporary philosophical thought that is no more than an updated version of myths, insofar as it always has at its core a more or less misrecognized mythological narrative. When applied to the sacrifice of Christ, the choice of the scientific method can reach only the "epistemological-ethical" conclusions already discussed, with no capacity to go further.

Confirmation that Girard's "reductionism" on the question of sacrifice does not arise from an insufficiency of the analysis may be found in Girard's own work, as Girard grasps and indeed does not shy away from admitting that sacrifice is in fact insufficient *as a concept*, that is, inasmuch as it inevitably ends up reducing the real, the existent, to itself, without ever being capable of containing it completely (J, 95). Yet—and this is the key point—this is all that Girard can admit while remaining faithful to his own premises and his own methodological choice, which, precisely in positing the transcendent *at the end* of its course of speculation, as a product of it, cannot accept the transcendent as presupposed. Therefore, Girard *suspends* the transcendent, but in so doing can neither thematize its phenomenology nor, even more prominently, include in his own theoretical horizon that which is essential in the Christian conception of transcendence: the Eucharist, the sacrifice of Christ. It is interesting to note how Girard takes dozens of pages to describe, in meticulous detail, the phenomenology of metaphysical desire and of "horizontal transcendence" without ever offering an analogous phenomenology of the imitation of Christ, of "vertical transcendence"; and yet this is the destination toward which all human beings should look. As already remarked by Adele Colombo,[7] at first, Girard held that the human being could pass from violence to love only through the message of the Word as codified in Scripture and through the action of the Spirit, that is, through the choice of Christ as mediator of desire. Only later did he add sacramental action, and hence the Eucharist, to this; but he added this only as praxis in life, without thematizing it.

It is correct to note in Girard's work an awareness of this speculative "void" in his own thought. If it is true that Girard started from what we might call a *frontal* contrast between Christianity and sacrifice, he now admits that it is possible to speak of a sacrifice of love on the part of Christ,[8] but *with no relation to ritual sacrifice*. In the past, for this same reason, he avoided any use of the term "sacrifice" in its conventional sense in reference to the New Testament and even eliminated from his scheme of the true revelation the Epistle to the Hebrews, which in fact makes extraordinarily intensive use of sacrificial symbolism. This position immediately appeared unsustainable to Girard's closest critics. In fact, such a position implied the exclusion of the

symbolic dynamic of the Eucharist, and the free recourse to sacrificial symbols present in the entire corpus of the letters of St. Paul.[9] Girard later recognized the intentional and active use of sacrificial symbology in the Eucharist,
and commendably withdrew his rejection of the Epistle to the Hebrews,
acknowledging that it was based on insufficiently thorough exegesis,[10] but
he did not entirely clarify the motivations or theoretical consequences of
these changes, because the questions in play cannot find plausible answers in
a purely "anthropological" human context.[11] In other words, Girard repudi-
ates his earlier refusal of the word "sacrifice" in a kenotic sense and declares
himself convinced that the crucifixion of Christ must be defined in terms of
(self)sacrifice.[12] He does so, significantly, at the very moment in which he
distances himself from the position of Gianni Vattimo, who underlines in
Girard's thought a conception of Christianity that would exclude recourse
to sacrificial symbology.[13] But this repudiation is not followed by a clarification of the redeeming nature of Christ's sacrifice. As argued above, Girard's
formulation of mimetic theory requires that Christ's death not be a *necessary*
event, but a consequence of humanity's refusal of his message. Thus salvation, Girard tells us, will follow the longer path, demonstrating the truth
of violence through the Gospels. But this does not yet mean that salvation
inheres in that specific death (if anywhere, it could lie in the *narration* of that
death), and the theme of the resurrection, to which Girard dedicates only a
few lines,[14] considering it as the opening of a truth that, in human terms, was
buried once and for all with the body of Christ, leaves the reader unable to
place Girard's version of the Passion coherently into the purely epistemological articulation of Christ's divinity.

2. Girard's Paradox

The problem of the absence of a kenotic dimension in Girard's thought is connected to another problem that has already been mentioned: insufficiency of
thought. If sacrifice, which is "the rationalization of a fortuitous chance,"[15]
does indeed generate human reason in its entirety, then reason, from its very
origins and even as far as its practical foundations, such as conceptualization
and language, is a sacrificial instrument.[16] The same mechanism that produced
philosophies also at one time produced myths—and today it produces the

thought that explains the origin of myths.[17] The Christian message demystifies sacrifice, showing it to be what it truly is, that is, the hidden engine of
human history. The transcendent here is, properly speaking, the cognitive
opening made possible by the Christian message; but even admitting that
humanity is ready to offer itself to that illuminating opening, how could
sacrifice be demystified using a logic and a language that, in the last analysis,
are in fact instruments created to reiterate the sacrificial mechanism? Girard
himself admits that "our own exercises in demystification" could even be
"cunning obstacles that our minds erect against the gospel revelation" (TH,
179). Even merely *speaking* of sacrifice would constitute *eo ipso* a betrayal of
the Christian demystification.

Why then embark on such an undertaking? Girard's answer is as follows: because after the Christian revelation, any accomplished mystification
is a mystification that can no longer be repeated in the future. What may
appear today to be a failure in the explication of truth may yet function
within a universal history of salvation: it becomes, provided that its memory
is preserved, a new limitation within which reason must stay so as not to fall
once again into the lie of the persecutors, and it therefore restricts reason's
sphere of action while also directing it toward truth. It is precisely through
the failures of reason that truth is able to emerge. Yet, at the same time, even
in the discourse that theorizes the lie of the persecutors and brings to light
the truth of the victims, the sacrificial mechanism is already dizzyingly at
work. Properly speaking, the only result that is not subject to the mystifica-
tions of sacrificial reason is the suspension of rational and linguistic activity:
the death of philosophy (TH, 525). There is no *logical* response to sacrificial
violence, for the obvious reason that any *logical* response would only blend
into the chorus of other violent voices, more or less hidden though they may
be. Silence, the most complete and total aphasia, thus seems to be the only
response, accompanied by a praxis that rejects the violence of sacred victim-
hood in the name of Christian love. As Girard himself seems to indicate,
commenting on the kiss that represents Christ's only response to the questions of the Grand Inquisitor in the famous episode of Dostoyevsky's *The
Brothers Karamazov*: "What to do in this case but to reaffirm the presence of
this love?" (RU, 130).

Therefore, the fundamental paradox of Girard's thought is this: the epistemological value of the Christian message places humanity at the threshold

of absolute knowledge (VS, 240–41). It is still situated in the world of reason, of thought; yet this thought opens us to transcendence, to a faith that refuses to be blind and unfounded abandonment. But, as we have seen, the instruments that should convey truth, reason and language, have been generated precisely to obscure that truth. Therefore, there can be only two possibilities. Either transcendence is a point of view that *still can* be attained thanks to the efforts of discursive reason—but in this case there remains the ineradicable doubt that every demystifying force may be in reality yet another obstacle intended to create obscurity—or transcendence *is* blind and unfounded abandonment.

Are there no other possible solutions? Is the only choice that Girard's thought offers us between Christian praxis, which in preaching silence overcomes even the most extreme form of mysticism,[18] and a discourse forever destined to be suspicious of itself to the point of risking irrelevancy? Perhaps there is theoretical space at least to hypothesize a third possibility: the economy of the transcendence of revelation.[19] Such economy would be a long and tormented journey from mystification to revelation, on problematic pathways that, in their failure, at the same time nonetheless confirm the tremendous value of a serious commitment to truth. Girard's recent clarifications on the use of the term "sacrifice" to describe the death of Christ may perhaps mitigate the perplexity surrounding the absence of kenotic sacrifice from his work, but they do not resolve its fundamental paradox of thought that remains forever inadequate to its own content. To speak of an economy of the transcendence of revelation alludes to the possibility of a form of thought that proves meaningful even (perhaps especially) when it encounters a limit, a barrier, when it fails—because from that failure emerges, as though a photographic negative, that which it cannot think of positively. It has not been possible, in this small space, to present an entirely serviceable hypothesis. What I must emphasize here is that Girard has not finished this argument, but has effectively begun it.

·   ·   ·

This short essay, written in 2004, represents a turning point in my engagement with mimetic theory. While on one hand some of the most prominent themes that featured in Intellectual Sacrifice *are still very much present in this essay (particularly the emphasis on the sacrificial nature of human reason and language and on the possibility of nonsacrificial thought), and hence it may be read in continuity with Part 1, on the other hand it also represents the opening of a (still internally) critical position that questioned some aspects of Girard's formulation of mimetic theory—specifically, the question of the divinity of Christ. The essays that follow may therefore be read as expressions of a "rupture" with an "orthodox" reading of mimetic theory, starting with the next essay, which is meant to be a thorough examination of Girard's "argument" for the divinity of Christ. However, they are also the expression of a continuity with the spirit, if not with the letter, of Girard's mimetic theory, and with the project, which already appeared in* Intellectual Sacrifice *and that featured more prominently in this essay, to establish a more direct dialogue between mimetic theory and the resources of Western philosophy—and particularly with philosophical hermeneutics.*

NOTES

1. For a wide-ranging survey of this problem, see Jean-Baptiste Fages, *Comprendre René Girard* (Toulouse: Privât, 1982), 156–61.

2. Thus runs the title of Paola Mancinelli's book, *Cristianesimo senza sacrificio: Filosofia e teologia in René Girard* [Christianity without sacrifice: Philosophy and theology in René Girard] (Assisi: Cittadella, 2001).

3. Compare Pierangelo Sequeri, "'Dare la vita' ed 'essere sacrificato': Il tema della singolarità cristologica nella prospettiva di R. Girard," *Teologia* 14, no. 2 (1989): 143–153, 153.

4. Compare Massimo Cacciari, *Dell'Inizio* (Milan: Adelphi, 1990), 561.

5. Thus Giuseppe Angelini is mistaken when he states that "love, to be at all, must be entirely separate from desire" ("Apologie postmoderne dell'amore: L'esempio di Girard e Levinas," *Teologia* 2 [2002]: 94–138, 108): Girard clearly indicates that, human nature being intrinsically mimetic, the only way to realize true love is not to pursue a hypothetical utopia free from all models, but to follow the only model that cannot transform into a rival because it is not solely human: Christ. See TH, 425–31.

6. Compare Cacciari, *Dell'Inizio*, 563.

7. Adele Colombo, *Il sacrificio in René Girard: Dalla violenza al dono* (Brescia: Morcelliana, 1999), 169. Concerning the textual examples of Girard's recognition of the importance of Eucharistic sacramental *praxis*, see TH, 235–37, 445, 198, 229.

8. "In the past, I was too exclusively insistent on the difference between the two [meanings of sacrifice]. . . . Christians are right to use the word "sacrifice" for Christ: they grasp that unity intuitively and, in any event, those who aren't ready to understand certain things will never be convinced by logical and anthropological arguments" (WTTB, 115). See also René Girard, "Not Just Interpretations: There Are Facts, Too," in *Christianity, Truth, and Weakening Faith: A Dialogue*, by Gianni Vattimo and René Girard, ed. Pierpaolo Antonello, trans. William McCuaig (New York: Columbia University Press, 2010), 88–108. Raymund Schwager underlines the

inescapability of the historical sacrifice of Christ in *Brauchen wir einen Sündenbock?* (Munich: Kosel, 1978), 32.

9. Compare Giuseppe Fornari, "Alla ricerca dell'origine perduta: Nuova formulazione della teoria mimetico-sacrificale di Girard," in *Maestri e scolari di non violenza*, ed. Claudio Tugnoli (Milan: Franco Angeli, 2000), 159.

10. Compare Rebecca Adams, "Violence, Difference, Sacrifice: A Conversation with René Girard," *Religion and Literature* 25, no. 2 (1993): 28–30, in which Girard, in relation to his interpretation of the Letter to the Hebrews in *Things Hidden*, admits: "I was completely wrong" (28). The need to revise the judgment on the Letter to the Hebrews was immediately supported by Raymund Schwager (see "Gewalt und Opfer," *Orientierung* 38 [1974]: 41–44). On the Eucharist, see the statement in René Girard, "La lotta tra Gesù e Satana: Conversazione con René Girard," in *La vittima e la folla: Violenza del mito e cristianesimo*, ed. Giuseppe Fornari (Treviso: Santi Quaranta, 1998), 159–60.

11. See Girard's own admission in ISS, 105.

12. This repudiation is achieved for the first time in René Girard, "Mimetische Theorie und Teologie," in *Vom Fluch und Segen der Sündenböcke: Raymund Schwager zum 60 Geburtstag*, ed. Józef Niewiadomski and Wolfgang Palaver (Thaur: Kulturverlag, 1995), 15–29. See also Girard, "Not Just Interpretations," 92–93.

13. Compare Gianni Vattimo, *Belief*, trans. Luca D'Isanto and David Webb (Stanford, CA: Stanford University Press, 1999); Vattimo, "Heidegger and Girard," in Vattimo and Girard, *Christianity, Truth, and Weakening Faith*.

14. See Girard, "Not Just Interpretations," 105.

15. Giorgio Rognini, "Al di là del sacrificio," *Hermeneutica* 5 (1985): 79–114, 109.

16. Compare Michel Serres, *Hermès V: Le passage du Nord-Ouest* (Paris: Minuit, 1980), 41.

17. Not only culture, as Angelini states, but reason itself thus appears "spoiled by this radical lie." See Angelini, "Apologie postmoderne dell'amore," 107–8.

18. Although Girard's thought may be regarded by someone as suggesting that Christianity is simply an antisacrificial praxis, Angelini's claim ("Apologie postmoderne dell'amore," 137) that such thought hides an "ideology that legitimates anarchic lifestyles" is frankly ridiculous.

19. Compare Eric Gans, "Le Logos de René Girard," in *René Girard et le problème du mal*, ed. Michel Deguy and Jean-Pierre Dupuy (Paris: Grasset, 1982).

Girard's Ontological Argument for the Existence of God

My main aim in this essay is to show that Girard's argument for Christ's divinity hides a variation of the classic ontological argument for the existence of God.[1] In order to do so, it is first important to distinguish three distinct hermeneutical approaches to Girard's mimetic theory: *internal and literal, internal nonliteral,* and *critical.* If we take an internal and literal approach, we find that Girard writes nothing about the ontological proof. If we take an internal and nonliteral approach to Girard, we can try to deduce what he might have thought about the ontological proof on the basis of his mimetic theory, thereby extending his thought while remaining within his theory. If we take a critical approach, we can interpret Girard from an external perspective and critically analyze analogies between the ontological proof and his mimetic theory on the assumption that there is no a priori reason why there cannot be a relationship between an argument (such as the ontological argument for the existence of God) and a thinker (such as Girard), even without that thinker's awareness and in spite of his intentions.

With respect to the internal and nonliteral approach, we should recall that, as I have clarified elsewhere,[2] Girard's mimetic theory posits a strong identity between religion and philosophy. Insofar as it is implicated in the mystification of reason, philosophy will never show the truth about scapegoating, exactly as a ritual ceremony, the only purpose of which is to perpetuate the original expulsion of the victim, will never be able to reveal the mechanism that produces it. In its origins, reason is a sacrificial tool. In order to demystify philosophy, reason would have to be above that which it demystifies, which is not possible insofar as the subject of the demystification is reason itself. Reason alone can never completely reveal its own origins (J, 124).

1. Girard's Argument for the Existence of God

The first phase of Girard's work culminates in *Violence and the Sacred*. The turning point of his thinking is contained in *Things Hidden*. Here Girard still claims that every religion is sacrificial. The Old Testament, he continues, is not, however, merely "mythological"; sometimes the chorus of the lynch mob, the devout followers of the jealous and violent Yahweh, is broken by a voice rising up in defense of the victim. Sometimes this is the victim himself, proclaiming his innocence, as in the book of Job. Christianity, for Girard, is an exception among religions insofar as the Gospels break with the violent sacred. On this view, Christ undergoes the collective lynching but refuses the role of the scapegoat and reveals the truth of mimetic victimage. But how is Christianity an exception? The Gospels revolve around Christ's Passion, which is the same drama narrated by every mythology: the collective murder of a scapegoat. The Gospels, however, are not myths in this sense, precisely because they lay the blame for the violence on the persecutors, not on the victim. They deny the ambivalence of the sacred in order to reveal the arbitrariness of sacrificial violence.

From Girard's arguments it can be deduced that the mechanism of mimetic victimage encompasses all of reason, language, and civilization. It cannot produce, at least not without "external" contributions, a doctrine, a hypothesis, or a theory able to demolish it. In order to denounce the mechanism, it is necessary to be outside the mechanism. Only someone who is free from the chains of the mimetic, who does not think according to the rules of violence and is extraneous to it, could do this. But the whole of humankind is the prisoner of this circle. No mere human could ever reveal the truth that we read about in the Gospels. The fact that the Gospels possess an authentic knowledge of violence reveals that its insight cannot be merely human. Therefore, according to Girard, Christ cannot be simply a man; he must also be divine. Girard writes: "To recognize Christ as God is to recognize him as the only being capable of rising above the violence that had, up to that point, absolutely transcended mankind. . . . We do not have to adopt the hypothesis of Christ's divinity because it has always been accepted by orthodox Christians. Instead, this hypothesis is orthodox because in the first years of Christianity there existed a rigorous (though not yet explicit) intuition of the logic determining the gospel text" (TH, 219).[3]

Although the Christian message is free of mystification, the Christian religion itself is not. Christianity has developed an internal sacred core: the death of Christ is interpreted as a sacrifice to the Father, the cruel God who requires the death of his Son to save humanity. Girard cites Anselm's theory of justification in this regard. Anselm, like most medieval thinkers, believes that God requires a precious and beloved victim to avenge his honor.

I contend that Girard's argument for the divinity of Christ, if properly reconstructed, is formally and logically equivalent to the classic structure of the ontological argument; and that Girard's argument cannot be considered valid without, simultaneously, considering the ontological argument (or at least a modern version of it: more on this later) equally valid.

For the sake of convenience, consider the first formulation of the ontological argument—that elaborated by Anselm of Canterbury. In the *Proslogion* Anselm gives two definitions of God. The first one, and the better known, is *id quo maius cogitari nequit*, "that than which nothing greater can be thought" (IQM). Later on, in chapter 15, Anselm gives another definition of God: *quiddam maius quam cogitari posit*, "something greater than whatever can be thought" (QM). The second is implicit in the first: God must be QM; otherwise he would not be IQM.

Anselm's demonstration of God's existence is based on the definition of God as IQM. The demonstration proceeds as follows:

> The one who denies the existence of God refers to God as IQM.
>
>   Therefore, the denier has the idea of God in mind (that is, God exists as an idea in the mind).
>
>   But the IQM cannot exist only in the mind, because an IQM that

exists would be greater than a being that exists only in the mind, and this is a contradiction.

Therefore, God exists.[4]

I will now formalize Girard's argument. Girard claims that the Gospels are the only texts in which we can read the truth about the victim. Christ, with his preaching, shows the arbitrariness of the scapegoat and thus completely demystifies the mimetic mechanism. But no human being could do this, because all are trapped in the mechanism; reason itself arose to perpetuate the victimary expulsion, and thus is unable to know and express the complete truth about the victim (that is, it is unable to do what Christ does). Thus, Christ is not simply a man; he also has a divine nature (that is, he is the Son of God). Therefore, God exists.

We note, in this argument, an insistence on the epistemological role played by Christ with his preaching. Christ is the only one who can tell the truth. Nobody else can. Thus, Girard's argument for the divinity of Christ, and the consequent conclusion about the existence of God, seems to be based on the following definition of Christ: "Someone who knows something greater than whatever one could think" (CQM). This definition is the "epistemological translation" of Anselm's definition of God as QM. Is the definition sufficient to demonstrate both that (1) Christ is not simply a man, and that (2) God exists?

1.1. Is Christ More Than Human?

Girard deduces that Christ is not simply a man from the definition of Christ as CQM. Nevertheless, there is an aporia in this passage. If Christ is the holder of a divine message (that is, "greater than whatever one could think"), this does not imply that this holder is the Son of God. Holding to Girard's premises, we could argue that God wanted the birth of a completely innocent man, extraneous to the mimetic rivalry that binds us all, without necessarily deriving from this that this man is the Son of God. Even if we accept Girard's tenet that the message of which Christ is the holder (CQM) cannot be of human origin, we cannot deduce his divinity from here. The very premises of Girard's mimetic theory do not make this theoretical move possible: according to those premises, in fact, the salvation of humankind seems to depend on a form of knowledge (the knowledge on mimetic victimage). Girard clearly emphasizes the epistemological and ethical dimensions of salvation:[5] Jesus saves because he tells the truth about the victim (and because he offers himself as the only model who cannot turn into a rival).

In passing, I want to emphasize that, according to the Christian tradition, it is not sufficient to say that Christ saves: Christ himself is salvation. The distance between the two affirmations is not negligible. If Christ merely saves, Christ differs from many other victims (Job, for example) because the presentation of the truth of his victimization, and of the lie of the persecutors, is clearer and more complete; the difference is, therefore, purely *quantitative*. If Christ is salvation, on the other hand, he is salvation because he is God, and his sacrifice thus assumes a decisive value; only in this case is the difference between Jesus and the other victims *qualitative*.[6] We cannot deduce the divinity of Christ from his definition as CQM because, even in the theoretical context of Girard's mimetic theory, it is possible to claim that Christ is more than human (1) if and only if it is possible to claim that God exists (2).

1.2. Does God Exist?

Can we demonstrate that God exists from the definition of Christ as CQM? A syllogism seems to lead in the desired direction:

MP: Christ is someone who knows something greater than whatever one could think (CQM).
mP: Only God could know something greater than whatever one could think.
C: Christ is God.

The question is, why can God alone know something greater than whatever one could think? There is no logical reason to affirm this, unless we surreptitiously assume the definition of God as the most perfect being, that is, the IQM. Thus:

Girard posits the definition of Christ as CQM.

He deduces (1) and (2) from CQM, but

(1) depends on (2), and
(2) implies the definition of God as IQM.

Therefore, (2) is true if and only if IQM is true—that is, only if the ontological argument works.

Let us go back to the ontological proof. The demonstration of God's existence is based on this definition of God as IQM. As is well known, Kant considers this proof either contradictory or impossible. It is contradictory if God's existence is already assumed in the concept of God. It is impossible if his existence is not previously assumed, because in that case the existence must be added synthetically to the concept, that is, through experience—but God is beyond experience.[7] The ontological proof, in Kant's view, seems to be convincing because it surreptitiously assumes in the definition of IQM that which has to be proved, namely God's existence. According to Kant, then, the ontological proof is invalid. We cannot deduce the existence of God from the definition of God as IQM.

A similar objection can be made against Girard's argument. Even in that case, in fact, we cannot assume the existence of God to be implicit in IQM—to do so would be to assume what remains to be demonstrated, that is, the existence of God. But if we do not assume the existence of God to be implicit in IQM, we must also admit that we cannot deduce that God exists from the definition of Christ as CQM.

2. Hegel, Ricoeur, and Mimetic Hermeneutics

The problems I have raised do not arise, I suggest, from any inadequacy in Girard's analysis. They arise, rather, from the *coherence* of his method. Girard often emphasizes his distance from contemporary philosophy. He contends that philosophy is properly a reiteration of a series of myths, having at its center the same narrative structures as mythology. Girard considers mimetic theory to be a scientific hypothesis. But the choice of this "scientific" method can lead solely to the epistemological and ethical conclusion we have seen. The definition of Christ as "someone who knows something greater than whatever one could think" is precisely what Girard can admit to while remaining faithful to his premises and his methodology. In fact, this account presents transcendence as the culmination of theory, which is why it cannot be accepted as its presupposition.

Girard nevertheless considers the divinity of Christ to be the central point in his theory. It may seem surprising that Girard, who is always critical of metaphysics, which he considers to be a myth, makes considerable, albeit unconscious, use of the ontological argument. Is he simply guilty of naïveté?

Let us put this question on hold for now, and recall that not all post-Kantian thinkers have rejected the ontological argument. For example, Hegel considers the ontological argument very positively. A necessarily brief analysis of the Hegelian reading of the ontological proof can provide helpful hints to understand its employment in the context of mimetic theory.

Hegel refuses Kant's confutation of the ontological proof.[8] It is mistaken, in Hegel's view, to compare an empirical object, such as the famous hundred thalers used in Kant's example, to God, and conclude that, as for the hundred thalers, so also for God existence can be ascertained only empirically. The main flaw that Hegel identifies in Kant's objection to the ontological proof is precisely this reductive account, that is, an account of reality that tends to treat equally empirical objects (such as the hundred thalers) and conceptual objects (in particular, the concept of God). In other words, for Hegel, Kant's "barbarous triviality"[9] lies in the fact that it is clear to everyone that concept and being are not necessarily united in finite beings. But the central point is that the ontological argument is concerned with infinite being, whose distinctive prerogative is precisely the necessary implication of its existence, its being.[10] In other words, for Hegel the starting point of the ontological argument is the concept of God as absolutely perfect being. The argument displays how religious consciousness can conceive the unity of finite and infinite. Hegel refuses Kant's objection because, although for finite beings there cannot be any necessary unity of concept and being, this unity is properly constitutive of God.

Hegel's argument appeared to many as a mere apology for the traditional ontological argument—or perhaps for its more modern formulation.[11] If that was the case, then Hegel's argument would be subject to the same objections raised against the ontological proof—most relevantly, Kant's objections. Actually, Hegel declares his dissatisfaction with the ontological proof in its traditional form,[12] precisely because of its alleged "linear" nature—that is, its pretension to be founded exclusively on an immediate certainty (the unity of being and concept). Hegel is always critical of *certainty* (*Gewissheit*): the "linear" proofs require a starting point perceived as "aproblematic," in the way the originary and subjective certainty (one of the early phenomenological stages of the *Phenomenology of Spirit*) considers its claims as aproblematic: the starting points are considered immediate rather than derived, or mediated. As Hegel argues on various occasions, the point of view of subjective certainty needs to be overcome not in the direction of Kantian skepticism, but in the direction of the development of a way of thinking that accepts the absence of absolute starting points and also, ultimately, the circularity of knowledge. Conceived as a moment of this "cognitive circle," then, the unity of being and thought is neither the same premise that we find in the traditional ontological proof, nor a religious dogma that must be accepted as such, but a coherent reconceptualized version of that starting point. Of course, someone might object that, if this is indeed the case, then nobody can get out of this circle and reach a "view from the outside." But perhaps Hegel would reply that this is precisely the point. In other words, the ontological argument expresses for Hegel precisely this circular structure that is distinctive of knowledge itself. In its Hegelian version, the ontological argument seems to make sense only when one embraces a specific hermeneutic horizon[13]—in the case of Hegel, that represented by the spirit which, in its process of self-consciousness, posits the idea of God as that idea in which thought and being are necessarily united.

Analogously, even the (implicit) use that Girard makes of the ontological argument might seem similar to the traditional version of the proof; but even in the case of mimetic theory, the ontological argument assumes its validity only if it is contextualized in a specific hermeneutic horizon. An example can be useful in clarifying this point. Consider once again the ontological proof in its original Anselmian formulation. For Anselm, "God exists" is a proposition that is true because it has been revealed, and that revelation is the central point of the history of salvation. This means that the proposition is true by authority: only after we have affirmed this truth can we prove it. For Girard, too, revelation is part of the history of salvation. Nevertheless—and this is the point—the history of salvation coincides with the history of interpretation. In fact, according to Girard, revelation did not end with the death and resurrection of Christ, but has continued since and continues to exercise its demystifying action. The Paraclete, the Spirit of truth of which the Gospel of John speaks (John 16:8–11), is the knowledge that progressively reveals itself in the world and continues the revelation of Christ.[14]

The birth of modern hermeneutics dates back to the Protestant Reformation: The awareness of the hermeneutical problem, substantially extraneous to previous conceptions of interpretation, appears in that historical context. The first application of the hermeneutic method is in the interpretation of the Judeo-Christian Scriptures: Flacius Illyricus emphasizes that interpretation reveals itself only if the interpreter approaches the texts not in an abstractly neutral way, but is animated by a religious sensitivity, by a preunderstanding of the truth of the text that searches and discovers its own confirmation. Such an affirmation fits with the Girardian view: texts have to be interpreted in light of principles that the Scriptures alone hold. It is interesting to note, however, that Johann Heinrich Ernesti distinguishes between "a theological hermeneutics" and "a profane hermeneutics." This distinction, from a Girardian perspective, generates the illusion that a text can express its truth—the truth of the victim—apart from the demystifying principles of the Scriptures. Even today we can distinguish between a "profane" hermeneutics, which asserts that there is an infinity of possible interpretations, and a "religious" hermeneutics, which leads to the unveiling of the only valid interpretation—that is, the only one that reveals the truth about the victim. It is evident, from Girard's texts, that when he criticizes hermeneutics, he refers to the latter and not the former. Indeed, the interconnection between the history of salvation and the history of interpretation really represents, in this sense, the key to grasping the place that the ontological argument occupies within Girard's mimetic theory.

In *Intellectual Sacrifice*, I have already distinguished between a "theological (or religious) hermeneutics" and a "profane hermeneutics."[15] I define "profane hermeneutics" as the philosophical position that emphasizes the equivalence of possible interpretations, instead of what distinguishes them. According to mimetic theory, this "respect for differences" legitimates the lynching of the innocents because it can lead us to think that the lie of the persecutors is one interpretation that is as valid as any other. As a result, this way of thinking leads toward the refusal of any knowledge and truth, basing itself on the principle that to believe in anything and to be violent are the same thing. According to Girard, profane hermeneutics holds itself to be closer to the truth by suspending the verdict about every truth. This is the reason why the truth, from this philosophical view, is the absence of every truth.

The philosophical text becomes the place in which the expulsion of the victim is continually repeated, and thereby ritualized. Philosophy never reaches a conclusion; for this reason it is possible to infinitely repeat the expulsion (see VS, 296).[16] Unveiling the sacred does not yet mean revealing the truth, but rather reproducing the lie on an interpretative level. Profane hermeneutics can be, therefore, the unveiling of the sacred, but not the unveiling of its lie. This is the case because a profane hermeneutics does not make use of the Gospels' revelation. It is the mirrorlike opposite of Anselm's position. On one hand, Anselm's argument is grounded solely on salvific revelation (history of salvation), ignoring any interpretative contextualization (history of interpretation); on the other hand, "profane" hermeneutics ignores the history of salvation (or better, it recognizes no salvation) and considers solely the history of interpretation.

Interpretation has always been relevant in the process of demystification. A "history of interpretation," that is, according to Girard, a progressive understanding of the truth of violence, is possible only as a result of Christian revelation. On the other hand, a "history of salvation" is possible only if the Scriptures are reinterpreted beyond their sacrificial interpretation. As I have already remarked in *Intellectual Sacrifice*, Paul Ricoeur's thought is, according to Girard, an example of what I call "religious hermeneutics"—that is, a demystification of mythical heritage made possible by the principles of interpretation provided by the Christ texts. The interpretation of myth opens a way to a knowledge that can discern the false from the true.[17] Hermeneutics, Ricoeur writes, is "one of the modes" by which "'modernity' transcends itself, as it is forgetfulness of the sacred."[18] In the context of a radical confrontation with modern consciousness, Ricoeur showed the presence of a residual mythical element that cannot be completely dissolved by thought. What if the presence of the ontological proof within Girard's mimetic theory was exactly this—a residual mythical element?

Even in the case of a positive answer to such a question, this does not mean that the presence of the ontological proof within mimetic theory should be eliminated (or "expelled . . .") at all costs. Human reason is a sacrificial instrument: once this presupposition has been accepted, we should make peace with the fact that the pathway of a demystifying thought will never be pure, in the sense of completely devoid of mythical remains: if our forms of thought are inevitably sacrificial, what we can do is to use those forms that allow us to progress in the path of demystification, while remaining aware of their origin, and hence of their limits.

3. Conclusion

From a logical point of view, Girard's argument is just as "fallacious" as Anselm's (or Descartes's, or Leibniz's) ontological proof. Nevertheless, I think that the "hermeneutic turn," already made by Hegel somehow, and then thematized in contemporary philosophical terms by Ricoeur, clarifies the substantial difference between Girard's argument and the classical formulation of the ontological proof. The history of salvation runs through the history of interpretation. Obviously, even religious hermeneutics must conform to the rules of logic. If it does not, it becomes exactly that which Girard abhors—profane hermeneutics. Girard does not say so explicitly, but I think it is clear that only an a priori choice that situates the ontological argument in a specific hermeneutic horizon can validate his argument. In fact, if we limit ourselves to a "mechanical" reading of Girard's mimetic theory and to an application of its premises, then coherence forces us to reject the ontological proof that is implicit in Girard's argument for the divinity of Christ. Effectively, Girard claims that he wants to remain faithful to a scientific paradigm, and even proclaims the "death of philosophy."[19] But if we consider the question in a broader perspective, then Girard's "ontological argument" has indeed a deep philosophical sense, insofar as it is indissolubly connected with the assumption that there is always a *wager* at the root of every philosophical position. We can wager for transcendence or for the absence of transcendence. From this point of view, Girard's thought does not require an "act of faith" (as Anselm's thought does); rather, it requires a wager, in Pascal's sense. Deriving the divinity of Christ from the definition of "someone who knows something greater than whatever one could think" means precisely to accept this wager. A wager "à la Pascal" is not a shift to some fideism; or, better, it is no more an act of faith than is the opposite choice. The wager shares with phenomenology—that phenomenology which constitutes the source of every authentic hermeneutics—a fundamental feature, that is, the capacity to reconquer "a second naïveté presupposing an initial critical revolution, an initial loss of naïveté."[20] Girard's argument could be considered "a second naïveté," based on a wager that manifests itself as interpretation. In this sense, I think we can speak of a "mimetic hermeneutics." In the contemporary context, dominated on the one hand by metaphysics as objective classification ("the God's-eye view") and, on the other, by a fascination with the equivalence of all possible interpretations (that is, the absence of truth), the perspective opened by Girard's thought can be fruitful for a philosophy that intends to reappropriate its own speculative vocation.

NOTES

1. Only a few studies have explored this issue; the most notable of them is Giuseppe Fornari, "La vittima e il corpo: La prova dell'esistenza di Dio nel pensiero di René Girard," *Filosofia e Teologia* 13, no. 2 (1999): 260–70.

2. See "Chapter 1: Intellectual Expulsion" in this volume.

3. See also: "If the Son of Man and the Son of God are one and same, it is because Jesus is the only person to achieve humanity in its perfect form, and so to be one with the deity" (TH, 216). See Fornari, "La vittima e il corpo," 263–64.

4. According to Graham Oppy, this is the conceptual (or hyperintensional) formulation of the ontological argument. See Graham Oppy, *Ontological Arguments and Belief in God* (New York: Cambridge University Press, 1995).

5. Girard himself admits this. See René Girard, *Les origines de la culture: Entretiens avec Pierpaolo Antonello et João Cezar de Castro Rocha* (Paris: Desclée de Brouwer, 2004).

6. See Massimo Cacciari, *Dell'Inizio* (Milan: Adelphi, 1990), 561.

7. Immanuel Kant, *Critique of Pure Reason*, trans. and ed. Paul Guyer and Allen W. Wood (Cambridge: Cambridge University Press, 1998), B667.

8. Georg Wilhelm Friedrich Hegel, *Enzyklopädie der philosophischen Wissenschaften im Grundrisse*, ed. Eva Moldenhauer and Karl Markus (Frankfurt am Main: Suhrkamp Verlag, 1970–71), vol. 1, *Logik*, §51.

9. Hegel, *Enzyklopädie*, vol. 1, *Logik*, §51.

10. On Hegel's conception of the ontological argument, see Paolo Diego Bubbio and Paul Redding, "Hegel and the Ontological Argument on the Existence of God," *Religious Studies: An International Journal for the Philosophy of Religion* 50, no. 4 (2014): 465–86.

11. For example, this is the opinion of Kevin J. Harrelson, *The Ontological Argument from Descartes to Hegel* (New York: Humanity Books, 2009), 219.

12. Hegel, *Enzyklopädie*, vol. 1, *Logik*, §193.

13. According to some recent interpretations, Hegel could be considered a hermeneutic thinker *ante litteram*. See Maurizio Pagano, *Hegel: La religione e l'ermeneutica del concetto* (Naples: Edizioni Scientifiche Italiane, 1992); Paul Redding, *Hegel's Hermeneutics* (Ithaca, NY: Cornell University Press, 1996).

14. See Vattimo, "Storia della salvezza, storia dell'interpretazione," *Micromega* 3 (1992): 107.

15. The most correct term to refer to the way of thinking that is opposed to "theological" or "religious" hermeneutics (the only really authentic hermeneutics, for Girard) would not be "profane," but rather the term that in common language constitutes its opposite, that is, "sacred." There is, in fact, a tendency in contemporary thought that is an unveiling of the sacred, but not an unveiling of the lie of the sacred.

16. See also Bruce Bassoff, "Interview with René Girard," *Denver Quarterly* 13, no. 2 (1978): 28–40.

17. I have examined this issue in Paolo Diego Bubbio, "Literary Aesthetics and Knowledge in René Girard's Mimetic Theory," *Literature and Aesthetics* 17, no. 1 (2007): 35–50.

18. Paul Ricoeur, *The Symbolism of Evil*, trans. Emerson Buchanan (New York: Harper and Row, 1967), 352.

19. "I do believe that philosophy has used up its resources. . . . I believe . . . that the end of philosophy brings with it a new possibility of scientific thinking within the human domain; at the same time, however strange this may seem, it brings with it a return to religious faith." DCC, 438.

20. This is Ricoeur's expression. He refers here to the thought of Gabriel Marcel. Paul Ricoeur, "Gabriel Marcel and Phenomenology," in *The Philosophy of Gabriel Marcel*, ed. Paul Arthur Schilpp and Lewis Edwin Hahn (La Salle, IL: Open Court, 1984), 491. A comparison between Girard and Marcel would be very fruitful. I focused my attention on the topic of the "choice of sense" in Marcel's thought in Paolo Diego Bubbio, "'If There Is a Plot': Gabriel Marcel and Second-Degree Reflection," in *Between Description and Interpretation: The Hermeneutic Turn in Phenomenology*, ed. Andrzej Wiercinski (Toronto: Hermeneutic Press, 2005), 55–70.

Mimetic Theory's Post-Kantian Legacy

I n the last few years, religion has increasingly become a subject of dispute. Two positions seem to be the most popular. On the one hand, outspoken atheists reject religion in the name of reason and science. On the other hand, we witness an increase in scholarship sympathetic with conservative Christian movements. In this chapter, I will use the term "new atheists" to refer to the former approach, and the term "new theists" to refer to the latter approach.

"New atheists" is a label that has become usual for identifying some thinkers such as Richard Dawkins, Sam Harris, and Quentin Smith. Atheism being a general term, a more detailed specification is necessary. The distinguishing feature of the "new atheism" seems to be a kind of "scientific atheism." To borrow Thomas Dixon's definition,[1] scientific atheism involves belief in three central doctrines. The first is antitheism. The second is scientism, conceived as the belief that "science, especially natural science" is "the most valuable part of human learning" because it is "the most authoritative, or serious, or beneficial."[2] Third, scientific atheists "recognise the need to develop an alternative worldview to replace supernaturalism and theism, in which to ground their interpretation of the results of natural science, their understanding of the origins and meaning of human life, and their ethical discourse."[3]

Providing a precise account of the "new theism" is much more difficult. If it is true that some scholars explicitly profess Evangelicalism, or at least some of its characteristics as identified by David Bebbington[4] (including conversionism, biblicism, activism, cruicentrism), and hence are often referred to as "Evangelic Christians," the term is only partly accurate, both because not all of them profess all these beliefs, and because the movement embraces a wider range of philosophical expressions. Sometimes they are referred to as "Christian nationalists," but this label is even less accurate, because it implies an emphasis on the political dimension of their philosophical activity, which, even assuming this as their ultimate goal, does not represent the philosophical justification for their reasoning. Rather, the distinguishing feature of what I call "new theism" seems to be a revived natural philosophy that welcomes rational proofs for the existence of a personal God and supernatural/religious explanations for scientific phenomena. This philosophical attitude is exemplified by (but not limited to) the theory of intelligent design. Intelligent design is the claim that "certain features of the universe and of living things are best explained by an intelligent cause, not an undirected process such as natural selection."[5] Thinkers such as William Lane Craig and Robert Koons seem to be committed to this notion.[6]

My claim is that the new atheists and the new theists are "enemy twins": they fight each other vigorously, but they need each other, as both of them build their identity in opposition to their adversary. They represent the last instance of mimesis in the cultural history of Western identity, as well as further evidence of that "escalation to the extremes" which drives the relationship between doubles. In fact, despite the frontal opposition that could lead one to think that these two positions have nothing in common, the standpoint of new theists and the standpoint of the new atheists mirror each other. They *have* something in common. They both assume that *religion is a theory*. They assume that philosophy can and/or should consider religion to be a system of theoretical propositions. ·

The assumption that religion is a theory seems to be based on a kind of metanaturalism.[7] Atheist philosophers profess a methodological naturalism, conceived as that approach which considers supernatural phenomena as nonexistent or not inherently different from natural hypothesis. On the other hand, the new theists profess a natural philosophy that welcomes supernatural explanations of natural phenomena. In both cases, religion is considered a theory, whose propositional content is then rejected (for it expresses something that does not exist, or that can be explained naturally) or assumed (for it is taken as the ground of natural phenomena).

In my view, the metanaturalism shared by the new atheists and the new theists is an account that is still dominant in the English-speaking world because the dominant philosophical tradition in the English-speaking world—so-called analytic philosophy—has rejected Kantian and post-Kantian perspectivism.

As is it known, according to Kant it is mistaken to take the ideas of the soul, the world, and God as constitutive: they are not cognitive objects, but "regulative principles which serve to guide the understanding through reason in respect of experience" by "using to their greatest perfection" the rules of reason.[8] Kant's *Religion within the Boundaries of Mere Reason* pursues this goal by removing religious claims from the realm of theoretical reason and referencing their significance to regulative and symbolic meaning.[9]

The whole history of German idealism from Kant onward can be read, as Paul Redding suggested,[10] as history of perspectivism. Perspectivism means first of all the renunciation of the idea that the world can be examined by the subject objectively, that is, from a God's-eye point of view.

Therefore, perspectivism can be considered to be the thread connecting the different moments of so-called continental philosophy: a process of radicalization of perspectivism that starts from Kant, goes through Schopenhauer and Kierkegaard, and has a fundamental moment with Nietzsche, whose emphasis on interpretation became central in the further developments of phenomenology, existentialism, and hermeneutics.

1. Post-Kantian Elements of Mimetic Theory

Prima facie, that tradition that has its origins in Kant's critical philosophy, then has a fundamental moment with Nietzsche, and then develops into contemporary philosophical hermeneutics, does not seem to have much in common with mimetic theory, especially if we consider the last outcomes of that tradition, which tend to question the knowability of truth and emphasize the necessity of an interpretative approach. Conversely, according to Girard, truth exists: it is the truth represented by the renunciation of metaphysical desire, the truth of the victim, which is revealed by the Gospels. Is religion a "theory of salvation," in Girard's view? The answer is positive only if we take the term "religion" in its sacrificial meaning—religion as a technique of catharsis. But from this point of view, the message of the Gospels is the opposite of a theory—on the contrary, it is the antitheory par excellence, because by revealing the truth of the victim it demystifies and makes the development of new sacrificial theories impossible.

A brief analysis of the notion of "the sacred" will show how much mimetic theory has in common with Kantian-hermeneutical perspectivism. We know that the sacred is sacrificial violence, a violence that is perpetuated in the narratives of the original event. Now, the point of view of mythical narratives is that of the persecutors: the victim is obviously presented as guilty. Furthermore, this point of view must be absolute: in fact, only if it is absolute, that is, universally shared, can it guarantee that unanimity that is fundamental for the efficiency of mimetic victimage. Therefore, the event is presented from a "detached" or "objective" perspective—that is, from the God's-eye point of view. The point is that, as Girard reminds us, the myth of detachment is "the greatest myth of all" (DDN, 270).[11] Conversely, the truth of the victim is perspectival: it contrasts the "absolute" point of view of the persecutors with an "alternative" point of view—a voice out of the chorus.

The peculiarity of Christianity lies, I argue, precisely in its fundamental perspectivism. As Chris Fleming has remarked, the writings of the Old Testament "narrate an ongoing *relationship* of a people with God, and, in so doing, exact not simply a critique or desymbolization of myth, but an ongoing process of *auto-critique*."[12] However, it is in the Gospels that perspectivism really comes to light, expressed by the image of a God who became man, whose earthly manifestation was temporally and geographically determined. What can better represent perspectivism than a God who becomes human and renounces the *God's-eye* point of view?

During a conversation between Girard and Gianni Vattimo, the latter claimed: "From René Girard I took the idea that God can only be a relativist . . . because the desacralizing thrust of Christianity (the extreme point of which is the Pauline *kenosis*, in other words the incarnation and humiliation) seems to me fundamentally to point toward the idea that God is not the content of a true proposition but is actually *someone* incarnated in Jesus Christ, and Jesus Christ is an exemplar of charity."[13] Leaving aside the first part of the claim—the appellative "relativist" attributed to God is questionable from Girard's perspective—Vattimo's affirmation can, in my view, be endorsed. Moreover, it might be argued that Girard echoes such claims when, in a later conversation, he maintains: "The idea that Christ is living interpretation seems highly valid to me."[14] It is against that "absolute" that is the sacred (i.e., everything that, by definition, refuses to be considered in perspective) that Christianity as living interpretation is opposed.

Mimetic theory belongs, I contend, to the Western tradition of Kantian and hermeneutical perspectivism, and does not share the metanaturalistic assumption of the new atheists and the new theists. The new theists obsessively look for supernatural explanations of natural phenomena. But Girard has taught us that the preference for supernatural explanations over natural causes means appealing to magical-persecutory causality, and that this causality has been slowly and laboriously abandoned thanks to the Gospels (S, 314). The new theists are still prisoners of the mimetic-victimary mechanism, and their attitude toward other religious traditions (a *sacrificial* attitude, as it reproduces the search for a scapegoat) is evidence of that.

But the new atheists too are still prisoners of the sacred. Science is their sacred. They do not realize that science has been made possible precisely by those Christian texts that they reject.[15] In order to avoid the "escalation to the extremes" that drives the relationship between doubles (the new atheists and the new theists), we need to affirm the perspectival feature of Western identity, something that can be done by a hermeneutical thought—as long as this thought is authentically hermeneutical. Here a distinction is necessary between perspectivism and relativism. Admittedly, Girard does not make such a distinction, and actually seems to consider perspectivism and relativism as equivalent—for instance, when he claims, in relation to the book of Job, "There are two truths, relatively speaking, in the sense of 'relativism' and 'perspectivism,' but there is only one when it comes to knowledge, and that is the truth of the victim" (J, 107). And yet Girard seems to overlook here that, in order for us to listen to the voice of the victim, we must have already endorsed (at least unconsciously) the epistemological principle according to which there is more than one perspective. This seems to be a trivial point, but actually it is not—especially in the context of mimetic theory, which has taught us that, for thousands of years, we have listened to only one perspective, to one "truth"—that is, to the voice of persecutors. In light of this background, the distinction between perspectivism and relativism now emerges as a need. Such a distinction mirrors the distinction I have drawn elsewhere, borrowing the terminology from the early hermeneutic thinker Johann Heinrich Ernesti, between a "theological" or "religious" hermeneutics, and a "profane" hermeneutics.

What Ernesti calls "profane hermeneutics"—that is, a form of hermeneutics that maintains that a text can express its truth (the truth of the victim) apart from the demystifying principles of the Gospel text—should rather be named, in the context of mimetic theory, "sacred hermeneutics." This kind of thought, in fact is "sacred" for at least three reasons. First, it is "sacred" because, as Girard stresses, it is the sacred that remains at the nondeconstructed core of that thought (TH, 64). Second, it is sacred in method: it is, in fact, ritual thought: it unveils the metaphysical pretensions of a reason that tries to impose an "absolute" point of view, but the sacred does not disappear: it enters into the sphere of the ritual of interpretation. Third, and most important, this thought is "sacred" because on this view there is still something absolute, unquestionable—properly "sacred": it is the myth of detachment. According to this myth, humankind today are supposed to be "disenchanted" enough to consider all truths equally valid. However, as Girard reminds us, "If we put the 'truth of the persecutors' on the same level as the 'truth of the victim,' there will very quickly be no difference or truth for anyone" (J, 107).

In other words, perspectivism is epistemologically superior to naturalism, because it rejects its presumption to look at the world "from the God's-eye point of view." However, within contemporary hermeneutics, which has welcomed perspectivism, one has to distinguish between a sacred hermeneutics and a theological hermeneutics. In fact, sacred hermeneutics feigns a detachment that, as Girard reminds us, "perpetuates the status quo, prolongs the occulting of the scapegoat, and makes us effective accomplices of the persecutors." "The true science of man," Girard continues, "is not indifferent" (J, 107). Therefore, theological hermeneutics is epistemologically superior to naturalism (both in its "neotheist" version and in its "neoatheist" version), but it is also superior to "sacred" hermeneutics. Theological, or religious, hermeneutics is a thought that does not expel truth in name of the myth of disenchantment, but looks for it, while at the same time stressing that truth is never absolute, but always perspectival. Mimetic theory itself belongs to this tradition.

Thus, relativism can be considered to be the last sacral vestige in this history of Western culture. This is the reason why theological hermeneutics is epistemologically superior to sacred hermeneutics: because it refuses to take the myth of disenchantment as sacred. Religious or theological hermeneutics is a thought more deeply secularized and secularizing than sacred hermeneutics, because for religious hermeneutics nothing is "sacred": not even the equivalence of all interpretation, not even detachment itself. In one of the public conversations that Girard had with Vattimo, Girard claimed: "We are in need of a good theory of secularization because secularization also entails the end of the sacrificial, and that is a development that deprives us of the ordinary cultural equipment for facing up to violence." And later on, Girard quoted a passage from Vattimo's work *Belief*, where Vattimo, referring to Max Weber, claims that "disenchantment has also produced a radical disenchantment with the idea of disenchantment itself." It is interesting to note that this is one of the occasions when Girard agrees with Vattimo without reserve.[16]

2. Perspectivism and the Wager on the Self

The core of theological hermeneutics is perspectivism, the same perspectivism that represents one of the most persistent (but often underestimated) roots of Western culture. To become truly *secularized*, Western culture should develop a progressive sharing of perspectivism, which entails renouncing a commitment to a specific perspective considered to be "absolutely true." The important distinction here is between *truth* (*Wahrheit*) and *truthfulness* (*Wahrhaftigkeit*), introduced by Kant in his essay *Concerning the Possibility of a Theodicy and the Failure of All Previous Philosophical Attempts in the Field*. If one still had doubts about mimetic theory's belonging to the tradition of Kantian perspectivism, a careful reading of this Kantian work (which has already been related to mimetic theory in a relatively recent essay by Michael Kirwan) would dissolve them all.[17] The knowledge to which theological hermeneutics can aspire does not depend on the subtlety of the arguments, but on faith in the truthfulness of one's claim.[18]

It is this truthfulness that should be the core of a truly secularized and secularizing thought. And this truthfulness is very much needed, because the sacred has not disappeared: it is all around us. James Alison has pointed out, for example, the very real danger of Ground Zero and the events of September 11, 2001, which have become respectively a "sacred space" and a "sacred event."[19] Reviewing Alison's book *On Being Liked*, Michael Kirwan explains: "He soberly reminds us of what we experienced . . . : a 'satanic' whirlpool of heightened emotion, a frenzied search for 'meaning,' and social mobilization towards intense and of course militaristic solidarity, which for mimetic theory can only mean one thing: the beginnings of the search for a scapegoat."[20] A passage written by Girard in 1978 now assume a new sense: "Either we are moving ineluctably toward non-violence, or we are about to disappear completely. . . . The genuinely new element is that violence can no longer be relied upon to resolve the crisis" (TH, 258).

The notion of truthfulness represents an important intellectual resource for confronting violence, disorder, and rivalry. Of course, recourse to the notion of truthfulness does not tell us what we should do in concrete. Obviously no form of violence, either real or intellectual, can play any role in this struggle, because as we know any alleged "destruction" of the mechanism through violence would merely constitute its continuation. It would be, to use the words of the Gospel (later used by Girard), to use Satan to expel Satan.[21] Satan is the symbol of sacrificial order: it represents the violence that expels itself through (sacrificial) violence to reestablish an order. But we should not forget that Satan is also the principle of disorder, expressed through disagreement and mimetic rivalry, that subsequently determines the establishment of a sacrificial order. It is in mimeticism that the sacred has its roots. The sacred is, first and foremost, the model, the mediator of desire, worshiped and hated at the same time. We know that a world where "Men Become Gods in the Eyes of Each Other" (DDN, 56), far from being a heaven, is the hell of mimetic contagion.

A real secularization, insofar as it coincides with a progressive sharing of perspectivism, must first happen on a personal and existential level. Therefore, I will devote the conclusion of this chapter to a clarification of what a hermeneutics should look like that, insofar as it is grounded on the intuitions of mimetic theory, can be considered to be a truly secularized philosophy. In order to carry out this analysis, let us go back to the very first principle of mimetic theory: "Once his basic needs are satisfied (indeed, sometimes even before), man is subject to intense desires, though he may not know precisely for what. The reason is that he desires being, something he himself lacks and which some other person seems to possess. The subject thus looks to that other person to inform him of what he should desire in order to acquire that being" (VS, 146). In other words, the subject cannot find the meaning of her or his own existence in her- or himself, and therefore imitates a model who seems equipped with the ability that the subject feels devoid of, that is, another human being strong enough to be able to create that "fullness of being" which the subject is lacking. Put differently, when subjects imitate a model, what they are really doing is looking for a preconstituted horizon of meaning in which they can integrate themselves, while waiting to grasp the secret of their model and hence to become themselves able to create a horizon of meaning.

The problem, in this dynamic, is not the aim of the subject, that is, becoming able to create a horizon of meaning, because this aim is absolutely human—or better, it is that which constitutes ourselves more deeply as human. The problem is the strategy that the subject adopts to accomplish such aim: in fact, no human can create a horizon of meaning by her- or himself. As Girard's illuminating analyses on the dandy and the snob have demonstrated, the pretended self-sufficiency is only a bluff: nobody really possesses that self-sufficiency, and to show it off is merely a strategy to attract disciples and secure a success through a clever use of mimetic techniques. It is a behavior that could be labeled "human, all too human," to borrow Nietzsche's expression—and indeed Nietzsche marked a fundamental stage in the process of secularization, inviting us to destroy our idols, to give up everything that we consider "sacred." Nietzsche, however, was mistaken in considering the resentment as a sickness limited to the weakest, and in indulging in the illusion of an absolute self-sufficiency outside the "herd." As Girard rhetorically asks: "Is it unfair, is it too cruel to point out that it was not Pascal who went mad but Nietzsche?" (DBB, 77).

If even the path indicated by Nietzsche is precluded from consideration, what alternative are we left with? I think that the reference to Pascal in Girard's quote could be considered more than a mere basis for comparison or a marginal reference. Healing from ontological sickness, and hence escape from mimeticism and the incipit of a fully secularized thought, is based on a *wager*. After all, this is precisely what happens, unconsciously, in the case of deviated transcendence: subjects wager on a model, in the hope that the imitation of their desires can confer on them that fullness, that self-sufficiency they feel devoid of. Conversely, the point is now to wager on a horizon of meaning, not the horizon of horizontal transcendence represented by various human models, but of vertical transcendence that, alone, can guarantee the development of an authentic self.

To develop an authentic self, finally free from the mimetic chains that make the subject consider "sacred" now this, now that model—a self, we might say, truly secularized—is possible: through an experience of *conversion*. It is an experience of conversion, for instance, that is described in Proust's episode of the madeleine: the "affective memory" gives back the authentic impression of things and of one's own existence (DDN, 80–81). "Recapturing the past is recapturing the original impression beneath the opinion of others which hides it; it is to recognize that this opinion is not one's own" (DDN, 38); it means, as remarked by Morigi, recovering "a straight access to the concreteness of the real."[22]

It is always a wager, a wager on a horizon of meaning: either the (illusory) horizon of deviated transcendence, or the horizon that is autonomously opened up by the subject thanks to an experience of conversion that constitutes, at the same time, an authentic secularization of the self in its intersubjective relationships. This "access to the concreteness of the real" has always as its precondition freedom from mimetic desire and the illusions that it imposes upon us: this is the reason why it has always assumed and it will always assume the immutable form of every radical change, that is, the form of a wager, on which every religious conversion is based.

In this context, even Girard's argument for the divinity of Christ and the existence of God can be read in a nontraditional perspective. It is not, in fact, the sign of a "metanaturalistic" conception of religion that mimetic theory would have in common with the "new theists." Rather, that argument expresses a "second naïveté" grounded on a wager that is manifested as interpretation. In this sense, I think it is perfectly legitimate to talk of a "mimetic hermeneutic theory" as an example of a fully secularized thought.

The further step for Western culture in confronting violence, disorder, and rivalry—to become, in other words, a truly secularized society—is to focus on a phenomenology of the conditions that allow the development of an authentic self. Eugene Webb, in the final chapter of *The Self Between*, makes in this respect some interesting (but partly undeveloped) remarks. One of them deserves to be mentioned here. Webb refers to the interpretation of Pentecost provided by Raymund Schwager. Schwager wrote:

> Peace as the fruit of the Spirit is clearly distinct from the unity that the scapegoat mechanism creates. The latter is nothing but a uniformity necessitated by the image of the common enemy. The Holy Spirit, on the contrary, gathers the people by respecting in each individually his or her singularity and freedom, and by unifying all, not *against* but *for* someone, *for* the Lord.
>
> In its account of the feast of Pentecost, the Acts of the Apostles stresses that the tongues of fire separated and descended on *each of the gathered persons* (Acts 2:3). In the same way it does not say that the miracle of tongues made all understand one language, but that the apostles began to speak in *foreign* tongues and that all in Jerusalem were amazed because everyone heard them speak in *his or her own mother tongue* (Acts 2:4–8). The Spirit produced a unified understanding while conserving full respect for existing differences.[23]

Webb remarks that the key idea here is the call for every human being to become, to borrow an expression from Kierkegaard, an "existent individual." And only an "existent individual" can generate around her- or himself a fully secularized intersubjective universe.

Of course, such a project is not merely a philosophical project, but mostly an existential one; and this is something that cannot be done from an armchair. After all, as Girard remarks, "It is not too difficult to recognize the accuracy of what I am saying in the abstract, which means to apply it to other people. It is a good deal harder to seek out the areas in which each of us operates . . . , to demystify our own feelings and not merely those of others, and to detect what is hidden behind our very passion for demystification" (TH, 398).

NOTES

1. Thomas Dixon, "Scientific Atheism as a Faith Tradition," *Studies in History and Philosophy of Biological and Biomedical Sciences* 33 (2002): 337–59.

2. Tom Sorrell, *Scientism: Philosophy and the Infatuation with Science* (New York: Routledge, 1991), 1, quoted in Dixon, "Scientific Atheism," 342.

3. Dixon, "Scientific Atheism," 342. As Dixon stresses, "This corresponds roughly to the fifth of Stenmark's five sorts of scientism, which he calls 'redemptive scientism,' that is, 'the view that science alone is sufficient for dealing with our existential questions or for creating a world view by which he could live.'" Compare Mikael Stenmark, "What Is Scientism?," *Religious Studies* 33, no. 1 (1997): 31.

4. David William Bebbington, *Evangelicalism in Modern Britain: A History from the 1730s to the 1980s* (London: Unwin Hyman, 1989).

5. Discovery Institute, "Top Questions—1. What Is the Theory of Intelligent Design?," http://www.discovery.org. The Discovery Institute's Center for Science and Culture is the hub of the intelligent design movement.

6. The Center for Science and Culture website, www.discovery.org, includes both William Lane Craig and Robert Koons as fellows.

7. The adoption of a naturalistic perspective also explains the rejection of the post-Kantian tradition, as Sebastian Gardner recently pointed out: "The kinds of philosophical positions most intensively worked on and argued about in non-historical, systematic analytic philosophy are predominantly naturalistic—and thus, on the face of it, not in any immediate and obvious sense receptive to the central ideas of German idealism." Sebastian Gardner, "The Limits of Naturalism and the Metaphysics of German Idealism," in *German Idealism: Contemporary Perspectives*, ed. Espen Hammer (New York: Routledge, 2007), 19.

8. Immanuel Kant, *Critique of Pure Reason*, trans. and ed. Paul Guyer and Allen W. Wood (Cambridge: Cambridge University Press, 1998), A320/B376.

9. Philip J. Rossi and Michael Wreen, eds., *Kant's Philosophy of Religion Reconsidered* (Bloomington: Indiana University Press, 1991).

10. Paul Redding, *Continental Idealism: Leibniz to Nietzsche* (New York: Routledge, 2009).

11. See also TH, 277: "The very detachment of the person who contemplates the warring brothers from the heights of his wisdom is an illusion." About this, see Eugene Webb, *The Self Between: From Freud to the New Social Psychology of France* (Seattle: University of Washington Press, 1993), 192.

12. Chris Fleming, *René Girard: Violence and Mimesis* (Cambridge: Polity, 2004), 123.

13. Gianni Vattimo and René Girard, "Faith and Relativism," in *Christianity, Truth, and Weakening Faith: A Dialogue*, ed. Pierpaolo Antonello, trans. William McCuaig (New York: Columbia University Press, 2010), 48.

14. Gianni Vattimo and René Girard, "Hermeneutics, Authority, Tradition," in Antonello, *Christianity, Truth, and Weakening Faith*, 64.

15. "The invention of science is not the reason that there are no longer witch-hunts, but the fact that there are no longer witch-hunts is the reason that science has been invented. The scientific spirit, like the spirit of enterprise in an economy, is a by-product of the profound action of the Gospel text." S, 204–5.

16. "I agree," Girard claims. René Girard and Gianni Vattimo, "Christianity and Modernity," in Antonello, *Christianity, Truth, and Weakening Faith*, 32. Compare Gianni Vattimo, *Belief*, trans. Luca D'Isanto and David Webb (Stanford, CA: Stanford University Press, 1999), 29.

17. Michael Kirwan, "Fuori dalle città, tra le città: René Girard e il male radicale," in *Male e Redenzione: Sofferenza e Trascendenza in René Girard*, ed. Paolo Diego Bubbio and Silvio Morigi (Turin: Camilliane, 2008), 133–49.

18. "One cannot always stand by the *truth* of what one says to oneself or to another (for one can be mistaken); however, one can and must stand by the *truthfulness* of one's declaration or confession, because one has immediate consciousness of this." Immanuel Kant, "On the Miscarriage of All Philosophical Trials in Theodicy," in *Religion and Rational Theology*, trans. and ed. Allen Wood, George Di Giovanni (Cambridge: Cambridge University Press, 1992), 34.

19. James Alison, *On Being Liked* (London: Darton, Longman and Todd, 2003).

20. Michael Kirwan, *Discovering Girard* (London: Darton, Longman and Todd, 2004), 119.

21. Compare Fleming, *René Girard*, 132.

22. Silvio Morigi, "Un essere 'vuoto di essere,' 'morale e risolutamente manicheo': Il demoniaco e la demonologia come 'sapere paradossale' in René Girard," in Bubbio and Morigi, *Male e Redenzione*, 172.

23. Raymund Schwager, *Must There Be Scapegoats? Violence and Redemption in the Bible* (San Francisco: Harper and Row, 1987), 220–21.

Mimetic Theory and Hermeneutic Communism

n the last fifteen years, Girard has engaged in a dialogue with the Italian philosopher Gianni Vattimo. Vattimo is famous for a philosophical approach
named *pensiero debole* (weak thought). "Weak thought" is basically concerned with arguing for philosophical antifoundationalism: drawing on the
philosophy of Nietzsche, Heidegger, and Gadamer, Vattimo advocates the
rejection of metaphysics and a reinterpretation of truth as the opening of
horizons. Vattimo has explained that he came to recognize a "completion"
of Heidegger in Girard by reading "the weakening of Being as its sole form
of manifesting itself beyond metaphysical oblivion" as "an analogon of the
dissolution of the violence of the sacred."[1] On this common ground, they have
reached similar (although not identical) conclusions about Christianity and
secularism, agreeing on the thesis that the process of secularization is a long-
term and ongoing effect of the Gospels.

In 2011, Vattimo authored, together with his student Santiago Zabala,
a book entitled *Hermeneutic Communism*.[2] Vattimo and Zabala argue that
communism, once it is separated from its metaphysical foundations (such
as an abiding faith in the immutable laws of history), is not only compatible
with, but is even the logical political implication of, the antifoundation-
alist stance drawn from the hermeneutic thought of Heidegger, Derrida,

and Rorty. To what extent is mimetic theory compatible with hermeneutic communism?

From an analysis of *Hermeneutic Communism*, it is possible to identify three main (interconnected) characteristics of Vattimo and Zabala's political proposal. The first is a critique of capitalism, which is deprecated, on substantially ethical grounds, as generating unacceptable inequalities, and regarded as collapsing at various levels—economic, technological, and political. The second characteristic of their political proposal is the weakened nature of the suggested form of communism: a communism that motivates a resistance to capitalism's inequalities yet intervenes against violence and authoritarianism by emphasizing the interpretative nature of truth. This leads to the third characteristic, that is, the affirmation of the *interpretative* nature of truth, as opposed to a dogmatic and *realist* account of truth, so that while the former represents a philosophical expression of capitalism, communism is regarded as the natural political expression of the latter.

I argue that as far as the first characteristic (the critique of capitalism) is concerned, Girard's mimetic theory and Vattimo and Zabala's hermeneutic communism are compatible. I then argue that the second characteristic (the weakened form of communism advanced by Vattimo and Zabala) is not in principle incompatible with mimetic theory, although some remarks by Girard need to be taken into account. These remarks pave the way for an analysis of the third characteristic; and in the context of this analysis I argue that the interpretative nature of truth, while it might be regarded as expressing a fundamental incompatibility between mimetic theory and hermeneutic communism, might also be considered the starting point for further inquiries aimed at considering the two theories as complementing each other.

1. (Absolute) Capitalism

The first aspect of Vattimo and Zabala's political proposal is a critique of capitalism. A system of "inequality, exclusion, famine, and economic oppression,"[3] capitalism violently oppresses the weak and the poor, and—they argue—it uses liberalism (a metaphysical system that sees the only substance in the power of the individual) as its justification. Additionally, while the capitalist market is supposed to ensure a prosperous economy, "The 2008 economic crisis demonstrated not only the extent to which states depend on financial markets but also their interest in the conservation of such a system,"[4] that is, a system of inequality and oppression. Is this reading of capitalism compatible with Girard's mimetic theory?

Girard has never provided a systematic critique of capitalism, but several remarks scattered through his writings indicate his position. A meaningful indication is already present in Girard's masterwork, *Things Hidden*, where he argues: "The real founders of capitalism . . . are the monkeys. All that capitalism, or rather the liberal society that allows capitalism to flourish, does, is to give mimetic phenomena a freer rein and to direct them into economic and technological channels. . . . The value of an object grows in proportion to the resistance met with in acquiring it" (TH, 295).

Everyone who is familiar with the basics of mimetic theory would easily realize that this judgment is consistent with Girard's thought in general, and it is the logical consequence of its premises. In fact, mimetic theory tells us that we desire an object only because that object is desired by somebody else (the *mediator* of desire), and that the more difficult it is to get an object, the more valuable it appears, as the resistance will be (mistakenly) interpreted by desiring subjects as a sign indicating the fundamental importance of that object in order to get that "something" they feel devoid of, and with which the owner of the desired object seems equipped. The hominization process begins when one human being starts to imitate the desires of another, that is, when a human being feels inferior and lacking: it is in this sense that monkeys are the real founders of capitalism. Of course, achieving fulfilment via acquisition of objects is an illusion (it cannot provide any real satisfaction), but an illusion so powerful that it permeates the totality of human life. Therefore, it should not come as a surprise that human beings have expressed a system of production that has its drive in the laws of supply and demand, as this is merely the economic translation of mimetic dynamics. Furthermore, liberalism is regarded by Girard as the political system that is established because "it allows capitalism to flourish." Both capitalism (as economic theory) and liberalism (as its corresponding political theory) are marked by a focus on the "I" and its independence; this is something that Vattimo and Zabala emphasize in their critique of capitalism, and there is no doubt that Girard would agree, as he has often indicated the mystifying nature of the romantic myth of the independence of the I.

Capitalism is also the expression of economic violence.[5] It has been said that capitalism is the economic translation of mimeticism; if this is true, then the presence of violence is not surprising, as mimetic relationships inevitably lead to violence. Lucien Goldmann's idea that "relations between people and things, and among people themselves, were 'replaced by a mediatized and degraded relation: the relation with purely quantitative exchange values'" (BE, 59)[6] is still a romantic idea, of which the political standpoint that criticizes contemporary financial capitalism—by invoking the return to a more "human" capitalism concerned with the real economy rather than with financial products—is a less sophisticated version. Exchange has never been "qualitative," but always "quantitative," and, Girard comments, "This feature has been aggravated by capitalist practices. We exchange goods so as not to exchange blows, but trading goods always contains a memory of trading blows" (BE, 59). Like a ritual, the capitalist market channels violence, but for this very reason it is also an *expression* of that violence: it is the extension of reciprocal violence by economic means. And we know that even the most perfect technique cannot control violence forever, and that sooner or later it will escape control.

Another expression that Girard uses to refer to this phenomenon is the "tendency toward extremes," which is one of the central notions of Girard's recent work, *Battling to the End*. Here the escalation to extremes is explored through the analysis of war advanced by the Prussian general Clausewitz. From Clausewitz, Girard draws the distinction between "absolute war" and "real war." "Real war," Girard explains, is "different from absolute war because it takes into account the dimensions of space and time: location, climate, various 'frictions,' fatigue, etc." (BE, 11). Modern wars tend to reduce, or even eliminate, these constraints, and as a consequence we "escalate to extremes," getting closer to "absolute war." Similarly, we might argue, historical capitalism has been somehow mitigated by spatiotemporal constraints that have prevented it from being "*absolute* capitalism." The globalized financial capitalism of present times is increasingly removing those constraints, and therefore it is getting closer to its prototypical version: absolute capitalism. From this point of view, the global financial crisis that started in 2008 can be conceived as a further step toward the escalation to extremes: "The apocalypse is nothing more than an abstraction made real, reality made consistent with its concept" (BE, 19). What we are witnessing is not a degeneration of capitalism: it is its accomplishment, real capitalism made consistent with its concept. Economic violence and political violence are not two separate phenomena, but two aspects of the same sacrificial crisis (BE, 20).[7]

The reference to politics is not marginal in this context, as Girard seems to be fully aware of the ambiguous relationship between capitalism and liberal democracy, which, since the Cold War, has usually been presented as mutual dependence, implying that there can be neither (liberal) democracy without capitalism, nor capitalism without (liberal) democracy. However, the end of the Cold War has made this opposition more problematic, and the ambiguities it hides more evident. "When we invoke our democratic principles," Girard asks, "are we talking about things like equality and elections, or are we talking about capitalism, consumption, free trade and so on?"[8] Such a distinction is important here, because while democracy is based on the "ultimate version of identity," that is, the Jewish and Christian notion of "fraternity" (BE, 45), "capitalism, consumption, free trade and so on" are expressions of mimetic victimage. Therefore, while (real) democracy should be encouraged, capitalism should be demystified as an expression of the mimetic system.

We might therefore conclude that, as far as the first aspect of Vattimo and Zabala's political proposal, namely, the critique of capitalism, is concerned, Girard's mimetic theory is compatible with hermeneutic communism. Of course being critical of capitalism does not imply an endorsement of communism; more fundamentally, it does not (necessarily) mean to claim that capitalism must be overthrown—a problematic claim because, if capitalism is, in its essence, the economic translation of mimeticism, and if mimeticism is what constitutes us as humans (and therefore cannot be eliminated), how might it be possible to hope for its overcoming? I will come back to this issue in the final section; now, it is appropriate to explore the compatibility of mimetic theory with the second aspect of Vattimo and Zabala's political proposal: weakened communism.

2. (Weakened) Communism

Girard's thought has sometimes been regarded as politically conservative. Partially this is due to the importance he attributes to the texts of the

Judeo-Christian tradition, an attitude that in some academic contexts is in itself sufficient to be called conservative. But beyond this, it is undeniable that when Girard mentions "communism" or "Marxism," this usually happens in the context of some critical remarks.

Girard is critical of communism insofar as he identifies it as one of those "ideologies of ressentiment" that provide us with new scapegoats, such as the father and the law for Freudianism, or the bourgeoisie and capitalists for Marxism. More specifically, Girard is critical of communism because he sees in it a form of *humanism*. Humanism is usually defined as a philosophical and ethical perspective that emphasizes the value of human beings, generally preferring a rationalist or empiricist approach over established doctrine or religious faith. As such, humanism has, in Girard's view, an ambiguous nature. On one hand, it is "the legacy of Christianity,"[9] insofar as it affirms the value of human life, condemns the violent sacred, and prefers anthropological explanation over superstitious sacrificial narratives. On the other hand, humanism (in Girard's account) dismisses Christianity as a religious superstition and, by looking for the divinity within humanity, prefers "horizontal transcendence" over "vertical transcendence," thus worsening the mimetic crisis.[10] The (violent) sacred does not disappear; it is only brought back to earth without being demystified. As Girard writes: "The humanists' scepticism seems to be the ultimate criticism of religion yet, in reality, it is its heir and, like all heirs, is only too interested in the perpetuation of the capital to be inherited not to respect it secretly" (J, 38). In their anxiety to affirm fraternity, some of the humanists, such as Feuerbach, did not realize that the deification of humanity leads to *more* rather than to *less* violence, and that, in this oversight, they "laid the groundwork for a disrespect of truth."[11]

Therefore, Marxism is indeed a transformation of Christianity,[12] and communism is still a humanism, but it is, in Girard's words, "a bogus humanism, the last and most incredibly foolish form."[13] The explanation that Girard adds to this definition is a bit simplistic, and yet it is indicative of his thought: "The communists had wanted to organize the world so that there wouldn't be any more poor people, and the capitalists had said that the poor were insignificant. The capitalists have prevailed."[14]

From here, we can deduce two things. The first is that Girard does not disapprove of communism for its intentions or agenda, but mainly for its extreme naïveté: we live in a mimetic world, and in a mimetic world the poor are irrelevant, as the Underground Man is irrelevant in Dostoyevsky's novel *Notes from Underground*. In both cases—economic irrelevance and psychological irrelevance—what appears clearly is that, in a mimetic world, only the powerful ones—those who have enough "mass"[15]—can win. This also explains Girard's claims that, in a capitalist world, the poor are "insignificant."

The second thing that can be deduced is that in Girard's view communism, properly speaking, "did not exist" (BE, 116). Historical communism, especially in its Soviet "incarnation," showed a "money-grubbing side": "It could not have," Girard argues, "any historical reality" (BE, 116) Some countries of the Eastern European bloc in the Cold War era showed some understanding of it when they coined the term, which was destined to become popular, "real socialism," implying that their policies represented what was realistically feasible, even if they did not conform to the Marxist concept of socialism. To draw a parallel with the argument I borrowed from Girard's analysis of Clausewitz to describe the current situation of capitalism, we might say that communism was never made consistent with its concept, and eventually it resulted "in terror."[16]

On the grounds of this brief analysis, it might seem difficult to argue for the compatibility between mimetic theory and any political theory that refers to itself as "communism." However, the entire critical analysis carried out by Girard is based on the specific assumption that communism is a form of humanism, something that, in Girard's view, brings some positive connotations, but mainly negative connotations, which are the ones that determine its final failure. Thus, before hastily concluding that there is no room for any compatibility, we should at least ask: to what extent is Vattimo and Zabala's hermeneutic communism a form of humanism?

Hermeneutic communism explicitly stands on behalf of the poor. Interestingly, Vattimo and Zabala refer to the expression "history of the winners," coined by Walter Benjamin. The history of the winners is the traditional history "of the oppressors," which Benjamin contrasts with the history "of the defeated" or "oppressed."[17] This idea fits with the Girardian distinction between the narrative of the scapegoaters ("the lie of the persecutors") and the alternative narrative of the scapegoat ("the truth of the victim"). From this point of view, hermeneutic communism is certainly a form of humanism insofar as it is a legacy of Christianity, affirms the value of human life against capitalist exploitation, and prefers a history sympathetic to the poor and the weak over the sacrificial history of the persecutors.

In Girard's view, the other characteristic of humanism is the preference for "horizontal transcendence" over "vertical transcendence." The drive of humanism is still the violent sacred, which is "brought back to earth," thus determining a worsening of ontological sickness. From this point of view, it would be difficult to argue that Vattimo and Zabala's communism is a humanism (according to Girard's definition), precisely because it is *herme-neutic*. The very first sentence of Vattimo and Zabala's book reads: "If Marxist philosophers until now have failed to change the world, it isn't because their political approach was wrong, but rather because it was framed within the metaphysical tradition."[18] Traditional communism was framed within the metaphysical tradition because of its positivist legacy, which is indeed "humanist" according to Girard's terminology: it is an approach that, in its ambition to get rid of the "vertical" sacred, eventually built up a new sacred *within humanity*. Thus it ended by providing new scapegoats (capitalists, the bourgeoisie, etc.) and by becoming violent. It is here that Heidegger's lesson becomes important for Vattimo and Zabala: when Heidegger argues that the history of Western thought has mistakenly articulated Being as a kind of ultimate entity (idea, substance, will to power—victory of the proletariat) and in this way forgotten Being *as such*, he is rejecting an idea of metaphysics that, in the context of mimetic theory, might well be identified with "deviated transcendence." Vattimo himself made this connection between mimetic theory and Heidegger's position in one of his writings, arguing: "The analogy between these two theories becomes evident if we consider that what motivates Heidegger's rejection of metaphysics is not a theoretical reason, as if metaphysics were a false description of Being for which we had to substitute a more adequate one. Heidegger's rejection of metaphysics ... is motivated by the violence by which it reduces Being—and particularly human existence—to measurable objectivity and rationalized mechanisms."[19] Consistently, Vattimo and Zabala's hermeneutic communism is presented as a deconstruction of the sacred, which is the reason why, to the question "What brings together communism and hermeneutics?" Vattimo and Zabala answer "the dissolution of metaphysics."[20] The weakened communism proposed by Vattimo and Zabala implies a rejection of both the violence of metaphysics *and* physical violence, as is evident from their refusal to consider revolution as a feasible political strategy.

Therefore, mimetic theory and hermeneutic communism agree on a criticism of traditional communism as being "too positivist." However, the "scientific pretext"[21] of traditional communism represents only *half* of Girard's critique. Communism was a bogus humanism, in Girard's view, not only because it was "too positivist" (in the sense that its pretense of providing a scientific account of a political strategy turned communism into the modern version of a myth, with new scapegoats and persecutors), but also because it was *not positivist enough*, insofar as in its naïveté it suggested the elimination of rivalry that grounds capitalism, thus failing to acknowledge that rivalry is a natural implication of distorted mimesis.

Here we appreciate the distance that separates the two positions and that seems to make them irreconcilable. On one hand, mimetic theory seems to suggest that capitalism cannot be overcome (are not the monkeys "the real founders of capitalism" after all?). On the other hand, hermeneutic communism is critical of realism, a position that seems to represent the basic epistemological framework of Girard's mimetic theory (at least insofar as it considers the mimetic nature of human beings as a *real* and natural *fact*, rather than as a matter of interpretation). The next section will therefore be devoted to an analysis of this issue in order to understand whether the two theories are effectively in this respect as irreconcilable as they prima facie appear to be.

3. "A Change Must Occur": Truth and Conversion

A fundamental aspect of Vattimo and Zabala's hermeneutic communism is its antirealism. "Metaphysical realism," defined as "the simple analysis and conservation of facts," is regarded by Vattimo and Zabala as the philosophical side of a "politics of description," whose essential theoretical features are "the violence of truth, the conservative nature of realism, and the winner's history." Truth is violent, they argue, because "it can easily become an imposition on our own existence" and "it implies an imposed description whose acceptance is assumed." Realism is conservative because its descriptive attitude (the "peaceful neutrality of metaphysics") implies a conservation of the status quo that resists any will to change. Lastly, realism implies a reference to that "winner's history" that neglects the poor and the weak, that is, the "victims of the politics of descriptions."[22]

All of this seems to be in stark contrast to mimetic theory, which Girard even labels, quite provocatively, a kind of "naïve realism" (J, 34). Mimetic theory presupposes a "realist" approach, Girard argues, insofar as it assumes it is possible to distinguish between "the lies of the persecutors," which always try to justify the search for a scapegoat, and "the truth of the victim." This also explains why Girard is so critical of relativism; and the philosophical hermeneutics advanced by Vattimo and Zabala might indeed appear guilty of relativism since, in its rejection of truth, it might be seen as perpetuating "the *status quo*," prolonging "the occulting of the scapegoat," and making us "effective accomplices of the persecutors" (J, 107). Interestingly enough, Vattimo and Zabala consider the neutrality of *realism* as justifying the oppression of victims, whereas Girard considers antirealist approaches, such as relativism, as guilty of the same justifying attitude. What is going on here?

We should not forget that one of the characteristic aspects of Girard's mimetic theory is the idea that the ability to distinguish between the lies of the persecutors and the truth of the victim is made possible by the revelation of the Gospels. Therefore, Girard supports a strong idea of truth.[23] Conversely, Vattimo and Zabala seem critical of any use of the word "truth," including the Christian one ("The truth will make you free," John 8:32). The confrontation between these two views might evoke the Johannine episode in which Jesus says to Pilate, "Everyone on the side of truth listens to me," and Pilate retorts: "What is truth?" (John 18:37–38). However, the issue is more complex than this evocative image suggests, and the core of it is, in my view, the question whether the position expressed by Vattimo and Zabala is really a relativistic one. Here I am advancing a suggestion, namely, that Vattimo's position, especially as it emerges from previous exchanges with Girard, rather than being defined as relativistic (entailing that all perspectives are equally valid), might be better seen as a form of *perspectivism* (implying that no way of seeing the world can be taken as definitely true). But even if it were considered a form of perspectivism, Vattimo's position would still not be compatible with mimetic theory: for Girard, there *is* a way of seeing the world that can be taken as definitely true. However, Vattimo's perspectivism is often implemented by an ethical preference for the weak and the poor. Vattimo and Zabala express a clear preference for hermeneutic communism over capitalism; and this preference is expressed not because hermeneutic communism is regarded as "truer" than capitalism, but because it is considered more able to guarantee justice and well-being for humankind. Significantly, Girard notes that Vattimo's slogan, "There are only interpretations" (a quote from Nietzsche), is often practically disregarded by Vattimo himself: faced with a choice between "the truth of the victim" and "the lies of the persecutors," Vattimo would not claim that all interpretations are equally valid, but would stand firmly for the truth of the victim—not in the name of *veritas*, but in the name of *caritas*.[24]

When it comes to a practical attitude to the poor and the weak ("victims," in the context of mimetic theory), Girard and Vattimo-Zabala are less distant than expected. This, however, does not solve potential disagreement on the concrete possibility of overcoming capitalism. In fact, in the context of mimetic theory, this possibility seems problematic: given that mimeticism is what constitutes us as humans, and therefore cannot be eliminated, how might it be possible to hope for its overcoming?

This is a specific case of a more general problem, namely, the possibility of overcoming mimeticism. Humans cannot disown their mimetic nature, because this is precisely what makes them *human*. Consistently, the Gospels do not preach an ethics of spontaneity and do not expect humans to give up imitation; rather, they recommend imitating the only model that cannot change into a fascinating rival. And this unique model is Christ because, thanks to his divine nature, he is not bound by chains of desire and violence and does not compete with those who imitate him, but he returns mimesis with love. Furthermore, the Gospels encourage humans to imitate Christ's desire to refuse every negative imitation.

Therefore, the only way to overcome mimeticism is through a process of conversion. The prototype of this experience is *religious* conversion; however, in a world that, as Oughourlian points out, "is secretly governed by the gospel revolution and reflects the extraordinary concrete character of this revolution," conversion does not necessarily need to be religious *in content*. As Girard maintains, "Even in the investigation of nature ... the great minds who have effected the most decisive intellectual breakthroughs have always apparently passed from one mental universe to another" (TH, 401).[25]

It might be argued that, as capitalism is a consequence of human mimetic nature, the only way to overcome it would be through a process of conversion that would not disown mimeticism, but would *reorient* it toward vertical transcendence. In other words, the overcoming of capitalism might occur not through collective political action, but only through a vast number of personal conversions. Ideally, these conversions should take the form of a religious conversion to Christianity—but not necessarily. As early as in *Deceit, Desire, and the Novel*, Girard presents conversion as an existential change (the renunciation of metaphysical desire) that allows the establishment of a different perspective, from which both the self and reality can be interpreted differently. Girard writes: "Repudiation of the mediator implies renunciation of divinity, and this means renouncing pride. . . . In renouncing divinity the hero renounces slavery. Every level of his existence is inverted, all the effects of metaphysical desire are replaced by contrary effects" (DDN, 294).

Does this have anything to do with Vattimo and Zabala's hermeneutic communism? I believe it does. A perspectival account of truth implies renunciation of the idea that the world can be examined by the subject objectively, that is, from an alleged God's-eye point of view. In the context of mimetic theory, persecutors claim to look at reality objectively, that is, from the point of view of God, a point of view that must be *absolute*. The scapegoating event is presented by persecutors from a "detached" and "objective" perspective, but, as Girard reminds us, the myth of detachment is "the greatest myth of all" (DDN, 111). Conversely, the truth of the victim is perspectival, because it contrasts the "absolute" account of persecutors with an "alternative" point of view, a discordant voice.[26] Therefore, conversion implies a "renunciation of divinity," which is not dissimilar to the *renunciation* of the idea of absolute truth (the God's-eye view), which Vattimo and Zabala maintain as fundamental in their political project. This switch of perspective (from the God's-eye view to a perspectival truth of the victim) might even been taken as grounding, I suggest, their account of "weakened communism." Their reading of Marx's claim that "philosophers have only *interpreted* the world in various ways; the point is to *change* it" seems to go in that direction, as it is taken as "evoking how, for interpretation to work, a change must occur."[27] To summarize: a personal experience of conversion leads to a "renunciation of divinity," which in turn, leads to embracing a perspective more sympathetic to victims; and the whole of these personal conversions might result in a radical change in society, politics, and the economic system.[28] To the extent that these elements are common to both mimetic theory and hermeneutic communism, the two theories can be considered as not incompatible.

It would not be appropriate to push for the compatibility of these two theories more than this. Furthermore, these reflections are not meant to underplay the distance that separates them, especially in relation to politics. Conversion, conceived as the rejection of violence and the reorienting of mimeticism, is the strategy indicated by Girard; however, Girard does not suggest what consequences a collective and broad conversion of humankind might have on politics.[29] Nevertheless, considering the premises of mimetic theory, it does not seem implausible to argue that a broad conversion would lead to an overcoming of capitalism and to a fairer distribution of resources. On the other hand, the elaboration of "hermeneutic communism" is only in its initial stages of development, and much could be done to elaborate it further.

As a conclusion, I think that, despite these limits and reservations, there is room for a fruitful dialogue between mimetic theory and philosophical hermeneutics, even on a political level. Both Girard and Vattimo agree, from different perspectives, on a central point: that the way the global economy and society are currently organized is no longer sustainable—a reality for which the current global financial crisis offers dramatic evidence. Vattimo and Zabala refer to economists' "blindness to the very possibility of catastrophic failures in a market economy,"[30] and Girard refers to the "heads of state, bankers, and soldiers who claim to be saving us when in fact they are plunging us deeper into devastation each day."[31] This situation urges us to do something. Vattimo and Zabala, paraphrasing Heidegger, claim that "only communism can save us," and suggest we regard communism as "the horizon of any possible liberation for the human being."[32] This claim will surely attract significant disagreement from scholars, and mimetic theory scholars will not be an exception. Still, I think they would agree that, to liberate humankind from devastation and apocalypse, a political and social engagement is needed—and this is definitely something that cannot be done from an armchair.

NOTES

1. Gianni Vattimo, "Heidegger and Girard: *Kénosis* and the End of Metaphysics," in *Christianity, Truth, and Weakening Faith: A Dialogue*, by Gianni Vattimo and René Girard, edited by Pierpaolo Antonello, translated by William McCuaig (New York: Columbia University Press, 2010), 85. For a critical reading of Vattimo's parallel between the "natural sacred" in Girard's thought and the violence of metaphysics, see Matthew Edward Harris, "Metaphysics, Violence and the 'Natural Sacred' in Gianni Vattimo's Philosophy," *Humanicus* 8 (2013).

2. Gianni Vattimo and Santiago Zabala, *Hermeneutic Communism* (New York: Columbia University Press, 2011).

3. Vattimo and Zabala, *Hermeneutic Communism*, 49. This expression is a quote from Jacques Derrida, *Specters of Marx*, trans. Peggy Kamuf (London: Routledge, 1996), chap. 3, "Existence Is Interpretation."

4. Vattimo and Zabala, *Hermeneutic Communism*, 58.

5. See Dumouchel and Dupuy, *L'Enfer des choses: René Girard et la logique de l'economie* (Paris: Seuil, 1979). Another "Girardian" critique of capitalism is included in Britton Johnston, "Temples of Debt: Capitalism as a Sacred/Sacrificial System" (paper presented at the Annual Meeting of the Colloquium on Violence and Religion [COV&R], Antwerp, Belgium, June 2001), brittondanna. files.wordpress.com/2008/01/templesofdebt.pdf.

6. Girard refers to Lucien Goldmann, *Towards a Sociology of the Novel*, trans. Alan Sheridan (London: Tavistock, 1975), 7.

7. Marx's claim that a class struggle always ends "either in a revolutionary reconstitution of society at large, or in the common ruin of the contending classes" might be interpreted in a mimetic sense—after all, every sacrificial crisis is always destined to end either in a reconstitution of the community, or in the common ruin of community members. Compare Karl Marx and Frederick Engels, *Manifesto of the Communist Party*, trans. Samuel Moore (London: Verso, 2012), 35.

8. René Girard, "Apocalyptic Thinking after 9/11," interview by Robert Doran, *SubStance* 37, no. 1 (2008): 20–32, 22.

9. Girard, "Apocalyptic Thinking," 28.

10. Girard calls this increasing preference for horizontal transcendence "ontological sickness." See DDN, 97.

11. René Girard and James Williams, "The Anthropology of the Cross: A Conversation with René Girard," in *The Girard Reader*, ed. James G. Williams (New York: Crossroad, 1996), 274.

12. Girard and Williams, "Anthropology of the Cross," 274.

13. Girard, "Apocalyptic Thinking," 28.

14. Girard, "Apocalyptic Thinking," 28.

15. Compare Jean-Michel Oughourlian, *The Genesis of Desire*, trans. Eugene Webb (East Lansing: Michigan State University Press, 2010), chap. 3.

16. Girard, "Apocalyptic Thinking," 28.

17. Vattimo and Zabala, *Hermeneutic Communism*, 40. See Walter Benjamin, "On the Concept of History," in *Selected Writings*, ed. H. Eiland and Michael W. Jennings, vol. 4, *1938–1940* (Cambridge, MA: Belknap Press, 2003), 391.

18. Vattimo and Zabala, *Hermeneutic Communism*, 1.

19. Vattimo, "Heidegger and Girard," 81.

20. Vattimo and Zabala, *Hermeneutic Communism*, 3.

21. Vattimo and Zabala, *Hermeneutic Communism*, 115.

22. Vattimo and Zabala, 14, 16, 18, 23, 137.

23. See Grant Kaplan, "An Interview with René Girard," *First Things*, November 6, 2008, www.firstthings.com.

24. If nobody has access to the "truth," then I have to "listen to others": "We don't reach agreement when we have discovered the truth, we say we have discovered the truth when we reach agreement. In other words, charity takes the place of truth." Gianni Vattimo, *Addio alla verità* (Rome: Meltemi, 2009), trans. William McCuaig, *A Farewell to Truth* (New York: Columbia University Press, 2011), chap. 2, "The Future of Religion," section 3, "For a Nonreligious Christianity."

25. Kirwan comments: "The content of the conversion is the same: a radical change of perspective." Kirwan, *Discovering Girard*, 81.

26. Someone might object that the truth of the victim is empirically true for Girard. However, this is just half of the story. Truth is incarnated in Christ, that is, God who becomes a victim and accepts human limitations. In Christ, God's being of love reveals true being and human negative mimesis. True being, then, is to become part of God's being in conversion. (I am grateful to Joel Hodge for drawing my attention to this point.)

27. Vattimo and Zabala, *Hermeneutic Communism*, 4.

28. Jun seems to suggest something similar when he argues that Girardian theory advocates "a series of on-going tactical interventions that resist sacrificial violence" and that "such interventions, if sufficiently widespread, would inevitably generate new forms of human social organization." Nathan Jun, "Toward a Girardian Politics," *Studies in Social and Political Thought* 14 (Fall 2007): 22–42, 38.

29. Some indications have been suggested by mimetic theory scholars, but Girard has rarely commented on them. See Wolfgang Palaver, "Political Implications of the Mimetic Theory," in *René Girard's Mimetic Theory*, trans. Gabriel Borrud (East Lansing: Michigan State University Press, 2013), 275–96.

30. Vattimo and Zabala, *Hermeneutic Communism*, 60; they quote Paul Krugman, "How Did Economists Get It So Wrong?," *New York Times*, September 6, 2009.

31. René Girard, "On War and Apocalypse," *First Things* 195 (2009): 17–22, 18–19.

32. Vattimo and Zabala, *Hermeneutic Communism*, 111.

The Self in Crisis

R esearch work in the humanities in general, and in philosophy in partic-ular, is today looked at with a certain degree of suspicion, for various, and sometimes even opposed, reasons. On one hand, work on subtle epistemological questions and/or historical analysis of the thought of past philosophers is regarded as a navel-gazing activity, otiose at best, wasteful at worst. On the other hand, when philosophy and intellectual analysis come to focus on popular culture phenomena, such as comics, movies, and TV programs, they are regarded as trivializing ideas and as committing them-selves to marginal and eventually unimportant work. One possible solution to this dilemma is to dismiss the critical role of the humanities in its entirety. Another possible solution is to try to show that it is actually possible to look at popular phenomena as instances of more profound dynamics currently operating at social, cultural, and psychological levels, and to make sense of them by subjecting them to a critical analysis that connects them with ideas and conceptual frameworks. Unsurprisingly, it is the latter strategy that is adopted here.

In this essay, two very popular American TV series are considered: *Mad Men* and *Homeland*. I approach them from the point of view of mimetic theory. My main goal, however, is not merely to pursue a mimetic analysis of these TV series, because I have a more specific focus: I argue that they are both concerned, in different ways and from different perspectives, with the question of the identity of the self and its crisis, conceived as a peculiarly modern phenomenon.

Someone might object that *Mad Men* and *Homeland* are "just" TV series, that they are commercial products, and that therefore their creators and writers are mostly concerned with retaining the audience by getting it interested in the development of the plot. This is obviously true. And yet this does not mean that, while they are trying to keep us in front of the TV, the show writers are not also (voluntarily or involuntarily, this is not relevant here) raising a timely issue: that of the *crisis* of the *self*. After all, ancient Greek tragedians such as Sophocles and Euripides were themselves interested in getting appreciation from their audiences, but this does not prevent us from considering them as expressing the Athenian culture of the fifth century B.C. at its highest level. I regard, again unsurprisingly, ancient Greek tragedies as being of a higher level of literary perfection than the scripts of *Mad Men* and *Homeland*; however, we should recognize that, Sophocles and Euripides not being around, TV series today play a social role quite similar to that played by tragedies in fifth century B.C. Athens.

The first section of this essay is devoted to *Mad Men* and the second to *Homeland*. I argue that the two shows represent two stages in the process of disintegration of the self, which here I consider from a mimetic perspective. In the third and final section, I address Girard's account of this process, and I consider his related and critical remarks on Hegel. As I find Girard's suggested solution of the problem of the disintegration of the self somewhat wanting, I therefore suggest that Hegel's philosophy, once reconstructed beyond Girard's own reading, might provide a more appropriate solution, while being not incompatible with mimetic theory.

1. "The Way That They Saw Themselves Is Gone": *Mad Men* and the Cracked Self

Mad Men is an American television series set in the 1960s.[1] The protagonist is Don Draper, the creative director of an advertising agency on Madison Avenue in New York City, and the series focuses on him and on the people in his professional and personal life. The series has received critical acclaim and has drawn a lot of attention—even from philosophy, as exemplified by the interesting collection of essays *Mad Men and Philosophy*.[2] However, none of the essays in the collection approaches *Mad Men* from the point of view of mimetic theory, which is quite surprising because, for a mimetic theory scholar, watching *Mad Men* is like a visit to a candy store for a kid.[3]

An entire essay could be written to analyze mimetic aspects and dynamics that affect all the characters in *Mad Men*. Let me mention some examples. Pete Campbell is an account executive who sees Don Draper as both a mentor and a hindrance to his advancement within the firm. Don is for Pete the model/obstacle in its prototypical form. Pete is a deeply mimetic character. When Ken Cosgrove, one of Pete's colleagues, gets a short story published in the *Atlantic*, Pete, who had so far showed no interest whatsoever in pursuing a career as a writer, suddenly dusts off an old story he had written about a talking bear and tries to get it published. He even goes as far as asking his wife to meet with an old boyfriend (who took her virginity) to help him get published (see the episode "5G").[4] However, Pete is far from being the only employee of the firm to be prone to mimetic contagion. On a different occasion, Harry Crane finds out that Ken Cosgrove earns one hundred dollars a week more than he ("The Benefactor"). Harry was not thinking of asking for a pay raise, but as soon as he becomes aware of this, he immediately starts to perceive his salary as being unacceptably low.[5] Both these episodes closely resemble (and ultimately have the same structure as) the situation of the protagonist of Dostoyevsky's *Notes from Underground*, who despises his schoolmates and is not interested in their company, until he discovers that they are organizing a dinner and that he was not meant to be invited; then suddenly he becomes obsessed by the reunion to the point of embarrassing himself by inviting himself to the dinner. This episode is used by Girard to emphasize the mimetic nature of desire, which longs precisely for that which others (the mediators of desire) possess, but whose possession is precluded from us (RU, 81). This is called by Girard "metaphysical desire," and metaphysical desire inevitably leads to the destruction of the self. This is precisely what happens to another *Mad Men* character, the British financial officer Lane Pryce, who is seduced by Don Draper's self-confidence and, despite his own lack of skills and weak temper, invests heavily in the new agency (Sterling, Cooper, Draper, and Pryce) to become

a partner, thus amassing a substantial debt, and eventually committing suicide. Lane's widow shows a remarkable awareness of the process that led her
husband to take his own life, when she addresses Don, saying, "You had no
right to fill a man like that with ambition" ("The Phantom"). And the list of
the situations featuring *Mad Men* characters in a struggle with the power of
mimetic desire could go on.[6] But here I am mainly interested in considering
Mad Men (and then *Homeland*) as instances of the crisis of the self, and for
that purpose, the character that should be analyzed in more detail is the
protagonist, Don Draper.

As the show's fans know, there is an obvious reason why Don Draper is
an interesting character from the point of view of the crisis of the self. In fact,
he stole his identity. Don's real name, we learn as the show progresses, is Dick
Whitman; and he is the illegitimate son of a prostitute. During military ser-
vice in the Korean War, Dick assumed the identity of Lieutenant Don Draper
after he was killed, by switching identification tags with him. From the early
episodes of the first season, it is clear that Don is an expert in how to use the
mechanics of mimetic desire. He knows the game. He even made a job out of
it. In one of the most often quoted lines of the show, Don remarks: "By love
you mean big lightning bolts to the heart, where you can't eat and you can't
work, and you just run off and get married and make babies. The reason you
haven't felt it is because it doesn't exist. What you call love was invented by
guys like me . . . to sell nylons" ("Smoke Gets in Your Eyes"). With his charm,
success, and obvious self-confidence, Don is a model (a mediator of desire, in
Girard's terms) for basically everyone around him. He is aware of that, and he
is happy to feed the attraction he exerts. Girard has a word for Don's strategy,
one that Don's "macho" ego would definitely not like: *coquetry*. Girard first
describes this dynamic in *Deceit, Desire, and the Novel*, in the context of his
analysis of Stendhal's *The Red and the Black*: Julien starts to show indifference toward Mathilde, and as a consequence her desire for Julien suddenly
escalates; it is Julien's "state of perceived self-sufficiency"[7] that makes Julien
so attractive to Mathilde. Julien is a coquette, which is Girard's term for
Freud's narcissist. Coquetry is "the enticing of desire from others by one who
does not intend to respond to that desire but to make use of it for his or her
own ends."[8] However, it is important not to forget that, as Girard writes, in
reality the coquette "has no more self-sufficiency than the man who desires
her" (TH, 370).

Mad Men fans are familiar with the graphics that accompany the show's opening music: the silhouette of a man, easily identifiable as Don, falling from a skyscraper; in the final sequence, we see "a tight shot of Don from behind, in which he initially appears to be still falling, but then the frame widens to reveal him sitting in a relaxed pose, his outstretched arm draped over the back of a couch, cigarette in hand."[9] This looks like an appropriate graphic representation of coquetry: self-sufficiency is just pretended, and in reality the coquette is as bound in the mimetic circle as anybody else: "The coquette's self-desire is mediated by those attracted to her at the same moment that their desire is mediated by the coquette's projected self-sufficiency."[10]

Let us take a closer look at the ways Don's self-desire is mediated by others. A prostitute's son, Don, thanks to a change of identity and to his undeniable skills, was able to climb the social ladder. He now wants to be what *others* want him to be: a highly successful and self-confident creative director. However, Don's inner self is far from being as confident as he usually pretends to be. He wants and needs others to see him as a successful businessman, because without the aura of self-sufficiency that is returned to him through others' imitation, he sees himself as nothing else but a "whore's child," as his stepmother used to call him.[11]

When his wife Betty eventually finds out that his real name is not Don Draper but Dick Whitman, and Don reveals his past to her, Betty asks, "What would you do if you were me? Would you love you?" Don replies, "I was surprised *you ever loved me*" ("The Gipsy and the Hobo"; emphasis added). This is a revealing moment: Don's fragile self, whom he has so far managed to shape externally in an attractive fashion, is now openly *cracked*—and Don *even seems to be relieved* by that. It is as if, after a long time, he is free to be himself again. After the crisis with his wife, Don makes a trip out to California to see Anna Draper, the widow of "the real Don" (the lieutenant killed during the Korean War), who several years earlier had discovered the identity theft but who eventually became a very close friend and confidante of Don/Dick. Anna appears to be Don's only true friend: she is the only one who knows Don's real self,[12] or at least the version of himself that is closer to an "authentic self." Referring to the disclosure of his past to his wife, Don entrusts Anna: "I could tell, the minute she saw who I really was, she never wanted to look at me again. Which is why I never told her" ("The Good News").

Now Don might seem free to be who he truly is, and might seem free to express his true self. *But he cannot.* He does not know what he really wants.[13] His self is irremediably cracked. Don knows far too well how mimeticism works to naively believe that one can easily get rid of mimetic mediation and *reconstruct* one's "true self." The point is—there is no "original self." In the context of an interesting conversation with some beatniks, friends of his mistress Midge, Don is criticized by one of them (Roy) because of his job: as an advertiser, he is contributing to the creation of "the religion of mass consumption." The dialogue continues as follows:

> DON: People want to be told what to do so badly that they'll listen to anyone.
> ROY: When you say "people," I have a feeling you're talking about thou.
> DON: And I have a feeling that you spent more time on your hair this morning (*points to Midge*) than she did. ("Babylon")

Roy is right: Don, even if he works in the industry of the "creation of desires," is not immune from mimetic contagion. But this is not a revelation for Don. The point is: *neither is Roy*, as Don ironically points out by referring to Roy's hairstyle, which he clearly copied from someone else to mark his belonging to an "alternative" and "dissenting" community.[14] Don here is rejecting Roy's pretense to a "look from nowhere." We all want to be original, to be "authentic"—this seems to be Don's argument—but what we end up being is merely a follower of another model. There is no escape from mimeticism.

Don's self is a cracked self. But perhaps this is not just about Don as an individual (or a character). The series is set in a specific historical moment (the 1960s), which featured a significant number of political and social changes that had a strong impact on individual adjustment in relation to values, gender roles, and self-perception. In one of his rare moments of disclosure, Don tells Peggy (a good copywriter and Don's protégée): "There are people out there who buy things, people like you and me. And something happened. Something terrible. And *the way that they saw themselves is gone.* And nobody understands that. But you do. And that's very valuable" ("Shut the Door, Have a Sit"; emphasis added). What is Don referring to here? Maybe the Cuban Missile Crisis, which according to the show's chronology happened less than a year earlier; or, more likely, the recent assassination of

President Kennedy. However, there might be something more. *People's self-perception* is changed. Peggy has good intuitions about what is going on, and this is what makes her so valuable to Don—not merely as a copywriter but, more importantly, as a companion.

Apart from Anna, Peggy seems to be the only person who understands Don. Don is clearly a mentor and a model for Peggy. However, unlike other employees who are Don's "disciples" (such as the aforementioned Pete Campbell, Harry Crane, and Lane Pryce), Peggy's imitation of Don is, to some extent, conscious, and more professional than personal. In a tense dialogue between the two, Peggy faces Don by telling him: "You know something. We are all here because of you. All we want to do is please you" ("Public Relations"). Peggy seems to be the only one able to look beyond Don's pretended self-sufficiency and see his cracked self. This is the reason why Peggy is so valuable to Don, but at the same time it is also the reason why he gets so easily irritated by her. Peggy's awareness of the mimetic nature of her relationship to Don is what ultimately leads her to leave the agency, stating: "I've reached a point where it's time for me to have a new experience." When Don tries to convince her to stay by offering her an open pay raise and saying, "You tell me the number. And I'll beat it," Peggy replies, "There's no number." Peggy leaves the agency because, she realizes, a close proximity with her mentor and model is now damaging rather than benefiting her.

Peggy understands that "the way people saw themselves is gone." It is not unlikely that Don, with this claim, is thinking not just in professional terms, but about himself personally. The way he saw himself is gone, but his self is cracked, and he does not know to what extent he can construct a new self (I will come back to this issue in the final section). In addition, Peggy understands that the way people saw themselves is gone also because she is very sensitive to all the changes her world is going through: the growing recognition of civil rights, changes in gender roles—and changes in politics. The world of *Mad Men* is the world of the Cold War: two superpowers maintaining a precarious equilibrium of rivalry. As we know, everything changed with the collapse of the Soviet Union in the early 1990s. And contrary to the optimistic expectations of the time, the post–Cold War world has been not less, but more, violent. That is the world of the other series that I consider here—our world: *Homeland*.

2. "Everyone's Not Me": *Homeland* and the Shattered Self

Homeland is an American political thriller television series set in our times.[15] The two main characters are Carrie Mathison, a CIA officer with bipolar disorder, and Nicholas Brody, a U.S. marine sniper. The plot opens with the release of Brody, who had been held captive by al-Qaeda for several years, and Carrie's belief that he was "turned" by the enemy and that therefore he could be a "dormant" terrorist.[16]

Both the characters have identity issues. Carrie is bipolar. She has a fluctuating personality. This makes her different. And somehow she *wants* to be different. In the series pilot, we witness a conversation between Carrie and her mentor and CIA supervisor, Saul Berenson, referring to the events of 9/11. Significantly, these lines are included in the soundtrack that opens every episode:

> CARRIE: I'm serious. I—I missed something once before, I won't . . . I can't let that happen again.
> SAUL: It was ten years ago. Everyone missed something that day.
> CARRIE: Yeah, *everyone's not me.* ("Pilot"; emphasis added)

Carrie is aware of her *difference*. Also, she feels she has a mission in life: she wants to *prevent violence*. It might be objected that, being a CIA agent, this is simply her job. However, the show makes clear that it is more than a job for Carrie. Later in the series, Maggie, Carrie's sister (who is also a medical doctor and is treating her for the bipolar disorder) tells her: "You say this is about patriotism, but we both know that's not the whole story. *Part of you wants to do this*" ("The Smile"; emphasis added). This is the reason why Carrie comes to believe that Brody is a threat to the United States: she doesn't want that violence to happen again. Her determination and persistence, however, make her appear paranoid.

The point is: Carrie is right. Brody has indeed been "turned" by the enemy. As we come to realize as the show progresses, after being tortured, Brody was sold to al-Qaeda commander Abu Nazir, who treated him kindly and asked him to teach his son, Issa, English. Brody becomes very attached to Issa, and is shocked when the boy is killed in an American drone strike. And he is even more shocked when the U.S. vice president Walden claims that no children were killed in the strike. It is this lie that makes Brody see things from a different perspective. As a U.S. marine, he was used to considering Americans as victims, and Islamic terrorists as persecutors. Suddenly he came to see Americans as persecutors. As a consequence, he converted to Islam and swore revenge on Walden. Therefore, Brody is effectively a dormant terrorist, whose mission is to kill the vice president in a suicide attack.

Brody conceals his "true" identity, or, better, he conceals what *he* came to see as his "true identity": he sees himself as the one who brings *justice*. This is clear from the videotape he makes before attempting his suicide attack (which will fail, first for technical problems, and then because Brody decides not to proceed after receiving a phone call from his daughter). In the video, looking at the camera, Brody states: "This is about *justice* for eighty-two children whose deaths were never acknowledged and whose murder is a stain on the soul of this nation" ("State of Independence"; emphasis added). Brody wants justice for the victims; he wants the persecutor to pay for his crime, and he builds his new "true" identity on this. But is it really justice that Brody is after, or is it just *revenge*?

Brody is very insecure and confused—much more than Don Draper! Watching the series, we see Brody change his mind several times. He decides not to detonate the bomb, but continues working for Nazir. When he is exposed, he agrees, on Carrie's suggestion, to become a triple agent for the CIA, but then he kills Vice President Walden (something that he does under Nazir's threat that he will kill Carrie if Brody doesn't comply, but it is also clearly something he enjoys doing).[17] In season 3, he agrees to be part of a CIA plot by seeking asylum in Iran, his mission being the assassination of the head of the Revolutionary Guard, but once the mission seems to have failed, he doesn't show up for an attempted extraction out of Iran, which raises doubts about his loyalty to the United States ("Big Man in Tehran"). Brody's identity is not just cracked. It is completely *shattered*. If Carrie has a fluid identity because of her bipolar disorder, Brody seems to have no stable identity at all.

And yet, from the outside, Brody's identity is perfectly clear. When he returns to the United States after eight years of captivity, he is unanimously celebrated as a hero—and Carrie's attempts to expose him are ridiculed: how could a *hero* be a *terrorist*? Later, a bomb hidden in Brody's car (unbeknownst to him) detonates and kills two hundred of the attendees at Walden's funeral;

and suddenly he becomes the most wanted and hated terrorist of the United States. A *hero* first . . . and then a *monster*. Brody becomes a *scapegoat*. No wonder everybody wants him dead. In the final episode of season 3 ("The Star"), Brody manages to kill the head of the Revolutionary Guard. The Iranian government is now after him; he could be extracted, but the CIA decides to *sacrifice* him as part of a deal with Javadi (the deputy head of the Revolutionary Guard, who secretly works for the CIA) to help him advance to a position of greater power. Brody is therefore killed in a public execution, surrounded by a crowd that celebrates his death. The following sequence is set a few months later. Saul Berenson's wife is reading the following news: "In a stunning development at the Geneva summit, Iranian diplomats have offered IAEA inspectors full and unfettered access to the regime's nuclear sites in exchange for the lifting of economic sanctions." The cycle is completed: the expulsion of the scapegoat has allowed the peace process between the United States and Iran to evolve.

Brody is depicted as a symbolic figure in the context of the mimetic rivalry between the Western world and fundamentalist Islam. As early as 2002, Girard had highlighted the essential mimetic nature of this conflict, writing: "Given their efficiency, the sophistication of the means employed, their understanding of the United States, and their training conditions, weren't the attackers a bit American themselves? The whole situation is entirely mimetic."[18] In their struggle for victory, the Western world and fundamentalist Islam end up using similar means—means that are highly technological, and extremely violent. We can mention two examples from *Homeland* here. First: Nazir's plan to assassinate Vice President Walden implies the retrieval of a serial number that corresponds to Walden's pacemaker, which is then used to manipulate the pacemaker wirelessly and induce a heart attack. Second: when Javadi, the deputy head of the Iranian Revolutionary Guard, kills his ex-wife and daughter-in-law, who live in the United States, he is not punished, because he is considered an asset by the CIA, which intends to employ him as a double agent back in Iran. This is one of the reasons why Brody is so confused. He cannot really distinguish between the two "rivals" in terms of good and evil. Girard makes a claim along these lines in *Battling to the End*:

> The Bush administration has done as it pleased in Afghanistan, as the Russians did in Chechnya. In return, there are Islamist attacks everywhere.

The ignominy of Guantanamo, the inhumane American camp for
presumed terrorists who are suspected of having ties with Al Qaeda, demonstrates the contempt for the laws of war. Classical war, which included
respect for the rights of prisoners, no longer exists. (BE, 67)

In the world of massive geopolitical mimetic rivalry in *Homeland*, everybody seems to consider Brody first a hero and then a monster, including his
wife—everybody but Carrie. Possibly thanks to her bipolar disorder,[19] Carrie seems to be able to grasp the psychological mechanisms behind Brody's
shattered self. When Brody is arrested and Carrie questions him, she starts
describing to him how he was systematically broken by Nazir and how
Brody's identity was rebuilt by him. Then she provides an explanation (or,
better, a set of explanations) for Brody's decision to not detonate the bomb:

> CARRIE: It was hearing Dana's [Brody's daughter] voice that changed your
> mind, wasn't it? She asked you to come home and you did. Why? Maybe
> because . . . Maybe because you suddenly understood that killing yourself
> and ruining Dana's life wouldn't bring Issa back. Maybe because you knew
> then how much you loved your own child. *Maybe because you were just
> sick of death*. That's the Brody I'm talking to. That's the Brody that knows
> the difference between warfare and terrorism. That's the Brody I met
> up in that cabin. That's the Brody I fell in love with. ("Q&A"; emphasis
> added)

Carrie realizes that Brody wanted justice for Issa, but she also realizes
that Brody's sudden change of heart did not depend on a weakness, but on
the intuition, prompted by the conversation with his daughter, that violence,
far from bringing justice, could only perpetuate violent rivalry. It is in the
hope of stopping violence through nonviolent means, which implies getting
Nazir arrested, that Brody agrees to become a triple agent for the CIA. The
relationship with Carrie seems to be the only thing that makes Brody overcome, at least temporarily, his involvement in mimetic rivalry.

However, as always when it comes to mimetic relationships, Carrie does
not hold a privileged God's-eye view. She might have a better understanding
of Brody's shattered self because of her own particular psychological condition, but she is as confused as anybody else. For instance, she seems to align

herself with the general opinion when, in order to convince Brody to become a triple agent for the CIA, she tells him that he will be a "real hero" and that all the bad things he has done so far would not matter, as it would all lead to the arrest of Nazir ("I'll Fly Away"). And in the final episode of the third season, a pregnant Carrie, who is still grieving Brody's death, is represented as not being sure whether she should accept the offer to become the CIA station chief in Istanbul, or be the mother of Brody's child. Brody's only escape from his shattered self is his death, and Carrie seems to be lost. Is there no redemption, no hope for a reconstruction of the self?

3. "It Was about Redemption": Girard, Hegel, and the Reconstruction of the Self

Both *Mad Men* and *Homeland* are concerned with a phenomenon typical of modernity that can be labeled the "crisis of the self." This is clearly a huge topic that cannot be exhaustively addressed here: the following remarks, therefore, are inevitably generic but they are meant to pave the way for a brief analysis of Girard's account of the self and its suitability.

Premodern conceptions of the self were organized around the idea of "fixed" identity roles (here one can think of, for example, the more rigid and hierarchical organization of society in the Middle Ages). Even Descartes, who claimed that everything must be doubted, considered the self the only substance whose existence was beyond doubt. However, the notion of the self started disintegrating soon thereafter. Progressively losing its fixity, the definition of the self became increasingly dependent on its relations with other selves. A critical moment in this process is represented by that triad of thinkers whom Paul Ricoeur called the "masters of suspicion," namely, Marx, Freud, and Nietzsche. They showed that what we usually regard as the integrity of our "self" is actually heavily determined by a set of ideological (that is, economically driven) and unconscious motives driven by the will to power. The self becomes fluid.[20] What in modernity becomes more and more evident is that, as Girard writes, "It is in the confrontation with otherness that the individual acquires self-consciousness. The self has no meaning except in the relation, *even when the relationship takes the form of a duel*" (BE, 97). Both Draper and Brody have very few authentic relationships, and, significantly, those that appear to be most meaningful often take the form of a duel (Draper with Peggy; Brody with Carrie). However, as we have seen, there is a difference between Draper's *cracked* self and Brody's *shattered* self. We might consider them as representing two different stages of the process of disintegration of the self.

Consider Don Draper in opposition to another character in *Mad Men*, senior agency partner Roger Sterling. Roger's self-perception is that of a late (or decadent) romantic hero, living his life as if he were "on shore leave" ("Long Weekend"): he thinks of himself as "thoroughly original."[21] Conversely, Don knows he is not original. A coquette is always aware that the pretended self-sufficiency is a strategy. When he does not have to show off his fake confidence, his ontological sickness becomes evident: he experiences that lack of being which mimetic desires falsely promise to fill. Don is unanimously considered a man who "has everything"; a guest at his daughter's birthday party points that out explicitly. And yet, a few hours later, Draper sits in his car "in front of a railway crossing, staring vacantly into the distance"[22] ("Marriage of Figaro"). What's the problem with Don Draper?

Unlike other characters, Don knows he is neither "original" nor "authentic." The point is: he knows the mimetic mechanism too well to believe that he can become authentic. In season 4, Don unveils his "true" identity to Faye Miller, a woman he is having a relationship with. She tries to convince him to stop living under cover:

FAYE: Listen, maybe it's not all about work. Maybe that sick feeling might go away if you'd take your head out of the sand about the past.
DON: You know it's not that simple.
FAYE: Of course it isn't. And you don't have to do it alone, but if you resolve some of that, you might be more comfortable with everything.
DON: And then what happens?
FAYE: Then you're stuck trying to be a person like the rest of us. ("Tomorrowland")

In this conversation, we can appreciate Don's reluctance to reveal his true identity to others. Although the concealment of his identity is certainly risky and stressing, there is an aspect of it that is very attractive to Don. If the identity of the self is always a farce (something that Don knows very well, and that the people around him constantly confirm), what's the point of being stuck in *one* identity? Every time the crisis of his self worsens, Don feels the temptation to "start over," to build a new identity.[23] Don's main fear is not to be exposed: it is, rather, to remain *stuck* in a fixed identity once he is exposed, because this would condemn him to stick to an identity that he does not perceive as authentic ("Dick Whitman" is just a name, not his "true identity"). As long as he plays a character (the successful businessman, the charming womanizer—that is, "Don Draper"), he can keep the hope that *maybe* one day he will become an authentic self. But as soon as he identifies with his character—be it Don Draper, Dick Whitman, or someone entirely different—he does not become "authentic." He becomes *that character*. Girard beautifully expresses this predicament when he writes: "Mimetic desire makes us believe we are always on the verge of becoming self-sufficient through our own transformation into someone else."[24] Mimetic desire is coessential with a process of disintegration of the self.[25] Consequently, a worsening of ontological sickness corresponds to a further disintegration of the self. Don Draper is a man of the sixties, and his self is seriously *cracked*; but Nicholas Brody is a man of the twenty-first century, and his self is irremediably *shattered*. Is there any solution to the disintegration of the self, or is this process irreversible?

According to Girard, freedom from mimeticism can be achieved through *redemption*, which is the final point of a process of *conversion*. Girard employs religious terminology, but it should be stressed that conversion does not always have to be religious in content (TH, 401). The process of conversion is usually tormenting, and often features an acute crisis, whose paroxysms can coincide with hallucinatory phenomena. In a *Mad Men*'s scene that (no irreverence intended) has an almost Dostoyevskian flavor,[26] Don is in bed with fever, and one of his previous mistresses, Andrea, apparently enters his flat, seduces Don, has sex with him, and then declares that he will continue meeting her because "he can't change who he is"; in response, Don chokes her to death. But this is merely a hallucination: Don awakens the next morning and realizes he had a fever dream. He says nothing of his vision to Megan (his new wife), and tells her she does not need to worry about him ("Mystery Date"). This might be Don's chance to start a process of liberation from the mimeticism in which he is trapped; however, he decides to go back to his usual, shattered self: a lost opportunity for redemption.

For Nicholas Brody, things are (unsurprisingly) even more difficult. While he is in Iran waiting for an extraction that will never happen, Brody questions the meaning of his actions, and especially his very recent assassination of the head of the Revolutionary Guard. Carrie replies with an interesting claim, and the following conversation ensues:

CARRIE: It was about redemption.
BRODY: In what universe can you redeem one murder by committing another?
CARRIE: You're a marine, Brody. The rules are different.
BRODY: I'm a lot of things. But I'm not a marine anymore. I haven't been for some time.
CARRIE: You were asked to do a mission on behalf of your country, and you did it.
BRODY: Is that what you tell yourself?
CARRIE: That's what I believe.
BRODY: Wind us up and point us in a direction?
CARRIE: If that's what you think, why'd you agree to do it in the first place?
BRODY: That is becoming less and less fucking clear. ("The Star")

They both have a point. Carrie sticks to the only element that defines her otherwise very fluid identity, namely, her desire to control violence. She believes that the assassination performed by Brody will have benefits in terms of the peace process, and, as we have seen, she is right. Therefore, from her point of view, Brody has redeemed himself. However, Carrie is right only in her "universe," the universe of mimetic victimage, where it is possible, effectively, to redeem one murder by committing another. She even appeals to Brody's military status: the idea that there are some individuals who have a monopoly on violence, for whom "the rules are different," is a classic assumption of a sacrificial society that seeks to control violence. But, as Brody points out, he no longer sees himself as a soldier. The lack of clarity to which Brody refers in his final statement is an expression of an existential failure: he failed to be a "true self," a "real human subject."[27] Can we analyze this problem in terms of Girard's mimetic theory?

Girard does not provide a systematic analysis of the "self."[28] However, on the basis of various references and reflections that can be found in his work, we can construct the following account. We are used to assuming the

Cartesian idea of the self as a self-sufficient substance. However, this idea does not correspond, in Girard's view, to the reality of the self, as it creates a false expectation of ontological self-sufficiency, which is nothing but an illusion. In Webb's words:

> It is the misguided will to be such an object-subject, that lures us to seek psychological fusion with figures of power, individual and collective, to try to find in the desires of rivals the secret of ontological self-sufficiency. It is what leads us to seek to be seen and admired by others: so that we can believe in our own substantial reality. It is also what leads us, in an extension of that effort, to try through relationships of domination and victimization to turn ourselves into gods.[29]

The substantial reality of the self is an illusion: the self is continuously being transformed through our (mimetic) relationships.[30] Building on Girard's insights, Jean-Michel Oughourlian defines this "interdividual self" as follows: "I have always thought that what one customarily calls the I or self in psychology is an unstable, constantly changing, and ultimately evanescent structure. I think . . . that only desire brings this self into existence. Because desire is the only psychological motion, it alone, it seems to me, is capable of producing the self and breathing life into it."[31]

In other words, the self is always unstable, because it is generated by desire. *First* there is mimesis, and *then* the self.[32] This is the reason why Oughourlian argues that the self must be conceived not in metaphysical but in functional terms: the self is merely "a function of its operations."[33] And since its operations are intrinsically mimetic, the self is constantly remodeled through interdividual relationships with the mediator. And this is where psychological dynamics acquire a historical dimension. The disintegration of the self, conceived as a modern phenomenon, is a self-feeding process that gets worse generation after generation: the more cracked the self of the model, the more shattered the self of the disciple. *Mad Men* seems to provide us with a clear description of this process when it shows us Don arguing: "Kids today, they have no one to look up to. 'Cause they're looking up to us" ("New Amsterdam").

To sum up: in Girard's view, one should renounce the idea of the (mimetically constructed) substantial reality of the self, and become a "real human subject." But what is a real human subject? Unfortunately, Girard is reticent on this point. He invites us to choose Christ as our model because, being divine, Christ is the only subject who does not respond to imitation with rivalry (TH, 219).[34] But is this enough to address the modern crisis of the self?

Although for space reasons I can provide only some brief remarks on this point, I believe that a crucial point in addressing Girard's account of the "real human subject" (and maybe in establishing a framework for the further development of the inquiry) is represented by Hegel's philosophy.

Girard's relationship to Hegel is a complex one, and deserves to be treated in more detail than can be done here. It is Girard himself who admits: "I felt an affinity with Hegel's philosophy" (BE, 30). As early as *Deceit, Desire, and the Novel,* Girard claims that "underground psychology" (the psychology of the mimetic subject) "parodies the Hegelian struggle for recognition" (DDN, 111). However—and this is the point—Girard seems to assume Kojève's reading of the Hegelian struggle for recognition,[35] with the master/slave dialectic as its prototype. Even Andrew O'Shea, one of Girard's best interpreters, and the author of a very acute study on mimetic theory and the notion of the self, seems to subscribe to this interpretation of Hegel when he marks the difference between the two thinkers by arguing: "The self, for Girard, is not a vehicle of *Geist* (as in the Hegelian dialectic), but rather must come to the humble realization that its historical becoming is also an illusion based on its belief in 'originality.'"[36] The self may well be a "vehicle of *Geist*" for Hegel, but the *Geist* is not merely, or primarily, the one that manifests itself in the power-exchange process of the master/slave dialectic, which is an early stage of the *Phenomenology of Spirit*; a much more advanced stage is the one represented by the "forgiveness and reconciliation" episode. Here a "hard-hearted judge" is represented as acknowledging that he is as historically located as is the beautiful soul, a move that allows reconciliation. But this is perfectly consistent with the "humble realization" of the self's historical becoming that O'Shea attributes (quite correctly, in my view) to Girard. Girard is right when he provides the following description of Hegel's philosophical enterprise: "To open up to the other, to get outside of oneself through alienation, is to prepare a return to oneself that provides true access to the real, access to real rationality free of any subjectivity" (BE, 38). Hegel's limitation, in Girard's view, was to give priority to the desire for recognition over the desire to acquire: "It is the desire to acquire, much more than the desire for recognition, that quickly degenerates into what I call metaphysical desire, whereby the subject seeks to *acquire the being* of his or her model" (BE, 31). Here Girard's thought becomes slightly ambiguous. Is the desire for being prior to the desire for the object, or vice versa? Girard seems to opt for the priority of the object when he describes the process by claiming: "He [the mediator] then becomes my model, to the point that I finally completely forget the object that I initially thought I desired" (BE, 31). Sticking to this description, one might summarize the process as follows: the subject experiences an existential lack; he or she tries to fill that lack with the possession of an object; then he or she forgets the object and tries to acquire the being of the model. Isn't this process a bit convoluted? Isn't Girard making a mistake similar to the one he identifies in Freud's account of the Oedipus complex—that is, opting for a complex explanation when a simpler one is at hand? (TH, 352–56). Wouldn't it be more appropriate to argue that the subject has a desire for the being (of the model), and that the desire for the objects (possessed by the model) is *secondary* to the being?

If we employ Hegelian terminology, we might say that the desire for recognition is the desire for being, because for an idealist such as Hegel there is no proper being for humans without mutual recognition (I am a human being because I am recognized as a human being by my peers).[37] Hegel too is not content with the Cartesian idea of the self as a self-sufficient and atemporal substantial reality. To think of the self independently of the world is an illusion. Hegel regards the self as a "mediated and achieved identity, which is realized through the process that Hegel calls 'World-history'"[38]—that is, it is a historical product. By the same token, Hegel would not dislike, I think, Girard's parallel between the (Hegelian) notion of the "return to oneself" through recognition and "Christ's death and resurrection" (BE, 28). What is missing in Girard's account, from a Hegelian perspective, is the *philosophical* moment linking the critique of the Cartesian notion of substantial reality with the religious representation of Christ. Hegel's theory of recognition is meant to be that philosophical moment. In a scene from the final episode of *Homeland* season 3 that is both "Girardian" and "Hegelian," Javadi (the incoming head of the Revolutionary Guard, secretly working for the CIA) addresses Carrie (who is desperate because of Brody's imminent execution) by mentioning everything Carrie has been through, and comments:

Why would anyone do that to themselves? Why would you? And I think I know now. It was always about Brody. That's what you care about. Maybe the only thing. Who Brody is, that's for Allah to know. But what he did, that's undeniable. It was astonishing . . . *Everyone sees him in your eyes now.* Saul. The President. Lockhart. Even me. ("The Star"; emphasis added)

Carrie wants others to see Brody through her eyes, so that, through the recognition of others, Brody can reconstruct his shattered identity on that recognition—because this is the only identity possible in a mimetic world. Beyond that, there is the higher recognitive moment represented by forgiveness and reconciliation. Rather than trying to win back an always-illusory substantial reality of the self, one should give up that illusion once and for all, and reject every mimetic relationship, maintaining a forgiving attitude toward others. In a nutshell, this is the philosophical/ethical meaning of Hegel's theory of recognition. Girard addresses recognition, but only in religious (rather than philosophical) terms, by maintaining that this can happen only through the imitation of Christ, the son of a nonviolent and forgiving God.[39] The content of the message, however, is the same. The reconstruction of the self (or redemption, in religious terms), can pass through the acceptance of our finitude only, and through an ongoing attitude of forgiveness and reconciliation. This is not an easy task. And yet, we have no alternatives, if we do not want to end up like Don Draper: in the final episode in season 6, in the very last sequence, Don picks up his children and shows them the now-dilapidated brothel he grew up in ("In Care Of"). While his daughter looks at him, he remains silent, stuck in front of the past, unable to rebuild his self.

NOTES

1. *Mad Men* was created and produced by Matthew Weiner. The series premiered on July 19, 2007, on the American cable network AMC and was produced by Lionsgate Television. The seventh and final season aired in 2015.

2. Rod Carveth and James B. South, eds., *Mad Men and Philosophy: Nothing Is as It Seems* (Hoboken, NJ: Wiley, 2010).

3. *Mad Men and Philosophy* features a chapter by George A. Dunn entitled "'People Want to Be Told What to Do So Badly That They'll Listen to Anyone': Mimetic Madness at Sterling Cooper" (20–33); however, it does not make any reference to Girard's mimetic theory. To the best of my knowledge, the only attempt to analyze *Mad Men* using mimetic theory is Christopher S.

Morrissey's conference paper "Mimetic Desire according to *Mad Men*," (paper presented at the Annual Meeting of the Colloquium on Violence and Religion [COV&R], University of Notre Dame, Indiana, United States, June–July 2010). (The paper's abstract is available on the conference website http://transformingviolence.nd.edu/assets/22954/morrisseyabstract.pdf.).

4. Compare John Fritz, "Pete, Peggy, Don, and the Dialectic of Remembering and Forgetting," in Carveth and South, *Mad Men and Philosophy*, 56: "We even get the feeling that it isn't success as a writer that Pete cares about, but the fact that Cosgrove succeeded and he failed. But Pete feels no qualms about forcing his wife into an incredibly awkward situation to satisfy his desire for success. When she does come through with an offer for publication in *Boys' Life*, Pete is further enraged because that isn't good enough for him."

5. Compare Robert White, "Egoless Egoists: The Second-Hand Lives of *Mad Men*," in Carveth and South, *Mad Men and Philosophy*, 91: "Crane's self-appraisal is based not on his actual job performance, but on how his paycheck compares to someone else's."

6. Compare White, "Egoless Egoists," 90: "Most, if not all, of the characters in *Mad Men* live second-hand lives. Betty Draper is a housewife and mother, not because this is her chosen profession (she would rather be a model), but because this is what was expected of women in 1960s America. Harry Crane's wife, Jennifer, is pleased her husband has become the head (and only member of) the television department at Sterling Cooper, not because this is good for him, but because this will impress her friends ("The Benefactor"). Peggy Olson smokes a cigarette and drinks beer while on a blind date, not because she likes cigarettes and beer, but in order to look "Manhattan" ("Indian Summer")." Although White does not make explicit reference to Girard, his remarks are definitely consistent with mimetic theory.

7. Chris Fleming, *René Girard: Violence and Mimesis* (Cambridge: Polity, 2004), 23.

8. Eugene Webb, *The Self Between: From Freud to the New Social Psychology of France* (Seattle: University of Washington Press), 111.

9. Dunn, "People Want to Be Told," 32.

10. Fleming, *René Girard*, 38.

11. "The adult Whitman/Draper accepted others' evaluation of him as the standard of his own self-worth, and so sought to manipulate how others saw him by taking on another man's identity." White, "Egoless Egoists," 92.

12. White, "Egoless Egoists," 87.

13. "For, even if he is a master at manipulating the desires of others, we see he is dramatically powerless to master his own desire, which is just as human, just as mimetic." Morrissey, "Mimetic Desire," abstract.

14. Compare George Teschner and Gabriel Teschner, "Creating the Need for the New: 'It's Not the Wheel. It's the Carousel,'" in Carveth and South, *Mad Men and Philosophy*, 129: "Don understands something about Roy that Roy doesn't understand about himself. Roy's values are no different from that of the 'middle class' that he rejects."

15. *Homeland* is developed and produced by Howard Gordon and Alex Gansa. It is based on the Israeli series *Hatufim* (English title: *Prisoners of War*), which was created by Gideon Raff. *Homeland* premiered on October 2, 2011, on the cable channel Showtime and is produced by Fox 21. *Homeland* was renewed for a fourth season (2014) and for a fifth one (2015), which featured a change of plot, now centered exclusively on Carrie's investigations after Brody's death at the end of season 3.

16. While there is, to my knowledge, no previous published work on *Homeland*, a book entitled *"Homeland" and Philosophy*, edited by Robert Arp, was in preparation for the Open Court's Popular Culture and Philosophy Series when I wrote the first version of this essay. It then appeared in print in late 2014.

17. WALDEN: (*gasping*) Call . . . an ambulance!
    BRODY: No.
    WALDEN clutches at the phone, but BRODY moves it away.
    WALDEN: What are you doing?
    BRODY: You still don't get it, do you? (*fierce whisper*) I'm killing you. ("Broken Hearts")

18. René Girard, "What Is Happening Today Is Mimetic Rivalry on a Global Scale," an interview with René Girard, conducted by Henri Tincq, trans. Thomas C. Hilde, *South Central Review* 19, nos. 2–3 (2002): 22–27.

19. While there is no evidence in the show explicitly supporting this hypothesis, I think it is interesting to consider the possibility that Carrie's bipolar disorder puts her in a unique position to understand Brody's identity crisis.

20. "Modernity frustrates the pursuit of integrity because it casts doubt on our received stories about who we are or what we should do." John Elia, "Don Draper, on How to Make Oneself (Whole Again)," in Carveth and South, *Mad Men and Philosophy*, 174. Teschner and Teschner, "Creating the Need," 134–35, talk about the "disintegration of the ego," presenting Don Draper as a Nietzschean nihilist.

21. "The romantic *vaniteux* does not want to be anyone's disciple. He convinces himself that he is thoroughly original" (DDN, 15). O'Shea comments: "The key to this structure is the Romantic figure who functions as a kind of archetype for autonomous being, standing apart and believing in his own separation, independence and, as Girard ordinarily understands it, his own selfhood." Andrew O'Shea, *Selfhood and Sacrifice: René Girard and Charles Taylor on the Crisis of Modernity* (London: Continuum, 2010), 39.

22. White, "Egoless Egoists," 93.

23. "If Don keeps his future open, he can always re-create himself again, as he once even proposes to do with Rachel Menken, the Jewish department store heiress ("Nixon vs. Kennedy"). Freedom from his past is Don's blessing as well as his curse." Elia, "Don Draper," 172.

24. René Girard, *Mimesis and Theory: Essays on Literature and Criticism, 1953–2005*, ed. Robert Doran (Stanford, CA: Stanford University Press, 2008), 265.

25. "Because the self is in some sense generated by its own recognition of and active attempts to achieve the good, mimetic desire necessarily involves a kind of depersonalization or disintegration. This is captured in part by Girard's insistence that the process of mimetic rivalry leads to a suppression of difference. In desiring the desire of another, the imitator becomes a passive hostage to the model. The model's selfhood, in turn, is threatened not only by the potential loss of the desired object, but of the desire itself." Nathan Jun, "Toward a Girardian Politics," *Studies in Social and Political Thought* 14 (Fall 2007): 36.

26. One can think of the breakdown that leads to a nine-day-long period of a lack of conscience, accompanied by hallucinatory phenomena, experienced by Arkadi (the protagonist of Dostoyevsky's novel, *The Adolescent*), which represents the starting point of his healing from ontological sickness.

27. "The real human subject can only come out of the rule of the Kingdom [of God]; apart from this

rule, there is never anything but mimetism and the 'interdividual.' Until this happens, the only subject is the mimetic structure" (TH, 199); the claim is made by Oughourlian.

28. Compare Jun, "Toward a Girardian Politics," 40.

29. Webb, *Self Between*, 243.

30. See Webb, *Self Between*, 237.

31. Jean-Michel Oughourlian, *The Puppet of Desire: The Psychology of Hysteria, Possession and Hypnosis*, trans. Eugene Webb (Stanford, CA: Stanford University Press, 1991), 11.

32. "Mimesis precedes consciousness and creates it by its action." Oughourlian, *The Puppet of Desire*, 6; compare Fleming, *René Girard*, 36.

33. Webb, *Self Between*, 233.

34. See Webb, *Self Between*, 232: "It is not clear exactly what Girard thinks a 'real human subject' could be understood to be. Even his positive references to the concept of a subject tend to be cast more in negative than positive terms, as when he explains the Christian doctrine of the divinity of Christ by saying that he is the only agent ('*sujet*' in the French) who is free from the controlling power of violence and therefore capable of radically nonviolent action."

35. The thought of Alexander Kojève had an influence on the development of Girard's mimetic theory, and in particular a strong influence on Girard's reading of Hegel. See George Erving, "René Girard and the Legacy of Alexandre Kojève," *Contagion* 10 (2003): 111–25.

36. O'Shea, *Selfhood and Sacrifice*, 45.

37. Here I am appealing to the so-called post-Kantian or revisionist approach to Hegel pioneered by Robert Pippin and Terry Pinkard—but I must acknowledge that this interpretation is still disputed. For a brief account of the dispute, see Paolo Diego Bubbio, "God, Incarnation, and Metaphysics in Hegel's Philosophy of Religion," *Sophia* 53, no. 4 (2014): 515–33.

38. Dennis Schmidt, *The Ubiquity of the Finite: Hegel, Heidegger, and the Entitlements of Philosophy* (Cambridge, MA: MIT Press, 1988), 50.

39. In the *Mad Men* episode set in the days of the Cuban Missile Crisis, Father Gill, a Catholic priest who recently discovered that Peggy gave birth, but gave the baby up for adoption, rebukes her, saying: "That is your guilt, Peggy. All that God wants is for you to reconcile with him. Don't, don't you understand that this could be the end of the world and you could go to Hell?" To this she replies: "I can't believe that's the way God is. Goodnight, Father" ("Meditations in an Emergency").

Hermeneutic Mimetic Theory

1. Paradoxes

In everyday language, the term "paradox" is used to refer to any claim or argument that contrasts with what is usually considered obvious. In a more specific and philosophical sense, a paradox is a claim or an argument that develops from apparently true premises and leads to a seemingly absurd (self-contradictory or logically unacceptable) conclusion. The term is also sometimes used in the context of religion to refer to a form of fideism professing a religious belief even when, or precisely because, that belief defies reason (as paradigmatically expressed by Tertullian's *Credo quia absurdum*). And then there is at least a third conception of "paradox," which is neither a simply logical paradox nor a necessarily religious paradox—although it could be argued that it features elements from both. The first proper account of this kind of paradox can be retrieved from Kierkegaard's *Philosophical Crumbs*, where Kierkegaard maintains that "the paradox is the passion of thought" (and he adds that "a thinker without a paradox is like a lover without passion"), and claims: "This is the highest paradox of thought, to want to discover something it cannot think." Considered in such a way, "paradox" is a fundamental characteristic of a form of thought that strives to think something to which thought has no proper or full access. As such, it retains something of a logical paradox, insofar as it is still related to that coincidence of self-reference and negation which is the source of semantic paradoxes in their classical form; however, it does not necessarily require a logical resolution, and actually such a logical resolution often turns out to be impossible. At the same time, it also retains something of a religious paradox, insofar as it affirms the limits of reason in front of content that transcends those limits; however, it is not necessarily religious, in the sense that its content is not limited to a supernatural revelation. In other words, according to this conception, a paradox is a *short circuit* of reason; it is, however, not only a problem but also, and perhaps especially, an opportunity: it signals that thought is *alive*, that reason is fulfilling its mission. In this sense, therefore, Kierkegaard calls that paradox "the passion of thought": because it is precisely when thought encounters a limit, a barrier, that it expresses itself according to its greatest capacity.[1]

Mimetic theory is a paradoxical form of thought in this sense. Not only is mimetic theory paradoxical because, as Henri Atlan and Jean-Pierre Dupuy indicate, there is a self-referential paradox at the heart of all mimetic figures—namely (as Chris Fleming puts it) the paradox according to which "it is because the Other appears to desire himself that I accept him as the object-model of my own desire";[2] nor is mimetic theory paradoxical only because sacrifice comes to be simultaneously the most blameworthy and the most sacred act; but, most fundamentally, mimetic theory is paradoxical because it shows that human reason is a faculty born to conceptualize (and hence express and then repeat) the founding event; then it tries to make use of that very same faculty in order to investigate its origin, to reveal the founding event, and to demystify mimetic victimage. This is precisely the paradox described by Kierkegaard, "the highest paradox of thought": "to want to discover something it cannot think."[3]

Most of the issues investigated in this book stem from this fundamental paradox. The idea that an intellectual sacrifice can represent the resolution of a sacrificial crisis in which the role of the scapegoat is assigned to a symbolic-cultural form is effectively one of the applications of that fundamental paradox, because it shows how a sacrificial reason always tries to perpetuate itself, even and perhaps especially when the desired object is nothing but truth itself. Girard's mimetic theory features an argument meant to display the divinity of Christ, and yet this argument is not fully consistent from a strictly logical point of view—unless one evaluates it against the background of a specific hermeneutic horizon. It is the paradox of a theory that, in pursuing a truth beyond any form of relativism, cannot but rely on a perspectival conception of truth, that is, the truth of the victim—thus displaying its belonging to the tradition of post-Kantian perspectivism; a theory that leads us to be suspicious of any kind of simplistic egalitarianism (if we are too "equal," that means we are very close to a crisis of undifferentiation), but that is not incompatible with a form of communism hermeneutically reinterpreted; and last, but not least, a theory that provides an interpretative key to address the crisis of the self in modernity, and then struggles to provide conceptual instruments for the overcoming of such a crisis.

Insofar as it acknowledges the self-referential nature of reason, mimetic theory has in itself the strength that makes it capable of addressing such paradoxes, as well as any other paradox it may encounter. Capable of addressing them, not *solving* them—actually, a paradox conceived in the sense outlined above cannot be properly "solved"; but it can be thought through, so that thought can move forward while learning something more about itself, its limits, and its potentialities.

It is my contention that the best way to make sense of such paradoxes is through a synergy of mimetic theory and philosophical hermeneutics. To realize and implement such a synergy in addressing the "mimetic paradoxes" mentioned above has actually been the overall goal (implicit at first, and then progressively more explicit) of the investigations that are the subject of the previous essays of this volume. In this final essay, my goal is to provide some insights for a more systematic treatment of such a synergy, and to clarify that such a synergy, far from being an artificial combination of theories extraneous to each other, actually is the explication of a much deeper, internal, and intrinsic relation.

However, two questions need to be answered before addressing the possibility of such a synergy more directly. First, what do we mean by philosophical hermeneutics? Second, how does mimetic theory traditionally consider philosophical hermeneutics?

To define philosophical hermeneutics is a huge task in itself, as it would require distinctions that are inevitably the result of philosophical discussions—it is, therefore, a task that cannot be pursued here. Hence, I will here use a definition that is partly standard and partly (inevitably) personal, and that relies on historical and theoretical considerations. By philosophical hermeneutics I therefore mean the philosophical movement that originated in Heidegger's hermeneutic phenomenology and that was reelaborated by him in terms of a hermeneutics of facticity that replaces traditional ontology. Such hermeneutics of facticity is centered on the question of human existence (addressed by Heidegger in terms of his existential analytic of *Dasein*): in this context, interpretation (*Auslegung*) is taken to be the concrete—and perhaps the only authentic—way of being in the world.[4] This philosophical project was then continued and somehow systematized by Gadamer, who adopted (with some variations) this view of ontology, and came to define hermeneutics as the attempt "to clarify the conditions in which understanding takes place";[5] importantly, such conditions include "prejudices and fore-meanings that occupy the interpreter's consciousness." As a result, "Understanding is always interpretation,"[6] and interpretation is never merely replicative, but is capable of discovering and producing meanings in the process of its development. Our consciousness is formed by the horizon of our prejudices and fore-meanings; but insofar as the interpretative act is not merely replicative, but also *productive*, it constantly contributes to the formation of our consciousness. Philosophical hermeneutics has also been developed by several other thinkers, most prominently French philosopher Paul Ricoeur and Italian philosopher Luigi Pareyson (and later Gianni Vattimo), sometimes with significant variations, but still endorsing, I believe, the fundamental insights mentioned above. From now on, whenever I mention philosophical hermeneutics, I therefore refer to this historical and theoretical tradition.

Now, how does mimetic theory consider philosophical hermeneutics? The view of mimetic theory on the subject is inevitably heavily influenced by the view of its founder, that is, René Girard. So the question becomes: how did Girard consider philosophical hermeneutics? If we look at Girard's main works, we realize that he rarely used the term "hermeneutics," and when he did, it was often in the generic, neutral sense of "theory of interpretation," without implying any of the philosophical insights mentioned earlier. He never addressed philosophical hermeneutics as a movement of thought, and he never cited Gadamer. He did consider some aspects of Heidegger's philosophy, of course; but when he did, most famously in *Things Hidden*, it was essentially to argue that the Being at the center of Heidegger's ontology, which in Heidegger's view has been forgotten by the Western tradition, is nothing but the sacralized victim (TH, 63–64).[7] It might also be argued that when Girard polemically targeted relativism, he was criticizing some contemporary streams of philosophical hermeneutics. From here, one might derive the conclusion that mimetic theory is theoretically opposed to philosophical hermeneutics. And yet, as I have striven to show since my 1999 work *Intellectual Sacrifice*, Girard's mimetic theory implicitly employs a hermeneutic method. This is particularly evident if we consider the hermeneutic circle, that is, the circularity according to which we comprehend something only if we have already obscurely precomprehended it. This conception has a long intellectual history, but philosophically it is very much connected with Kant's transcendental idealism, which clarified that we should move on from the old metaphysical question about the knowledge of objects, and rather focus on the conditions under which objects can become knowable to us. In other words, knowledge is possible only on the grounds of a precognition that determines the circular nature of that knowledge. Kantian perspectivism was then amended by Hegel, who was the first thinker to outline that those conditions of precognition are also historical and cultural. In contemporary philosophical hermeneutics, the hermeneutic circle has come to express the need to thematize such transcendental (historical, cultural, linguistic) conditions that make possible the cognitive connection between subject and object. Now, it is not difficult to see that the hermeneutic circle lies at the very roots of mimetic theory, for which the central question is not about the knowledge of our desires (from a mimetic standpoint), nor about the truth of the victim (from a victimary standpoint), but rather about the conditions under which we can realize that our desires result from mimetic activity, and the conditions under which we come to recognize the victim as such. Any awareness of mimetic and victimary relationships is possible on the grounds of a precognition that, in Girard's view, derives (directly or indirectly) from the Christian revelation; in other words, if and when we are able to recognize a victim, it is because we already know what a victim is. But the conditions under which we become capable of acknowledging our mimetic nature or of recognizing a victim as such are not ahistorical; and not only because the Christian revelation itself was a historical event, but also, and perhaps more important for the sake of this argument, because the effects of the Christian revelation have slowly but constantly had an impact on human civilization.

Interpreted from a mimetic angle, the entire history of culture can be interpreted as the intersecting of the hermeneutic circle with the vicious circle of self-referential reason.

The reference to the Christian revelation is of course of the highest importance here. The extent to which the Christian revelation operates as a precomprehension (or, which is the same, as a hermeneutic key), effectively constitutes the separation between a religious hermeneutics and a profane (or "sacred") hermeneutics—a distinction that I have often appealed to in my writings on mimetic theory included in this volume. While profane hermeneutics can lead, and sometimes does lead, to relativism, religious hermeneutics leads to perspectivism; and, as I argued in the second essay in Part 2, mimetic theory is intrinsically perspectival. However, an important qualification needs to be introduced here: religious hermeneutics must be perspectival (it cannot be relativistic, because it would fail to recognize the truth of the victim, and it cannot be objectivistic, because it would cultivate the illusion of a "God's-eye view" of the world—in both cases, it would represent a return to the sacred), but a form of hermeneutics does not necessarily have to be "religious" in content to embrace perspectivism. What I mean by this is that perspectivism, considered as a philosophical approach to the world (philosophical in the broadest and most concrete sense of the term, insofar as, once taken seriously, it informs not only our epistemological commitments, but also, and perhaps more importantly, our ethical commitments, including everyday acts and behaviors), can be embraced by anyone, without necessarily requiring a commitment to the Christian faith (or to any other religious creed, for that matter). It might be objected that the cultural and epistemic roots of perspectivism lie in the Christian revelation, whether one acknowledges them or not—an objection that has its validity especially, but not exclusively,[8] in the context of mimetic theory. However, this does not prevent someone from endorsing such a position without acknowledging those roots that reach down, from the point of view of mimetic theory, to its foundation (I will come back to this issue concerning the question of conversion in the final section of this essay).

Against this background, one might expect to see intellectual synergies being realized, or at least a significant amount of cultural dialogue happening, between mimetic theory and philosophical hermeneutics—if not by Girard, definitely from some of the several brilliant scholars who have been active in this field. And yet mimetic theory has remained remarkably silent in this respect. This silence is even more surprising if one considers that Girard himself often engaged in intellectual dialogues with the Italian hermeneutic thinker Gianni Vattimo;[9] and while the recorded dialogues often highlight intellectual disagreements between the two (especially on the conception of truth), they also offer insights into the synergy between mimetic theory and philosophical hermeneutics, providing a significant amount of material to be considered, reflected upon, and possibly developed. And yet, there seems to be a widespread reluctance among mimetic theory scholars to engage in this kind of dialogue. I am aware that I am generalizing here, and there are some notable exceptions;[10] but even when dialogue does take place, mimetic theory scholars seem to be preoccupied with emphasizing the distance between the two positions, rather than their synergies. Why so?

There might be several reasons behind this reluctance, including those of belonging to different disciplinary fields, personal inclinations, a tendency to remain faithful to the letter (rather than to the spirit) of Girard's original insights, and probably many others. Without denying any of these reasons, here I want to advance another possible explanation, which is not meant to be applied to an individual scholar or set of scholars in particular, but rather to the overall reluctance that I mentioned earlier. The explanation I am suggesting derives from the application of a principle that Girard himself suggested. In *Things Hidden*, he addresses the (typically modern) phenomenon according to which we *despise* imitation. Artistic, literary, and—we might add—philosophical movements constantly struggle to present themselves as unique: any potential resemblance with another cultural form or movement is seen as a weakness and a lack of "originality." However, the search for originality at all costs is itself mimetic: each cultural form strives to be more "unique" than any other, not realizing that in trying to do so it is actually imitating the desire to be "unique" of any other cultural form, in a never-ending circle (we can call this the "uniqueness paradox"). In Girard's own words: "Our art and literature take great pains to resemble nothing and no one— mimetically" (TH, 17). Now, consider the possibility that something along similar lines is happening in mimetic theory scholarship as well—would that be so unlikely? After all, there is an undeniable proximity between mimetic theory and philosophical hermeneutics; according to a mimetic logic, it would make perfect sense for a (cultural) subject to try to distance itself from another (cultural) subject, and all the more so if the other (cultural) subject presents characteristics that point to that proximity. Moreover, if we consider that mimetic theory is still a young discipline that only recently has acquired (partially, with a consensus that is far from universal, and definitely not without a significant amount of struggle) the status of a "respectable" field of investigation, it would be only natural to expect some reluctance to show any proximity with another, older, already established approach—a reluctance determined by the fear of losing its own uniqueness and autonomy.

It might be objected that, even assuming the originary proximity between mimetic theory and philosophical hermeneutics that I postulated above, the analogy with the "uniqueness paradox" outlined by Girard is not entirely appropriate, because—so would say someone who fully endorses Girard's mimetic theory in all its aspects and implications—there is a sense in which mimetic theory, unlike any other cultural form or philosophical movement, is indeed unique in its recognition of mimetic victimage and its acknowledgment of the Christian revelation as the only truly demystifying force. Let us assume this is indeed the case: if so, then mimetic theory should not underestimate itself, and should give up any hesitation in getting closer to a cultural form (philosophical hermeneutics) with which it has so much in common. If the uniqueness of mimetic theory is not delusional but, unlike that of other cultural forms, substantial, that uniqueness would not dissolve in proximity with philosophical hermeneutics. In short, mimetic theory has everything to gain, and nothing to lose, in a mutual embrace with philosophical hermeneutics.

It is against this background that I endorse what I call "hermeneutic mimetic theory" (hereafter, HMT). In my view, HMT means, first, acknowledging the hermeneutic roots of mimetic theory, and second, using the hermeneutic component of mimetic theory to clarify its opacities and to advance investigations in the field. I will now consider these two aspects in more detail.

First, HMT means acknowledging the hermeneutic roots of mimetic theory. I have already addressed this point on various occasions, and also here in this essay: I have outlined how relevant hermeneutic perspectivism is for mimetic theory, and that both mimetic theory and philosophical hermeneutics are culturally linked with the tradition of Kantian and post-Kantian perspectivism. Here, however, I want to add and underline two additional points. First, mimetic acts are, as Schweiker puts it, "generative of a world":[11] I take this as meaning that, from the point of view of mimetic theory, our entire symbolic and cultural world is generated through mimetic acts; we give value and meaning to physical and nonphysical (ideal) objects through such acts; we literally *build* our (cultural) world through such acts. And of course this also means that any act that resists horizontal transcendence (by embracing, as Girard suggests, Christ as model) also generates a world—which is not, however, the world of violent reciprocity, but the world of the reciprocity of love. Structurally, this is an insight that, as Schweiker remarks, belongs to philosophical hermeneutics, and more specifically, to Gadamer: during our very brief definition of philosophical hermeneutics, in fact, we have already emphasized the conception of consciousness as being formed and shaped through interpretative acts. Mimetic acts are interpretative acts: acknowledging this allows us to use the resources of philosophical hermeneutics to explore how mimetic acts generate both our self and, relatedly, our symbolic and cultural world (I will come back to the important issue of the self in the next section). Second, acknowledging the hermeneutic roots of mimetic theory does not mean regarding it in a position subordinate to philosophical hermeneutics; rather, it means highlighting the common Christian roots of both mimetic theory and philosophical hermeneutics. This is an instance where the extent to which both mimetic theory and philosophical hermeneutics could benefit from their mutual encounter would be most apparent. Vattimo, in his book *Belief*, maintains that he had been able to fully articulate his long-lasting intuition of the dependence of philosophical hermeneutics upon the Christian revelation only after his encounter with Girard's mimetic theory. Hermeneutics is, in Vattimo's view, the philosophical practice that endorses a perspectival standpoint, which is modeled on the Christian kenosis.[12] This is actually a paradigmatic example of how the encounter of mimetic theory with philosophical hermeneutics is not "passive," but can generate something new: HMT.

Second, HMT means using the hermeneutic component of mimetic theory to clarify its opacities and to advance investigations in the field. The open assumption here is that, as I have previously argued, hermeneutics (as I have conceived it) is not an extraneous set of philosophical tenets to be juxtaposed with the insights of mimetic theory, because a hermeneutic component is already embedded in mimetic theory, for the reasons that I presented above.

Therefore, when I suggest "using" the hermeneutic component of mimetic theory, what I am really suggesting is extending that hermeneutic component out of the "safe zone" of mimetic theory so that it might benefit from the contributions of philosophical hermeneutics in terms of both methodologies and previous insights. An example of how this process could take place is represented by the conception of sacrifice. While Girard's analysis of sacrifice has been invaluable in showing how the scapegoating mechanism operates, mimetic theory scholars are nonetheless familiar with the problem of Girard's apparent denial of the possibility of unselfish and altruistic sacrifice—including, very prominently, Christ's sacrifice. As is well known, Girard clarified its conception, opening mimetic theory to the possibility of an act of sacrifice that is not exclusively suppressive or (which is the same) masochistic. The question here is, of course, not primarily terminological: it matters little if to refer to an altruistic sacrifice we keep using the same term, adding some qualifications to it (sacrifice as withdrawal, as a "making room" for others), or we use another term entirely (such as "kenosis"). What matters is that there is, undeniably, more going on in relation to "sacrifice" than Girard was originally willing to concede. And here is where the hermeneutic component of mimetic theory could be fruitfully extended, and philosophical hermeneutics could complement mimetic theory. Ricoeur, for instance, has taught us the inexhaustible nature of symbols; and we should never forget that, as Girard himself remarked, "true sacrifice" exists "only in minds distorted by Platonic essentialism" (J, 95), and that—as already discussed in Part 1—such "symbols," even when they are the object of a process of demystification, "may also be cunning obstacles that our minds erect against the gospel revelation" (TH, 179). Symbols, as Ricoeur reminds us, are inexhaustible; and to display a symbol, in terms of Ricoeur's phenomenological hermeneutics, means "to display the multiple and inexhaustible intentions of each symbol, to discover intentional analogies between myths and rites, to run through the levels of experience and representation that are unified by the symbol."[13] Even sacrifice, as a symbol, is inexhaustible: it is a paradoxical notion—it can be violent scapegoating and it can be loving kenosis—and admitting the inexhaustibility of sacrifice does not mean weakening Girard's insights, but rather enriching them, making them even more relevant to our concrete reality.

I have mentioned only one example of the fruitfulness of HMT; other examples could be drawn,[14] and even with respect to the question of sacrifice, much remains still to be done. But it is about the conception of the self that HMT could, I contend, really show its fruitfulness in terms of advancing the discipline, and it is therefore to this aspect that I will turn in the next section.

2. Mimetic Hermeneutics of the Self

As I argued in the previous section, there is a mimetic hermeneutics that mimetic theory always already employs, although it is not always explicitly thematized. The HMT that I am advancing here is not only identified by a more conscious and explicit use of mimetic hermeneutics, but also by two important qualifications. The first qualification concerns the mimetic desire of the object as secondary to being. The second qualification concerns the self-critical nature of HMT itself. Both qualifications are relevant in terms of the conception of the self.

Consider the first qualification. As I argued in the preceding essay, when it comes to the relation between the desire for the object and the desire for the being of the mediator—that is, whether the desire for being is prior to the desire for the object, or vice versa—Girard is somewhat ambiguous. Such ambiguity probably depends on whom he is trying to dissociate himself from: Freud or Hegel.[15] In his early works, Girard is keenest to distance himself from Freud, and therefore he grants priority to the desire for the being of the mediator, in relation to which the desire for the object is regarded as secondary. Later on, and presumably as a reaction to criticisms that saw him as producing a theory of mimetic desire in the wake of Alexandre Kojève (whose thought is essentially a reelaboration of Hegel's philosophy), Girard became preoccupied with distancing himself from Hegel, almost suggesting the priority of the desire of the object over the desire for the being of the mediator—effectively presenting a more "Freudian" version of mimetic theory. Of course Girard is never either "Freudian" or "Hegelian," and yet the balance between the two poles of the relation remains somehow unresolved. It is also important to clarify whether the "priority" that is at stake here is temporal, ontological, or both.

It might be helpful to focus on infant development here. It might be objected that it is difficult to argue that an infant who is, say, three weeks old, is suffering ontological incompleteness (unless one adopts a kind of Lacanian model of ego development, which is also a possibility); but it is equally difficult to argue that the infant imitates desires for objects. And yet infants are mimetic—as Meltzoff's work has recently underscored.[16] The objection here, in other words, is that it seems more commonsensical to argue that the child in the nursery desires the object, and not the "being" of the other child—and that it is only the adult, who has been inducted into the symbolic, who desires someone else's being. And yet it is indeed possible to see things the other way around—and more convincingly, in my view. Logically speaking, nothing prevents one from assuming that the desire for being precedes the desire for objects in human life, *even for infants*: after all, one can suffer ontological incompleteness even if one is not conscious of it. In this light, one might indeed argue that the child does want the being of the mediator (whether the mediator be another child, or one of the child's parents), although the child is not aware of it and therefore focuses on something that her or his mind can grasp—that is, a concrete, physical object (a toy, for example). Once children become adults and inducted into the symbolic, they could possibly (that is, not necessarily) become aware of the metaphysical nature of their desire—at least to some extent. This is still a hypothesis, and someone might wonder how we would know that this is indeed the case. In other words, why should this hypothesis be preferred over the alternative? I think the answer is twofold—both empirical and theoretical. From an empirical point of view, Meltzoff has demonstrated that imitation starts within a few hours, or at least within a few days, of birth. Now, it would be difficult to explain such mimetic behavior without postulating a fundamental drive behind each and every desire for objects. Postulating an ontological lack of being is neater than the alternative. And to support such a conclusion, one could refer to a Lacanian psychoanalytic approach, and see the child's ontological lack of being as constitutive of the development of the ego. But Lacan's psychoanalysis is not enough. In order to really address the ontological lack of being, psychoanalytic analysis would need to be complemented by a phenomenological and hermeneutic analysis—a hermeneutics of the self.

This is an extremely important point, I contend, for the future of mimetic theory. In fact, if desire is taken to be primarily object-focused, it is difficult to avoid a neopositivistic drift. If the object-relation is taken as valid, then metaphysical desire would become a mere psychological phenomenon, whose reality depends solely on the subject's illusion. As a consequence, metaphysical desire should be treated psychologically on an individual level, leaving little room for any existential improvement. Conversely, if desire is taken to be indicative of a lack of being, then metaphysical desire is a phenomenon concerning the human as such, and needs to be explored (also) philosophically. From the point of view of the interpretation of Girard's work, the latter choice would mean opposing the "Freudian" reading of desire. It would not mean fully endorsing the "Kojèvian" reading, though; it means rather reconnecting mimetic theory to its post-Kantian roots—even its Hegelian roots. Most of the concerns that Girard had about an excessively "Hegelian" reading of metaphysical desire, in fact, were related to a Kojèvian reading of desire. Kojève's conception of desire strongly relied on his reading of the Hegelian master-slave episode. However, as Hegel scholarship has demonstrated in the last couple of decades, Kojève's interpretation does not do justice to Hegel's philosophy. As I argued in the preceding essay, once Hegel's philosophy is reconsidered in light of his theory of recognition, his conception of desire becomes compatible with Girard's conception of desire. From a broader point of view, and in terms of HMT, to define metaphysical desire as a phenomenon concerning the human as such actually means regarding it as the most fundamental element in the constitution of the self. Therefore, a mimetic hermeneutics of the self is, I contend, the most appropriate approach to deal with such an issue.

What does a mimetic hermeneutics of the self look like? As I see it, it is just the development of Girard's conception of the self, complemented by the insights of other mimetic theory scholars. The notion of the self (*le soi*) is introduced by Girard in his early works devoted to the analysis of the mimetic nature of human relationships carried on through an exploration of literature. Girard's conception of the self presents influences from Kojève,[17] Sartre,[18] and Lacan.[19] The early phase of Girard's work is characterized by a preoccupation with the relationship between "self" and "other." In the elaboration of his central thesis of the mediated nature of desire, Girard engages in a "debunking of subjectivity"[20] that takes the form of an attack on those literary and philosophical forms that endorse conceptions of spontaneous desire and of the autonomy of the self. In Girard's view, "The Self is not an object alongside other selves, for it is constituted by its relation to the Other and cannot be considered outside of this relation" (RU, 43). This is an implication of Girard's central assumption that every human being is characterized by a "lack of being" (VS, 146) and therefore imitates an "Other" in order to get that "something" she or he feels devoid of, and with which the "Other" seems equipped. From here, Girard develops a type of psychology that is "interdividual" (Girard's neologism), that is, a psychology that considers the formation of personal identity as deriving from mimetic relationships. "Desire chooses its objects through the mediation of a model; it is the desire of and for the other, which is nonetheless identical to a furious longing to center everything around the self" (DBB, 39). The idolatry of the Other is never altruistic, but is always motivated by an innate impulse to "be a self," which (paradoxically) can exclusively be realized through the imitation of models. This also explains "the regular alternation between an imaginary omnipotence of the self in solitude and the real omnipotence of the other in society" (DBB, 78). The self is always an "interdividual" self, because it is constituted by (and effectively is nothing but) a set of mimetic relationships.

Therefore, the self can be grasped only by an interdividual psychology centered on desire, and not by an "individual" psychology centered on the subject. In fact, there is no "subject" as such, and all the philosophical and psychological theories that assume, to various degrees, the autonomy of the subject are destined to fail. Hence, Girard's theory of the self implies both an antisubjectivist stance, and a hypostatization of desire: "If desire is the same for all of us, and if it is the key to the system of relationships, there is no reason not to make it the real 'subject' of the structure—a subject that comes back to mimesis in the end. I avoid saying 'desiring subject' so as not to give the impression of relapsing into a psychology of the subject" (TH, 303). In other words, as Erving remarks, "The self is coextensive with the structure of mimetic desire. Since Being cannot be pried apart from desire, and since our desires are always mediated by another's, the self is a relational and dynamic phenomenon rather than an essential, objectively real, and autonomous source of intentions."[21]

In the context of his critique of Freud (TH, 352–92), Girard argues that it is the principle of interdividual psychology that should be employed to explain the formation of the self in children. The child starts imitating her or his parents and, later, other children and models. In some cases, however, and if the imitation goes too far, the child is denied access to the objects of desire (this is what happens, for example, if the male child desires his mother): the "disciple" of a model, in fact, always runs the risk of turning into her or his rival. The child thus learns that there are roles, rules, and boundaries that the child is expected to respect. Such roles, rules, and boundaries are effectively social constructs (originally wrapped in a religious package, and effectively coinciding with religion, and later expressed in a more secularized form, which nonetheless maintains its religious core) that are meant to avoid or limit the turning of mimesis into rivalry.[22]

Because the cultural order is always the expression of mimetic relationships *and* of techniques that humans have developed to prevent the potentially disastrous consequences of a mimetic crisis (that is, the peak of the process of undifferentiated and uncontrolled imitation within a community), the identity of the self is, as shown by O'Shea, first and foremost about the difference conferred by the cultural order.[23] The identity of the self, therefore, is never "stable," but is always the temporary outcome of an ongoing process. From a psychological point of view (the point of view of the single individual), the identity of the self is constantly changing, consistent with changes in the dynamics of the self's mimetic relationships (the self is disappointed by a model, finds new models, etc.). From a historical point of view, the identity of the self is also changing, consistent with the changes of the cultural order in which the subject lives and the challenges that her or his community is to face and that depend on the specific phase of the cycle of mimetic violence that the community is going through. The only fixed point in the development of the self is, therefore, consistency with the psychological and historical logic of mimetic desire.[24]

Girard's interdividual psychology of the self has been developed by Jean-Michel Oughourlian. Oughourlian argues that "what one customarily calls the I or self in psychology is an unstable, constantly changing, and ultimately evanescent structure. . . . [O]nly desire brings this self into existence. Because desire is the only psychological motion, it alone . . . is capable of producing the self and breathing life into it."[25] The self is always unstable, because it is generated by desire. *First* there is mimesis, and *then* the self: "Mimesis precedes consciousness and creates it by its action."[26] The self is a function of imitation and repetition, a result of mimetic learning, and it is organized around patterns of desire. Because such patterns can change over time, a given individual may have a multiplicity of personalities or "selves," some of which may be radically discontinuous with others. These insights can be used, in Oughourlian's view, to explain psychological phenomena such as hypnosis or possession. The hypnotic subject is "*constituted* and *moved* by the other's desire";[27] similarly, possession consists essentially of a mimetic operation so intense that one loses one's ordinary sense of independent selfhood in it, and identifies one's thoughts, feelings, and desires with those of another (either a real one or a culturally defined imaginative other). On these grounds, the aim of psychological therapy becomes a critical acceptance of mimetic relationships.[28]

If Oughourlian has established the psychological side of mimetic theory's conception of the self on solid grounds, it is the philosophical side, I contend, that is still wanting. In a recent article, Erving addresses the similarities between Girard's and Kojève's conceptions of the self. He argues that both Girard and Kojève theorize the self as "a quasi-empirical phenomenon that cannot be reduced to an essence"; the self is defined by desire, an "anti-essentialist phenomenon" that is not ultimately directed at objects but at the Being of another, and that is inevitably violent, for "it seeks to establish the Self through the negation and appropriation of an Other."[29] Through his excellent analysis, Erving has confirmed, in my view, that the theoretical grounds of Girard's conception of the self are closer to a Kojèvian/Hegelian interpretation than to a "Freudian" reading of desire. However, Ervin also argues that Kojève "anticipates Girard in signaling a significant departure from Hegel, for whom the self desires the self as an object."[30] Here my view diverges from Erving's. In fact, as I have argued elsewhere,[31] for Hegel the self desires the self only as a *mediated* object; that is, the self is always already mediated through recognition. This is something that Kojève, with his emphasis on the master-slave dynamic, completely missed, because, in his reading, Hegel is seen as regarding the self as desiring the self as an external object, a *gegenstand*, literally "that which stands over against"; this, however, reflects the standpoint of consciousness in a very early phenomenological phase—one that, we might argue, is structurally similar to the stage of unconscious mediation in the context of mimetic theory: but in order to achieve the status of a fully conscious free self, consciousness must go, for Hegel, through more advanced phenomenological stages, and most notably, through forgiveness and reconciliation—a stage that is actually similar to the process of *conversion* in the context of mimetic theory (more on this soon).

The lack of development of the philosophical dimension of the conception of the self in the context of mimetic theory has also been pointed out by O'Shea, who has devoted an entire book to selfhood, bringing Girard into dialogue with Charles Taylor. O'Shea identifies a "highly problematic discontinuity in selfhood at the heart of Girardian theory."[32] Girard's early work on the self is clearly characterized by a strongly critical attitude (or even hostility) toward views of stable selfhood and identity. Such hostility, O'Shea argues, is based on a "deep division between two radically different 'selves' that he [Girard] 'postulates'":[33] the individual (the literary hero) must "die" to a false (mimetic) self and be born to a true (nonmimetic) self. However, the "rebirth" seems to O'Shea to be absent in Girard's later "anthropological" work. Although I would not go as far as arguing, as O'Shea does, that this absence is due to a scapegoating of that "self who must die"—a scapegoating that is concealed, in O'Shea's view, in *Deceit, Desire, and the Novel*—I agree with him that Girard's hypostatization of desire can be problematic. The problem, as I see it, is that the more desire is hypostatized, the less room is left for the self. If we make desire the absolute protagonist of mimetic theory, we lose sight of the self. However, we need both. The self must be conceived as a product of (metaphysical) desire—but, in turn, (metaphysical) desire can exist in the self only. Antisubjectivism is not necessarily incompatible with a proper conception of the self; but it is certainly necessary to overcome a radical hypostatization of desire to make a fully developed conception of the self possible.[34]

The second qualification of hermeneutic mimetic theory, which I announced at the beginning of this section, concerns its self-critical nature. This is actually very much connected with the previous qualification. If it is true that the self is (constantly) generated by metaphysical desire, and that—as I argued in the previous section—interpretative and mimetic actions produce meanings, then it is also essential to be aware that even the interpretative acts that mimetic theory performs (including, of course, the interpretative acts that I am performing right now as I write) are inevitably governed by the same logic of metaphysical desire.[35] This is, of course, nothing but the application of the principle of the self-referentiality of reason to the agency of the self. But in the context of hermeneutic mimetic theory, it is possible to combine self-critical reflection on the limits of mimetic reason and of the mimetic self (the *pars destruens*, as it were) with a more positive hermeneutics of the self (the *pars construens*). Here I am appealing to the combination, suggested by Paul Ricoeur in *Freud and Philosophy*, of a hermeneutics of suspicion and a hermeneutics of reminiscence.[36] HMT is a hermeneutics of suspicion insofar as it remains critically alert to its self-referential nature: as such, it is a form of thought that proves meaningful even, and perhaps especially, when it encounters a barrier, a limit—as in the case of Kierkegaard's paradox, the encounter with something that cannot be properly thought actually signals that thought is fulfilling its mission. But HMT is also a hermeneutics of reminiscence, that is, a hermeneutics that does not stop at its critical nature; it also pursues a phenomenology of the self—that is, a hermeneutics based not only on the demystification of mimetic illusions, but also on the restoration of meaning. I think this is consistent with the "spirit" (if not with the "letter") of Girard's work. In fact, Girard has always been critical of postmodern attempts to overcome traditional "metaphysics of the subject" by developing a "philosophy of pure difference": a "philosophy of pure difference" cannot, by definition, produce a phenomenology of the self; accordingly, "it does not constitute a real rupture with the past" (DBB, 117). Girard, referring to the philosophy of Gilles Deleuze, argues that "there are two sides to the exclusive emphasis on difference: the first, critical, is directed against metaphysical identities and the second is more metaphysical than ever, because it is aimed against the new use of identity made possible by symbolic disintegration, the identity with the other and not with the self, the mimetic reciprocity of the doubles" (DBB, 117). I think Girard is right here: "symbolic disintegration" (a hermeneutics of suspicion, in the terminology we have employed above) makes possible a "new use of identity" that effectively opens up to a hermeneutics of meaning. It is important that mimetic theory not make, in an attempt to distinguish itself from postmodern philosophies, precisely the same mistake that characterizes those postmodern philosophies—that is, giving up the possibility of pursuing a phenomenology of the self in terms of a hermeneutics of meaning.

All these reflections might still sound very abstractly "philosophical" from the angle of mimetic theory—a theory that is constitutively characterized (and rightly so, in my view) by a constant struggle to grasp the concreteness of the world and of human relations. Therefore, we should ask: what is the starting point of such a phenomenology of the self, of such a hermeneutics of meaning? The answer to this question is effectively theoretical and practical at the same time (and actually there should be no such distinction in the context of mimetic theory). The answer is *conversion*.

The term "conversion," from the Latin *convertere*, "to turn about," immediately recalls a religious dimension. And there is no doubt that Girard often uses the term in its markedly religious meaning. However, the meaning of conversion is broader—even for Girard himself. As Oughourlian points out in *Things Hidden*, the awareness about the mimetic nature of our self, which is at the beginning of any possible hermeneutics of the self, "is only truly accessible through an experience similar to what has traditionally been called religious conversion, though there may be no reason to avoid describing it in rational terms at the same time"; and to this remark, Girard replies by referring to the "investigation of nature," and pointing out that any "decisive intellectual breakthrough" can be described in terms of conversion, conceived as a "passing from one mental universe to another" (DCC, 400–401). This is, after all, very consistent with the use of the terminology that is employed in the Gospels; for instance, in Mark 1:15, when Jesus is reported as addressing the crowd by saying "Repent" or "turn away from your sins," the Greek term used is μετανοεῖτε, which literally means "Change your hearts and minds" or, even better, "Change your point of view," "Turn your point of view around." Conversion, in the context of mimetic theory, is first and foremost conversion of the self, which, to use O'Shea's words, "gives up the illusion of its separateness and embraces its dependence on the other for its true identity—a conversion that is the result of a 'sublime lucidity.'"[37]

And here is another paradox of mimetic theory—probably the greatest paradox of all. It is a paradox that was already outlined by Oughourlian in *Things Hidden*. Commenting on the experience of conversion that Girard has just outlined, Oughourlian argues:

> There is a paradox here. In a world that is secretly governed by the gospel revolution and reflects the extraordinarily concrete character of this revolution, as well as the desacralization it brings about and the way in which it brings to light the most hidden mechanisms of human culture, the type of experience you describe may indeed reproduce the immemorial process of religious conversion, but for the first time it need not rely on divine agency, as can be seen by the great works of literature that reflect it. Such reliance will seem all the more unnecessary because there are already quite enough concrete results—both literary (like Proust) and non-literary—so that reference to any transcendence besides that of the knowledge being acquired

will appear superfluous or even antithetical to the truth embodied in that knowledge. (TH, 401)

This is indeed a paradox in the Kierkegaardian sense that we have used since the beginning of this essay: on one hand, mimetic theory seems to be centered around the discovery that our world is secretly governed by the gospel revolution, so that its mission becomes to find more and more new evidence in support of that discovery; on the other hand, all the "concrete evidence" that can be retrieved seems to work independently of any transcendence or supernatural revelation, thus making it seemingly superfluous (I will call it the "Oughourlian paradox"). How can a hermeneutic mimetic theory deal with this paradox?

3. Hermeneutic Mimetic Theory as Philosophy of the Threshold

According to Girard, the Gospels represent a demystification of mimetic violence, and reveal the nature of interdividual psychology. Christ did not ask his disciples to stop imitating a model (which would be impossible), but he invited them to imitate the only model who, being divine, cannot turn into a rival: Christ himself. Christianity therefore introduces the possibility of a new model of the self, one that is no longer consistent with the logic of mimetic desire, and potentially able to build up intersubjective relationships centered on love rather than on mimetic rivalry. As Girard put it: "The fact that there is a new type of individual in Christianity is the most important thing in the world. The Christian person is new and would have been viewed by traditional cultures as subversive. . . . Jesus is a real person in the Christian sense."[38]

The Christian revelation has groundbreaking and ongoing effects on the development of the self in the Western world, because it breaks the cycle of mimetic violence that has repeated itself over and over since the beginning of human civilization. It seems reasonable, therefore, to look at the development of the self into a Christian "person" in modernity as the model for a hermeneutic mimetic theory of the self. This is, for instance, the pathway attempted by Gil Bailie, who in a recent essay has argued that postmodernity is "setting up questions to which Christianity has answers."[39] In fact, Christ "is a person who emphatically insists that he exists only to bear witness to another person, a person whose life is therefore iconic in the extreme, an icon of the invisible God";[40] Bailie therefore contrasts "the self" as "the secular simulation of the person," which is "inevitably idolatrous," with "the person in the original Christian sense of the term": the uniquely Christian form of personhood cannot be regarded "as a concession to a regrettable mimetic propensity in fallen creatures, for Jesus' own personhood was as defined by his Trinitarian consubstantiality with the Father as Christian personhood is defined by the Imitatio Christi."[41]

Bailie's approach is a very interesting one, and it is certainly consistent with the premises of mimetic theory. Here, however, I want to focus on a more fundamental question, that is, the paradox with which I concluded the previous section (the "Oughourlian paradox"). The paradox is not only internal to mimetic theory, for it has important implications for the way in which mimetic theory is regarded "externally," and ultimately for its success. Admittedly, a theory that argues that the only true conversion away from violence and mimetic rivalry is made possible by the Christian revelation, which, in turn, is made possible by a supernatural event (God's incarnation, in Christ), is destined not to be welcome either by those who do not believe in any supernatural explanation or by those who believe in a different religious revelation. A theory that argues that, because of the paradox outlined earlier, there are already quite enough concrete results so that reference to any transcendence appears superfluous, certainly does not help its own cause, if that very theory simultaneously advocates for the need to an appeal to transcendence. Of course, one could counterobject that if the transcendence now appears superfluous, that is precisely because of the demystifying effect of the gospel revelation: but this simply points back to the paradox. The crucial point here is represented by the divinity of Christ. As is known, Girard argues that Christ must be not only human, but also divine, so that the initial demystification of mimetic victimage can be explained. In the second essay in Part 2, I have shown that this argument is not, strictly speaking, logically rigorous, because it basically hides a version of the ontological proof for the existence of God. In light of such considerations, and for the future of the discipline (that is, mimetic theory), there seem to be, prima facie, only two options. The first is a quasi-fideistic endorsement of the divinity of Christ considered as coessential with the fundamental principles of mimetic theory. The second is a "weakened" form of mimetic theory that focuses on its psychological, anthropological, and sociological aspects, but refuses any religious or supernatural aspect. This is a distinction that mirrors the split between the so-called right Hegelians and left Hegelians shortly after Hegel's death. In this sense, we might even refer to "right Girardians" and "left Girardians." Most of the (more or less) "orthodox" mimetic theory scholars may be considered to be "right Girardians" according to this definition; but the group of "left Girardians" is growing—already in 2010, in their interesting article "The Reception of René Girard's Thought in Italy: 1965–Present," Casini and Antonello noted the use of "Girard's paradigm in a 'formalist' or rather 'lay' sense, that is, stripped of the religious aspects of his reflections and insights" by a group of political philosophers and scholars of social theory, including among others Luigi Alfieri, Maria Stella Barberi, Roberto Escobar, and Roberto Esposito;[42] and there is no doubt this is an attitude that has spread across different countries. The use of the term "weakened" to refer to this religion-free version of mimetic theory might induce someone to connect it with Vattimo's "weak thought"—but this would be misleading. As appears clear from his book *Belief*, as well as from many others of his works, for Vattimo transcendence is not necessarily a form of metaphysics:[43] it becomes such, however, if and when it is organized within a metaphysical system, that is, when it ceases to be a personal experience of faith and is regarded as a fundamental structure of reality independent of the human subject. Vattimo is a hermeneutic thinker; as such, he would never easily dismiss transcendence—although he would probably regard the use of the ontological argument as a metaphysical element. And isn't metaphysics, after all, the greatest myth of all?

The reference to Vattimo's hermeneutics seems to suggest that perhaps we do not have only two options—that is, the fideistic endorsement of the "right Girardians" and the anthropological transcendence-free approach of the "left Girardians." Already in my *Intellectual Sacrifice*, I advanced the idea of a form of thought that, back then, I labeled "knowledge in faith," defining it as the *pars construens* of the critical principle of Christian revelation—that is, as the recapitulation of every stage of intellectual symbolism, but always already read from the perspective of their revealing end. I am still convinced of the validity of that definition; but in time I have become more aware that

"Knowledge in faith" is still a form of religious philosophy, that is, a form of philosophical inquiry that, while it remains rational, gets most or all of its value and meaning from the transcendent. Moreover, "Knowledge in faith" does not significantly help us with the predicament of assigning a place to the divinity of Christ in the context of mimetic theory.

There is, I contend, another model according to which this paradox can be rethought; it is the perspectival model that originated in the German idealist tradition and that has found in contemporary philosophical hermeneutics its theoretical fulfillment. Consider, for instance, Hegel's philosophy of religion: once interpreted beyond the misinterpretation of left and right Hegelians, in fact, Hegel's philosophy of religion can be regarded as addressing a content that is objective without being metaphysical, that is, a content that takes into account the way in which we have achieved a specific set of knowledge as part of that same knowledge.[44] For instance, as I have already suggested in the second essay in Part 2, the argument for the divinity of Christ can be regarded not as metaphysically true, but as valid within a specific hermeneutic horizon—the horizon of the "truth of the victim," to use the terminology of mimetic theory (and this is indeed another great paradox!). But the reference to Hegel's philosophy of religion is useful for another reason. Unlike a view that is sometimes mistakenly attributed to Hegel, he never considered religion to be fully exhausted in or made superfluous by the "superior" form of philosophy. For Hegel, religion and philosophy express the same content in two distinct forms: religion in the form of representation (*Vorstellung*), and philosophy in the form of the concept (*Begriff*). Similarly, we might think of the Oughourlian paradox in these terms: the same content is expressed in a religious form through the argument for the divinity of Christ and the recommendation to follow Christ as the model for imitation; but at the same time, the same content can be expressed in a more philosophical form through a hermeneutics of the self that does not necessarily require a reference to transcendence.

It is important to underline that Christian representations and a hermeneutics of the self are not two separate forms, but are connected or held together by a liminal space—a *threshold*. I borrow this expression from the French twentieth-century philosopher Gabriel Marcel, who considered himself a "philosopher of the threshold," that is, in his own words, "a philosopher who kept himself in rather uncomfortable fashion on a line midway between

believers and nonbelievers so that he could somehow stand with believers
..., but also speak to nonbelievers, make himself understood by them and
perhaps help them."⁴⁵ Significantly, Marcel makes this claim in the context
of a conversation with Paul Ricoeur; and there is a sense in which Ricoeur's
entire hermeneutics can be defined as a "philosophy of the threshold," insofar
as Ricoeur addresses, for example, Christian symbols in their uniqueness,
without necessarily requiring the commitment of faith. It is thanks to this
fundamental perspectival attitude that philosophical hermeneutics can provide the resources for mimetic theory to clarify the space of its engagement
with religion. HMT, therefore, does not give up the Christian revelation,
but thematizes it in a hermeneutic context that eliminates any temptation
to return to a metaphysics that always hides in itself the violent sacred. The
most appropriate model for this kind of philosophical work is, in my view,
represented once again by the hermeneutics of Paul Ricoeur. "How shall we
get beyond the 'circle of hermeneutics'?," Ricoeur wonders, and he answers:
"By transforming it into a *wager*." Ricoeur describes the threefold process for
the recovery of meaning through the wager as follows: "I wager that I shall
have a better understanding of man and of the bond between the being of
man and the being of all beings if I follow the *indication* of symbolic thought.
That wager then becomes the task of *verifying* my wager and saturating it,
so to speak, with intelligibility. In return, the task transforms my wager: in
betting on the significance of the symbolic world, I bet at the same time *that*
my wager will be restored to me in power of reflection, in the element of
coherent discourse."⁴⁶ A three-stage process: wager, verification, and trans-
formation.⁴⁷ An interpretative act is always, from its very inception, a wager
on meaning; then one must bring about that meaning, one must "make it
true" and real (from the Latin *verus-facere*, to make true); and if this process
is successful, then the world is actually changed, or transformed, as a result
of the wager.

Considered in this sense, the threshold is the place of the wager par
excellence: it is the place where the wager on meaning can become the
wager on transcendence. At this point, one might ask whether there can be,
from the point of view of mimetic theory, any authentic meaning (that is,
a meaning that does not belong to the sphere of mimetic victimage) at all,
without vertical transcendence. Provocatively, I contend that the answer to
this question is inevitably positive. If, in fact, we assume the standpoint of

someone who does not have any faith commitment to any transcendence in general, and to Christianity in particular, but who endorses HMT as it was outlined earlier, then we must admit that that approach actually manages to achieve meanings. Someone who, conversely, endorses mimetic theory in all its "orthodox" aspects—including, that is, faith in the divinity of Christ and in the everlasting effects of the gospel message—will consider the "lay" hermeneutic work all the more valid, because she or he will recognize in it the signs of the history of salvation, which operates sometimes without the awareness of human agents and interpreters.

HMT, as I conceive it, can involve everyone, "arousing interest, if not consent"—to use the expression of another "philosopher of the threshold," the Italian hermeneutic thinker Luigi Pareyson.[48] As a conclusion, I want to remark, once again, that the theoretical move I have talked about in this section is not the umpteenth scapegoating of Christianity. Christian symbolism is still at the center of HMT in all its uniqueness, which is at the same time a hermeneutic uniqueness and a practical uniqueness—a hermeneutic uniqueness because, as pointed out by Ricoeur, Jesus "is an Event that exceeds the resources of our phenomenology of images";[49] a practical uniqueness, because, as remarked by Vattimo, "the fuller realization of its truth" is "kenosis, the abasement of God,"[50] and this kenosis is the model for *caritas*, love and openness toward the other. Whether one, at the threshold, decides to make the leap of faith is an irreducibly personal decision (or, better, wager). But inhabiting that threshold, thinking about the paradox through the encounter of mimetic theory and hermeneutics, is already an important wager: a wager on a (philosophical) thought considered to be an irrevocable, rigorous, sometimes tragic, but always existentially grounded search for Meaning.[51]

NOTES

1. Søren Kierkegaard, *Philosophical Crumbs*, in *Repetition and Philosophical Crumbs*, trans. M. G. Piety (Oxford: Oxford University Press, 2009), 111. I addressed this conception of paradox, and used it for a hermeneutic analysis of the notion of sacrifice, in my book *Il sacrificio: La ragione e il suo altrove* (Rome: Citta Nuova, 2004). For a historical and theoretical analysis of such a conception of paradox, see Claudio Ciancio, *Il paradosso della verità* (Turin: Rosenberg and Sellier, 1999).

2. Chris Fleming, *René Girard: Violence and Mimesis* (Cambridge: Polity, 2004), 38.

3. Eric Gans employs the category of paradox in another specific sense in the context of his

generative anthropology: "Paradox is a structure of language; it cannot be conceived without the sign. But neither can the sign be conceived without paradox. . . . The sign that is in the world represents the world it is in; the sign that stands above the world remains within the world of the sign." Eric Gans, *Signs of Paradox: Irony, Resentment, and Other Mimetic Structures* (Stanford, CA: Stanford University Press, 1997), 10. There is a sense in which Gans's conception of paradox is not so distant from Kierkegaard's, insofar as for Gans paradox maintains itself in a perpetually deferred form, thus representing a form of "short circuit" of language. Unfortunately, there is no room here for a critique of Gans's conception of paradox. The category of paradox is also used by Piero Burzio, *Il paradosso del sacro: Bataille, Girard, Klossowski, Marion* (Milan: AlboVersorio, 2010). Burzio, however, links paradox explicitly to the notion of the sacred, and then he uses such a notion to interpret Girard (and other thinkers). My Kierkegaardian conception of paradox is simultaneously broader (because it is not limited to the sacred) and narrower (because it refers to the specific dynamic according to which reason "wants to discover something it cannot think").

4. Jeff Malpas and Hans-Helmuth Gander, eds., *The Routledge Companion to Hermeneutics* (New York: Routledge, 2014).

5. Hans-Georg Gadamer, *Truth and Method*, trans. Joel Weinsheimer and Donald G. Marshall (New York: Continuum, 2004), 295.

6. Gadamer, *Truth and Method*, 306.

7. See the chapter "Historical Forms of Mystification," in this volume.

8. In *Sacrifice in the Post-Kantian Tradition* (Albany: SUNY Press, 2014), one of my central contentions is that the cultural roots of philosophical perspectivism have to be retrieved in the Christian "kenotic" tradition. In that context, I pursued this analysis without any direct reference to mimetic theory.

9. See Gianni Vattimo and René Girard, *Christianity, Truth, and Weakening Faith: A Dialogue*, ed. Pierpaolo Antonello, trans. William McCuaig (New York: Columbia University Press, 2010).

10. See, for instance, Matthew Edward Harris, "Metaphysics, Violence and the 'Natural Sacred' in Gianni Vattimo's Philosophy," *Humanicus* 8 (2013).

11. William Schweiker, "Sacrifice, Interpretation, and the Sacred: The Import of Gadamer and Girard for Religious Studies," *Journal of the American Academy of Religion* 55, no. 4 (1987): 791–810, 804.

12. Gianni Vattimo, *Belief*, trans. Luca D'Isanto and David Webb (Stanford, CA: Stanford University Press, 1999). See Harris, "Metaphysics, Violence." Harris writes: "Not much evidence is provided by Vattimo for this identification [between Christianity and the principle of weakening], but it is possible to go back through the history of Christianity and find examples which back up his claims, such as how Aquinas' theology in the thirteenth century could be interpreted as a 'twisting' of Aristotle which weakened his philosophy" (1). I think that Harris here overlooks the fact that for Vattimo the evidence for such identification does not need to be retrieved in specific "weakening" of philosophical systems, but rather more generally in the ethical kenotic principle that informs the epistemological attitude of philosophical hermeneutics.

13. Paul Ricoeur, *The Symbolism of Evil*, trans. Emerson Buchanan (New York: Harper and Row, 1967), 353.

14. Another example of the fruitfulness of HMT is represented by the political implications of mimetic theory: as I tried to show in the essay "Mimetic Theory and Hermeneutic Communism" in this volume, the encounter of mimetic theory with recent hermeneutic reflections on politics,

such as Vattimo's and Zabala's manifesto for "hermeneutic communism," can actually advance the possibilities of fruitfully applying mimetic theory in the political field.

15. I am very grateful to Chris Fleming, who suggested this explanation to me in an email conversation in July 2016.

16. See Andrew N. Meltzoff, "Out of the Mouths of Babes: Imitation, Gaze, and Intentions in Infant Research; the 'Like Me' Framework," in *Mimesis and Science: Empirical Research on Imitation and the Mimetic Theory of Culture and Religion*, ed. Scott R. Garrels (East Lansing: Michigan State University Press, 2011), 55–74.

17. See George Erving, "René Girard and the Legacy of Alexandre Kojève," *Contagion* 10 (2003): 111–25.

18. See Claudio Tarditi, *Al di là della vittima: Cristianesimo, violenza e fine della storia* (Turin: Marco Valerio, 2004).

19. Eugene Webb, *The Self Between: From Freud to the New Social Psychology of France* (Seattle: University of Washington Press, 1993).

20. Andrew O'Shea, *Selfhood and Sacrifice: René Girard and Charles Taylor on the Crisis of Modernity* (London: Continuum, 2010), 16.

21. Erving, "René Girard," 118.

22. See James G. Williams, "René Girard without the Cross? Religion and the Mimetic Theory," *Anthropoetics* 2, no. 1 (1996): "One of the most important functions of culture and religion is to furnish differences—roles, rules, institutions, etc.—which will alleviate this potential harm to relationships."

23. O'Shea, *Selfhood and Sacrifice*, 9.

24. The consistency of mimetic desire with psychological and historical logic is the only fixed point in the development of the self—at least until the Judeo-Christian Scriptures, and particularly the revelation of the Gospels, introduce a significant change; more on this later.

25. Jean-Michel Oughourlian, *The Puppet of Desire: The Psychology of Hysteria, Possession and Hypnosis*, trans. Eugene Webb (Stanford, CA: Stanford University Press, 1991), 11.

26. Oughourlian, *The Puppet of Desire*, 6.

27. Oughourlian, *The Puppet of Desire*, 234.

28. Webb contextualized Girard's notion of the interdependency of the self and the other and its development as a psychosociological model by Oughourlian in the broader tradition of the French reception of psychoanalysis, which he sees centered around the central idea of a "self between." The self is constantly being "formed and reformed by the shifting pattern of its interdividual relations" (Webb, *Self Between*, 137) with real others and idealized models. The self is merely "a function of its operations" (233). The substantial reality of the self is an illusion: the self is continuously being transformed through our relationships (237).

29. Erving, "René Girard," 116.

30. Erving, "René Girard," 117.

31. Paolo Diego Bubbio, *God and the Self in Hegel: Beyond Subjectivism* (Albany: SUNY Press, 2017).

32. O'Shea, *Selfhood and Sacrifice*, 23.

33. O'Shea, *Selfhood and Sacrifice*, 14.

34. The unacknowledged nature of such scapegoating is regarded as playing an active role in Girard's antisubjectivism; O'Shea makes the case that "Girard's hypostatizing of desire, which arises from his hostility toward subjectivity, has ominous similarities with Schopenhauerian Will and is difficult if not impossible to relate to Christian agape" (O'Shea, *Selfhood and Sacrifice*, 23). Also, because of such hypostatizing of desire and his related antisubjectivism, and by insisting that identity is "first and foremost about difference that can only be conferred by the cultural order," Girard ends up "undermining the conditions of the ethical whereby an individual can take a stand in relation to a community and the cultural forces that prevail there" (11).

35. Schweiker makes a similar point, I think, when he argues: "Thus, while a mimetic hermeneutic seeks to interpret the matrix of power and meaning in the dynamics of a religious tradition, it is also self-critical through the awareness that its own path is one of under-standing and illusion." Schweiker, "Sacrifice, Interpretation," 805.

36. Paul Ricoeur, *Freud and Philosophy*, trans. Denis Savage (New Haven: Yale University Press, 1970), 32–36.

37. O'Shea, *Selfhood and Sacrifice*, 28.

38. René Girard and James Williams, "The Anthropology of the Cross: A Conversation with René Girard," in *The Girard Reader*, edited by James G. Williams (New York: Crossroad, 1996), 278.

39. Gill Bailie, "The Imitative Self: The Contribution of René Girard," in *The Self: Beyond the Postmodern Crisis*, ed. Paul C. Vitz and Susan M. Felch (Wilmington, DE: ISI Books, 2006), 6.

40. Bailie, "The Imitative Self," 6.

41. Bailie, "The Imitative Self," 21.

42. Federica Casini and Pierpaolo Antonello, "The Reception of René Girard's Thought in Italy: 1965–Present," *Contagion: Journal of Violence, Mimesis, and Culture* 17 (2010): 139–74, 153.

43. Harris is, therefore, mistaken when he argues that Vattimo "cannot but see" transcendence "as a form of metaphysics." Harris, "Metaphysics, Violence," 19.

44. See Bubbio, *God and the Self in Hegel*.

45. Gabriel Marcel, "Conversation between Paul Ricoeur and Gabriel Marcel," in *Tragic Wisdom and Beyond*, trans. Stephen Jolin and Peter McCormick (Evanston, IL: Northwestern University Press, 1973), 240.

46. Ricoeur, *The Symbolism of Evil*, 355.

47. Compare Sebastian Purcell, "Hermeneutics and Truth: From *Aletheia* to Attestation," in *Hermeneutics and Phenomenology in Paul Ricoeur: Between Text and Phenomenon*, ed. Scott Davidson and Marc-Antoine Vallee (Dordrecht: Springer, 2016), 189.

48. "Nell'interesse, se non nel consenso." Luigi Pareyson, "Il nulla e la liberta come inizio," in *Ontologia della liberta* (Turin: Einaudi, 1995), 462.

49. Ricoeur, *The Symbolism of Evil*, 269.

50. Vattimo, *Belief*, 47.

51. With the last sentence, I deliberately paraphrase the final sentence of my book *Il sacrificio: La ragione e il suo altrove*, as I still believe in what those words were meant to express—and I think they are even more meaningful in the context of a discussion about the future of mimetic theory.

Bibliography

Adams, Rebecca. "Violence, Difference, Sacrifice: A Conversation with René Girard." *Religion and Literature* 25, no. 2 (1993): 9–33.

Agacinski, Sylviane, Jacques Derrida, Sarah Kofman, Ph. Lacoue-Labarthe, Jean-Luc Nancy, and Bernard Pautrat. *Mimésis des Articulations*. Paris: Aubier-Flammarion, 1975.

Alison, James. *On Being Liked*. London: Darton, Longman and Todd, 2003.

Angelini, Giuseppe. "Apologie postmoderne dell'amore: L'esempio di Girard e Levinas." *Teologia* 2 (2002): 94–138.

Arp, Robert, ed. *"Homeland" and Philosophy: For Your Minds Only*. Chicago: Open Court, 2014.

Attili, Grazia, Francesca Farabollini, and Patrizia Messeri, eds. *Il nemico ha la coda*. Florence: Giunti, 1996.

Bailie, Gill. "The Imitative Self: The Contribution of René Girard." In *The Self: Beyond the Postmodern Crisis*, ed. Paul C. Vitz and Susan M. Felch, 3–24. Wilmington, DE: ISI Books, 2006.

Bandera, Cesareo. "The Double Reconciled." *MLN* 93, no. 5 (1978): 1007–14.

Bassoff, Bruce. "Interview with René Girard." *Denver Quarterly* 13, no. 2 (1978): 28–40.

Bebbington, David William. *Evangelicalism in Modern Britain: A History from the 1730s to the 1980s*. London: Unwin Hyman, 1989.

Benjamin, Walter. "On the Concept of History." In *Selected Writings*, edited by Howard Eiland and Michael W. Jennings, vol. 4, *1938–1940*, 389–411. Cambridge, MA: Belknap Press, 2003.

Bottani, Livio. "La Mimesi, la violenza e il sacro: Nota sul pensiero di René Girard." *Filosofia* 38, no. 1 (1987): 53–56.

Bubbio, Paolo Diego. "Ermeneutica: Ancora pensiero sacrificale? Heidegger, Derrida e Ricoeur secondo il pensiero di René Girard." *Annuario filosofico* 15 (2000): 449–81.

———. "Girard and Anselm: Ontological Argument and Mimetic Theory," *Analecta Hermeneutica* 2 (2010).

———. *God and the Self in Hegel.* Albany: SUNY Press, 2017.

———. "God, Incarnation, and Metaphysics in Hegel's Philosophy of Religion." *Sophia* 53, no. 4 (2014): 515–33.

———. "'If There Is a Plot': Gabriel Marcel and Second-Degree Reflection." In *Between Description and Interpretation: The Hermeneutic Turn in Phenomenology*, edited by Andrzej Wiercinski, 55–70. Toronto: Hermeneutic Press, 2005.

———. "Il circolo auto-referenziale del Logos sacrificale: Spunti gnoseologici del pensiero di René Girard." *Filosofia* 51, no. 1 (2000): 36–63.

———. *Il sacrificio: La ragione e il suo altrove.* Rome: Citta Nuova, 2004.

———. "Il sacrificio intellettuale: René Girard e la filosofia della religione." *Filosofia e Teologia* 13, no. 3 (1999): 545–61.

———. "Literary Aesthetics and Knowledge in René Girard's Mimetic Theory." *Literature and Aesthetics* 17, no. 1 (2007): 35–50.

———. "Mimetic Theory and Hermeneutics." *Colloquy* 9 (2005).

———. "Oblazione e paradosso: L'evoluzione del pensiero di René Girard." *Iride* 41 (2004): 151–61.

———. *Sacrifice in the Post-Kantian Tradition: Perspectivism, Intersubjectivity, and Recognition.* Albany: SUNY Press, 2014.

———. "Secolarizzare il male: La teoria mimetica e *L'adolescente* di Dostoeveskij." In *Male e redenzione: Sofferenza e trascendenza in René Girard*, edited by Paolo Diego Bubbio and Silvio Morigi, 17–39. Turin: Edizioni Camilliane, 2008.

Bubbio, Paolo Diego, and Silvio Morigi, eds. *Male e redenzione: Sofferenza e trascendenza in René Girard.* Turin: Edizioni Camilliane, 2008.

Bubbio, Paolo Diego, and Paul Redding. "Hegel and the Ontological Argument on the Existence of God." *Religious Studies* 50, no. 4 (2014): 465–86.

Burzio, Piero. *Il paradosso del sacro: Bataille, Girard, Klossowski, Marion.* Milan: AlboVersorio, 2010.

———. "Mito, tragedia, romanzo in René Girard," *Rivista di estetica* 43 (1994): 41–68.

Cacciari, Massimo. *Dell'Inizio.* Milan: Adelphi, 1990.

Carveth, Rod, and James B. South, eds. *Mad Men and Philosophy: Nothing Is as It Seems.* Hoboken, NJ: Wiley, 2010.

Casini, Federica, and Pierpaolo Antonello. "The Reception of René Girard's Thought in Italy: 1965–Present." *Contagion* 17 (2010): 139–74.

Ciancio, Claudio. *Il paradosso della verità.* Turin: Rosenberg and Sellier, 1999.

Colombo, Adele. *Il sacrificio in René Girard: Dalla violenza al dono.* Brescia: Morcelliana, 1999.

Deguy, Michel, and Jean-Pierre Dupuy, eds. *René Girard et le problème du mal.* Paris: Grasset, 1982.

Derrida, Jacques. "La Pharmacie de Platon." In *La Dissémination*, 71–197. Paris: Seuil, 1972. Translated by Barbara Johnson as "Plato's Pharmacy," in *Dissemination*, 61–172 (London: Athlone Press, 1981).

———. *Specters of Marx*. Translated by Peggy Kamuf. London: Routledge, 1996.

Dixon, Thomas. "Scientific Atheism as a Faith Tradition." *Studies in History and Philosophy of Biological and Biomedical Sciences* 33 (2002): 337–59.

Doutreloux, Alexandre. "Violence et religion d'après René Girard." *Revue Théologique de Louvain* 7 (1976): 182–95.

Dumouchel, Paul, and Jean-Pierre Dupuy. *L'enfer des choses: René Girard et la logique de l'economie*. Paris: Seuil, 1979.

Dunn, George A. "'People Want to Be Told What to Do So Badly That They'll Listen to Anyone': Mimetic Madness at Sterling Cooper." In *Mad Men and Philosophy: Nothing Is as It Seems*, edited by Rod Carveth and James B. South, 20–33. Hoboken, NJ: Wiley, 2010.

Dupuy, Jean-Pierre. *Ordres et désordres: Enquête sur un nouveau paradigme*. Paris: Seuil, 1982.

Elia, John. "Don Draper, on How to Make Oneself (Whole Again)." In *Mad Men and Philosophy: Nothing Is as It Seems*, edited by Rod Carveth and James B. South, 168–88. Hoboken, NJ: Wiley, 2010.

Erving, George. "René Girard and the Legacy of Alexandre Kojève." *Contagion* 10 (2003): 111–25.

Fages, Jean-Baptiste. *Comprendre René Girard*. Toulouse: Privât, 1982.

Ferraris, Maurizio. *Differenze: La filosofia francese dopo lo strutturalismo*. Milan: Multipla, 1981.

———. *Storia dell'ermeneutica*. Milan: Bompiani, 1988.

Fleming, Chris. *René Girard: Violence and Mimesis*. Cambridge: Polity, 2004.

Fleming, Chris, and John O'Carroll. "On Romanticism," *Anthropoetics* 11, no. 1 (2005).

———. "Revolution, Rupture, Rhetoric." *Philosophy and Social Criticism* 38, no. 1 (2012): 39–57.

Formenti, Carlo. "La guerra e il sacro." *Alfabeta* 60 (1984): 23–24.

———. *Prometeo e Hermes*. Naples: Liguori, 1986.

Fornari, Giuseppe. "Alla ricerca dell'origine perduta: Nuova formulazione della teoria mimetico-sacrificale di Girard." In *Maestri e scolari di non violenza*, edited by Claudio Tugnoli, 151–201. Milan: Franco Angeli, 2000.

———. "La vittima e il corpo: La prova dell'esistenza di Dio nel pensiero di René Girard." *Filosofia e Teologia* 13, no. 2 (1999): 260–70.

Fritz, John. "Pete, Peggy, Don, and the Dialectic of Remembering and Forgetting." In *Mad Men and Philosophy: Nothing Is as It Seems*, edited by Rod Carveth and James B. South, 53–65. Hoboken, NJ: Wiley, 2010.

Gadamer, Hans-Georg. *Truth and Method*. Translated by Joel Weinsheimer and Donald G. Marshall. New York: Continuum, 2004.

Gans, Eric. "Le Logos de René Girard." In *René Girard et le problème du mal*, edited by Michel Deguy and Jean-Pierre Dupuy, 172–214. Paris: Grasset, 1982.

——. *Signs of Paradox: Irony, Resentment, and Other Mimetic Structures*. Stanford, CA: Stanford University Press, 1997.

Gardner, Sebastian. "The Limits of Naturalism and the Metaphysics of German Idealism." In *German Idealism: Contemporary Perspectives*, edited by Espen Hammer, 19–49. New York: Routledge, 2007.

Garin, Eugenio. *Medioevo e rinascimento*. Rome-Bari: Laterza, 1954.

Gilson, Étienne. *History of Christian Philosophy in the Middle Ages*. London: Sheed and Ward, 1955.

Girard, René. "Apocalyptic Thinking after 9/11." Interview by Robert Doran. *SubStance* 37, no. 1 (2008): 20–32.

——. "La lotta tra Gesù e Satana: Conversazione con René Girard." In René Girard, *La vittima e la folla: Violenza del mito e cristianesimo*, edited by Giuseppe Fornari. Treviso: Santi Quaranta, 1998.

——. "La meurtre fondateur dans la pensée de Nietzsche." In *Violence et vérité: Autour de René Girard*, edited by Paul Dumouchel, 597–613. Paris: Grasset, 1985.

——. "La violence et le religieux." Interview by L. Schneiter. *Construire*, September 30, 1981, 20–21.

——. *Les origines de la culture: Entretiens avec Pierpaolo Antonello et João Cezar de Castro Rocha*. Paris: Desclée de Brouwer, 2004.

——. "Lévi-Strauss, Frye, Derrida and Shakespearean Criticism." *Diacritics* 3 (1973): 34–38.

——. *Mimesis and Theory: Essays on Literature and Criticism, 1953–2005*. Edited by Robert Doran. Stanford, CA: Stanford University Press, 2008.

——. "Mimetische Theorie und Teologie." In *Vom Fluch und Segen der Sündenböcke: Raymund Schwager zum 60 Geburtstag*, edited by Józef Niewiadomski and Wolfgang Palaver, 15–29. Thaur: Kulturverlag, 1995.

——. "Not Just Interpretations: There Are Facts, Too." In Gianni Vattimo and René Girard, *Christianity, Truth, and Weakening Faith: A Dialogue*, edited by Pierpaolo Antonello, translated by William McCuaig, 88–108. New York: Columbia University Press, 2010.

——. "On War and Apocalypse." *First Things* 195 (2009): 17–22.

——. "Rite, Travail, Science." *Critique* 380 (1979): 20–34.

——. "Superman in the Underground: Strategies of Madness; Nietzsche, Wagner and Dostoevskij." *MLN* 92, no. 6 (1976): 1161–85.

——. "Vers une définition systématique du sacré." *Liberté* (Montreal) 15, nos. 3–4 (1973): 58–74.

——. "What Is Happening Today Is Mimetic Rivalry on a Global Scale." Interview by Henri Tincq. Translated by Thomas C. Hilde. *South Central Review* 19, nos. 2–3 (2002): 22–27.

Girard, René, and Raymund Schwager. *Correspondence, 1974–1991*. Edited by Scott Cowdell, Chris Fleming, Joel Hodge, and Mathias Moosbrugger. Translated by Chris Fleming and Sheelah Treflé Hidden. New York: Bloomsbury Academic, 2016.

Girard, René, and James Williams. "The Anthropology of the Cross: A Conversation with René Girard." In *The Girard Reader*, edited by James G. Williams, 261–88. New York: Crossroad, 1996.

Goldmann, Lucien. *Towards a Sociology of the Novel*. Translated by Alan Sheridan. London: Tavistock, 1975.

Guillet, Jacques. "René Girard et le sacrifice." *Études* 351 (July 1979): 91–102.

Harrelson, Kevin. *The Ontological Argument from Descartes to Hegel.* New York: Humanity Books, 2009.

Harris, Matthew Edward. "Metaphysics, Violence and the 'Natural Sacred' in Gianni Vattimo's Philosophy." *Humanicus* 8 (2013).

Hegel, Georg Wilhelm Friedrich. *Enzyklopädie der philosophischen Wissenschaften im Grundrisse.* Edited by Eva Moldenhauer and Karl Markus. Frankfurt am Main: Suhrkamp Verlag, 1970–71.

Heidegger, Martin. *Einführung in die Metaphysik.* Tübingen: Max Niemeyer, 1953. Translated by Ralph Manheim as *An Introduction to Metaphysics* (New Haven: Yale University Press, 1968).

———. *Vorträge und Aufsätze.* Pfullingen: Günther Neske, 1954.

Hessen, Johannes. *Religionsphilosophie.* 2 vols. Munich: Ernst Reinhardt, 1955.

Huizinga, Johan. *The Autumn of the Middle Ages.* Chicago: University of Chicago Press, 1997.

Johnston, Britton. "Temples of Debt: Capitalism as a Sacred/Sacrificial System." Paper presented at the Annual Meeting of the Colloquium on Violence and Religion (COV&R), Antwerp, Belgium, June 2001. http://brittondanna.files.wordpress.com/2008/01/templesofdebt.pdf.

Jun, Nathan. "Toward a Girardian Politics." *Studies in Social and Political Thought* 14 (Fall 2007): 22–42.

Kant, Immanuel. *Critique of Pure Reason.* Translated and edited by Paul Guyer and Allen W. Wood. Cambridge: Cambridge University Press, 1998.

———. "On the Miscarriage of All Philosophical Trials in Theodicy." In *Religion and Rational Theology*, translated and edited by Allen Wood and George Di Giovanni, 19–37. Cambridge: Cambridge University Press, 1998.

———. *Religion and Rational Theology.* Translated and edited by Allen Wood and George Di Giovanni. Cambridge: Cambridge University Press, 1992.

Kaplan, Grant. "An Interview with René Girard." *First Things*, November 6, 2008. www.firstthings.com.

Kearney, Richard. "Le mythe chez René Girard: Un nouveau bouc émissaire." In *Violence et vérité: Autour de René Girard*, edited by Paul Dumouchel, 35–49. Paris: Grasset, 1985.

Kierkegaard, Søren. *Philosophical Crumbs.* In *Repetition and Philosophical Crumbs*, translated by M. G. Piety, 83–173. Oxford: Oxford University Press, 2009.

Kirwan, Michael. *Discovering Girard.* London: Darton, Longman and Todd, 2004.

———. "Fuori dalle città, tra le città: René Girard e il male radicale." In *Male e Redenzione: Sofferenza e Trascendenza in René Girard*, edited by Paolo Diego Bubbio and Silvio Morigi, 133–49. Turin: Camilliane, 2008.

Krugman, Paul. "How Did Economists Get It So Wrong?" *New York Times*, September 6, 2009.

Lochet, Louis. "René Girard: Une gnose?" *Cahiers Universitaires Catholiques*, May–June 1979, 46–47.

Malpas, Jeff, and Hans-Helmuth Gander, eds. *The Routledge Companion to Hermeneutics.* New York: Routledge, 2014.

Mancinelli, Paola. *Cristianesimo senza sacrificio: Filosofia e teologia in René Girard.* Assisi: Cittadella, 2001.

Marcel, Gabriel, "Conversation between Paul Ricoeur and Gabriel Marcel." In Gabriel Marcel, *Tragic*

Wisdom and Beyond, translated by Stephen Jolin and Peter McCormick, 217–57. Evanston, IL: Northwestern University Press, 1973.

Marx, Karl, and Frederick Engels. *Manifesto of the Communist Party.* Translated by Samuel Moore. London: Verso, 2012.

Meltzoff, Andrew N. "Chapter 3: Out of the Mouths of Babes; Imitation, Gaze, and Intentions in Infant Research—the 'Like Me' Framework." In *Mimesis and Science: Empirical Research on Imitation and the Mimetic Theory of Culture and Religion*, edited by Scott R. Garrels, 55–74. East Lansing: Michigan State University Press, 2011.

Morigi, Silvio. "Un essere 'vuoto di essere,' 'morale e risolutamente manicheo': Il demoniaco e la demonologia come 'sapere paradossale' in René Girard." In *Male e redenzione: Sofferenza e trascendenza in René Girard*, edited by Paolo Diego Bubbio and Silvio Morigi. Turin: Camilliane, 2008.

Morrissey, Christopher S. "Mimetic Desire according to *Mad Men*." Presented at the Annual Meeting of the Colloquium on Violence and Religion (COV&R), University of Notre Dame, IN, United States, June–July 2010. http://transformingviolence.nd.edu/assets/22954/morrisseyabstract.pdf.

Oppy, Graham. *Ontological Arguments and Belief in God.* New York: Cambridge University Press, 1995.

O'Shea, Andrew. *Selfhood and Sacrifice: René Girard and Charles Taylor on the Crisis of Modernity.* London: Continuum, 2010.

Oughourlian, Jean-Michel. *The Genesis of Desire.* Translated by Eugene Webb. East Lansing: Michigan State University Press, 2010.

———. *The Puppet of Desire: The Psychology of Hysteria, Possession and Hypnosis.* Translated by Eugene Webb. Stanford, CA: Stanford University Press, 1991.

Oughourlian, Jean-Michel, and Guy Lefort. "Psychotic Structure and Girard's Doubles." *Diacritics* 8, no. 1 (1978): 72–74.

Pagano, Maurizio. *Hegel: La religione e l'ermeneutica del concetto.* Naples: Edizioni Scientifiche Italiane, 1992.

Palaver, Wolfgang. *René Girard's Mimetic Theory.* Translated by Gabriel Borrud. East Lansing: Michigan State University Press, 2013.

Pareyson, Luigi. "Il nulla e la libertà come inizio." In *Ontologia della libertà*, 439–62. Turin: Einaudi, 1995.

Poulet, Georges. *Études sur le temps humain.* Paris: Plon, 1950.

Purcell, Sebastian. "Hermeneutics and Truth: From *Aletheia* to Attestation." In *Hermeneutics and Phenomenology in Paul Ricoeur: Between Text and Phenomenon*, edited by Scott Davidson and Marc-Antoine Vallee, 175–96. Dordrecht: Springer, 2016.

Ravera, Marco, ed. *Il pensiero ermeneutico.* Genoa: Marietti, 1986.

Redding, Paul. *Continental Idealism: Leibniz to Nietzsche.* New York: Routledge, 2009.

———. *Hegel's Hermeneutics.* Ithaca, NY: Cornell University Press, 1996.

Ricoeur, Paul. *Freud and Philosophy.* Translated by Denis Savage. New Haven: Yale University Press, 1970.

———. "Gabriel Marcel and Phenomenology." In *The Philosophy of Gabriel Marcel*, edited by Paul Arthur Schilpp and Lewis Edwin Hahn, 471–94. La Salle, IL: Open Court, 1984.

———. "Philosopher après Kierkegaard." *Revue de théologie et de philosophie* 13, no. 4 (1963): 303–16.

———. *The Symbolism of Evil*. Translated by Emerson Buchanan. New York: Harper and Row, 1967.

Rognini, Giorgio. "Al di là del sacrificio," *Hermeneutica* 5 (1985): 79–114.

Rossi, Philip J., and Michael Wreen, eds. *Kant's Philosophy of Religion Reconsidered*. Bloomington: Indiana University Press, 1991.

Schmidt, Dennis. *The Ubiquity of the Finite: Hegel, Heidegger, and the Entitlements of Philosophy*. Cambridge, MA: MIT Press, 1988.

Schneider, Matthew. "Mimetic Polemicism: René Girard and Harold Bloom contra the 'School of Resentment.' A Review Essay." *Anthropoetics* 2, no. 1 (1996).

Schwager, Raymund. *Brauchen wir einen Sündenbock? Gewalt und Erlösung in den biblischen Schriften*. Munich: Kosel, 1978. Translated by Maria L. Assad as *Violence and Redemption in the Bible* (San Francisco: Harper and Row, 1987).

———. "Gewalt und Opfer." *Orientierung* 38 (1974): 41–44.

Schweiker, William. "Sacrifice, Interpretation, and the Sacred: The Import of Gadamer and Girard for Religious Studies." *Journal of the American Academy of Religion* 55, no. 4 (1987): 791–810.

Sequeri, Pierangelo. "'Dare la vita' ed 'essere sacrificato': Il tema della singolarità cristologica nella prospettiva di R. Girard." *Teologia* 14, no. 2 (1989): 143–53.

Serres, Michel. *Hermès V: Le passage du Nord-Ouest*. Paris: Minuit, 1980.

Simon, Alfred, ed. "Discussion avec René Girard." *Esprit* 429 (1973): 528–63.

Sorrell, Tom. *Scientism: Philosophy and the Infatuation with Science*. New York: Routledge, 1991.

Tarditi, Claudio. *Al di là della vittima: Cristianesimo, violenza e fine della storia*. Turin: Marco Valerio, 2004.

Teschner, George and Gabriel Teschner. "Creating the Need for the New: 'It's Not the Wheel. It's the Carousel.'" In *Mad Men and Philosophy: Nothing Is as It Seems*, edited by Rod Carveth and James B. South, 126–40. Hoboken, NJ: Wiley, 2010.

Troisfontaines, Claude. "L'identité du social et du religieux selon René Girard." *Revue Philosophique de Louvain* 78 (1980): 71–90.

Valadier, Paul. "Bouc émissaire et révélation chrétienne selon René Girard." *Études* 357, no. 7 (1982): 251–60.

Vattimo, Gianni. *Addio alla verità*. Rome: Meltemi, 2009. Translated by William McCuaig as *A Farewell to Truth* (New York: Columbia University Press, 2011).

———. *Credere di credere*. Milan: Garzanti, 1996. Translated by Luca D'Isanto and David Webb as *Belief* (Stanford, CA: Stanford University Press, 1999).

———. "Heidegger and Girard: *Kénosis* and the End of Metaphysics." In *Christianity, Truth, and Weakening Faith: A Dialogue*, by Gianni Vattimo and René Girard, edited by Pierpaolo Antonello, translated by William McCuaig, 78–87. New York: Columbia University Press, 2010.

———. "Storia della salvezza, storia dell'interpretazione." *Micromega* 3 (1992): 106–10. Reprinted in

Dopo la cristianità: per un cristianesimo non religioso, by Gianni Vattimo, 63–74 (Milan: Garzanti, 2002).

Vattimo, Gianni, and Santiago Zabala. *Hermeneutic Communism.* New York: Columbia University Press, 2011.

Webb, Eugene. *The Self Between: From Freud to the New Social Psychology of France.* Seattle: University of Washington Press, 1993.

White, Michael. *Rivals: Conflict as the Fuel of Science.* London: Secker and Warburg, 2001.

White, Robert. "Egoless Egoists: The Second-Hand Lives of *Mad Men.*" In *Mad Men and Philosophy: Nothing Is as It Seems,* edited by Rod Carveth and James B. South, 79–94. Hoboken, NJ: Wiley, 2010.

Williams, James G. "On Job and Writing: Derrida, Girard, and the Remedy-Poison." *Scandinavian Journal of the Old Testament* 7, no. 1 (1993): 32–50.

———. "René Girard without the Cross? Religion and the Mimetic Theory." *Anthropoetics* 2, no. 1 (1996).

Wolfson, Harry Austryn. *The Philosophy of the Church Fathers.* Cambridge, MA: Harvard University Press, 1964.

Index